Credit Where It's Due

Julia Ann Parzen
Michael Hall Kieschnick

Credit Where It's Due

Development Banking
for Communities

Temple University Press
Philadelphia

Temple University Press, Philadelphia 19122
Copyright © 1992 by Temple University. All rights reserved
Published 1992
Printed in the United States of America

Library of Congress Cataloging-in-Publication Data
Parzen, Julia.
    Credit where it's due : development banking for communities /
Julia Ann Parzen and Michael Hall Kieschnick.
      p.   cm.
    Includes index.
    ISBN 0-87722-811-6
    1. Development banks—United States. 2. Community development—
United States. I. Kieschnick, Michael. II. Title.
HG1976.U6P37 1991
332.2′8′0973—dc20   90-48881

To Daniel and Frannie, who sympathized,

and

to the development bankers, who are doing the real work

Contents

List of Tables

List of Tables

Acknowledgments

The writing of this book was funded by the Joyce Foundation, the Ford Foundation, the John D. and Catherine T. MacArthur Foundation, and the Charles Stuart Mott Foundation through the Center for Urban Economic Development at the University of Illinois at Chicago. Comments on the manuscript were received from Jason Kravit, Michael Annes, Edward Best, Marc Klyman, Vincent Hillery, Laura Henze, Larry Litvak, Mary Houghton, William Schweke, Martin Eakes, Robert Friedman, Cliff Rosenthal, Richard Schramm, Greg Ramm, Jean Pogge, Jane Baker, and Beth Siegel. Michael Barker provided extensive editorial assistance, which also improved the substance of the material. Editha Paras prepared much of the Glossary. Trude Parzen provided research and production assistance.

1
Introduction

COMMUNITIES HAVE always had to be creative and flexible to find capital to support business and housing development. As the supply of capital from the federal government has declined in the last decade, private financing has become more important to community development. Foundations have offset a small part of the decline, religious organizations and individuals have taken on a more important funding role, and capital has been pried loose from local financial institutions through negotiation and confrontation.

The growth in private funding of community development has helped a new breed of financial institution to emerge, one created explicitly to promote community economic development. Private suppliers of capital—and, at times, public sources also—are depending more and more on the expertise and the economies of scale these "development banks" offer. The expanding supply of private capital is allowing such institutions to grow in size and to proliferate, with the result that development banking is becoming an important tool of economic development at the community level. If development banks continue to grow and spread, they can be the catalyst for a new financial system that more actively promotes community economic development.

It is particularly important now to explore the role of development banking in the economy because of the crises in banking and insurance. General Accounting Office estimates are that the total cost of the savings and loan bailout will be as high as $500 billion, or $2,000 for every person in America.[1] The House Banking Committee's current estimate of the total cost of recapitalizing the bank insurance fund and closing down failed banks is $235 billion.[2] According to a report issued by Congressman John Dingell of Michigan, the current state of the insurance industry bears a close resemblance to the situation in the early stages of the savings and loan crisis. The menaces facing these sectors have demonstrated that all is not well with the current system. Confidence in financial institutions that are given broad latitude to make good lending decisions has dropped. Support is growing for a reassessment of what kinds of financial institutions should be offered access to government guarantees and insurance and for what purposes. Development banks have characteristics that make them worthy of attention from policy makers trying to fix the financial system and from financial institutions trying to fix themselves. Like other financial institutions that have weathered these hard times, development banks generally are small, serve basic lending markets they understand, pay a great deal of attention to managing risk and costs, ignore investment fads, and are driven by a desire to serve their customers. In addition, development banks are finding ways to address the credit needs of communities and borrowers that other financial institutions shun.

This book explains why development banks have an important role in economic development, reviews the elements of successful development banking, provides a blueprint for how such banks can be effective development vehicles, and suggests a program for building a financial system that promotes community economic development. Later in this chapter, we introduce the notion of economic development and the role of capital in community economic development. We explain why development banking has emerged and begin to flesh out the basic model of a development bank. In Chapter 2, we present the evidence that interventions in financial markets are required to promote community economic development. We rely on a conceptual analysis of how capital markets work (and do not work), studies that have researched local capital gaps, and an evaluation of the trends in capital markets. The chapter ends with a summary of the implications of the condition of capital markets for community development. Chapter 3 explores the factors that contribute to or limit development-bank effectiveness in promoting economic development. Even though there is not a large base of evaluative data on which to rely, we can still determine a great deal about the essential characteristics of development banks that have achieved some longevity while serving developmental markets. In Chapter 4, we address how development banks assess the need for their services, establish goals, and evaluate their performance. Because development banks are hybrids, part financial institution and part development organization, their goal setting is especially complex and important to their success. The chapter focuses most on the process through which they identify markets and come to terms with conflicts between serving these markets and surviving. Chapter 5 describes the various models adopted by development banks and their pros and cons as development vehicles. We try to show that a strong case can be made for each of the models, but our preference for commercial banking is very clear. In Chapter 6, we turn our attention to the sustainability of development banks. We explore the feasibility of self-sufficiency for each kind of development bank and look at whether there is something short of self-sufficiency that can suffice and is supportable. Chapter 7 covers the risk of development banking and the experience of development bankers with how to manage that risk. We present evidence that the risk of losses from development lending is lower than mainstream financial institutions perceive. In part, this is because established bankers do not understand the deals, but it is also because development banks have been resourceful and, sometimes, extremely innovative in the ways that they manage risk. In Chapter 8, we present the reasons that developmental lending can cost more than conventional lending. We then analyze the cost structure for a set of development banks and explore how development banks minimize their costs. Chapter 9 describes how development banks manage capital and how they price their financial services. We explore why most development banks are highly leveraged and the implications of this for their role in economic development. We also review their sources of capital and the relationship between a development bank's target cost of capital and its access to capital. We then look at the flip side of capital sources (i.e., how capital is allocated to borrowers), and make a case for market-rate pricing. Market pricing is not generally the rule in development banking, but it is becoming more common for the excellent reasons we describe. In Chapter 10, we offer a plan for achieving the full potential of development banking, including specific steps for development bankers, mainstream financial institutions, government agencies, and foundations.

Our Goal

Economic development is an increase in economic activity (more or better jobs, housing, or public services) that results in a wider distribution of the quantities being measured (income is more evenly distributed, the housing stock is not simply in a few very large homes) and an economy that is capable of sustaining the higher level of activity in the future from its own resources. Economic growth is not the same thing as economic development. Economic growth can result in higher income, but greater poverty, and can be maintained solely by the continuous injection of aid from outside sources.

How to respond to the plight of losers is a key issue in economic development. Given the competitive dynamics of our international economy, achieving even the greatest possible overall level of growth will generate losers among individuals, businesses, industries, and communities. We do not subscribe to the large body of literature asserting that efforts to encourage economic development should be implemented solely at the national level through a mix of tax, monetary, and spending levels set in such a way as to maintain the highest sustainable growth rate for the national economy. Losses are unavoidable and indeed desirable in economic competition, but successfully adjusting to losses is appropriate as a goal of public policy. Economic-development policies seek to stimulate overall growth while putting individuals and tangible capital left idle by the losses back into the competitive economy.

Ownership is integral to the notion of economic development. It has become commonplace to describe economic development by citing the old parable that you can feed someone for a day by giving them a fish, or you can feed someone for life by teaching them how to fish. This may be true. But the twentieth-century postscript to the story is that what really matters is who owns the pond with the fish. There is surely a difference in the sustainability of future growth between two communities, one with all of its tangible assets owned by distant investors and one with a significant degree of local ownership. The absence of local ownership implies either a lack of local capital or a lack of confidence in local investing on the part of local owners of capital—and neither is consistent with a policy of economic development. Of course, there is good reason to oppose xenophobic versions of self-help. External capital, if attracted to the right investments, can accelerate development and create local wealth. Conversely, it is hardly wise to demand that all local capital be invested in the local community.

Economic development can be achieved through a variety of activities, the most important of which is business development. While business development is the focus of this book, we also include two areas of secondary concern—housing development and programs to increase the financial resources in the hands of community residents. Good housing enhances the attractiveness of communities and the environment for economic development. Housing development helps create business opportunities in construction, management, and maintenance and can create wealth for low-income residents. Furthermore, because community organizations have been more successful in promoting housing development than business development, a way to diversify the risk of the latter is to balance it with housing activities. Financial programs that reduce the leakage of household incomes from communities (usually by enabling people to earn more on their savings or to pay less for loans) contribute to economic development by increasing the savings available for reinvestment, the resources individuals have to increase their well-being, and the purchasing power that can be used at businesses in the community.

The Role of Capital

How capital flows through the economy affects the potential for economic development.[3] Capital is needed to acquire equipment, build housing, or create infrastructure. While it cannot make nonviable projects into viable ones, lack of capital on appropriate terms can prevent viable projects from succeeding and stunt economic development. The potential sources of capital to fuel economic development are the real sectors of the economy—households, federal, state, and local governments, nonfinancial businesses, and foreign entities. For quite some time, households have been the source of capital for all sectors of the economy. In both 1978 and 1988, households were net savers, and businesses and the federal government were net borrowers. State and local governments, constrained by the requirement to balance annual budgets, were generally neutral. Tables illustrating this distribution, and the points made in the following paragraphs concerning the flow of funds, can be found at the end of this chapter.

While households provide most of the savings in the U.S. economy, only in a limited sense do they make the decisions about who will receive capital. The great majority of the funds flowing between and among real sectors pass through financial institutions, which reallocate the funds among real sectors. Overall, the degree of involvement in financial transactions by financial institutions has stayed relatively constant in recent years at between 85 percent and 87 percent of all funds.[4]

Historically, two types of financial institutions have facilitated the transactions of the real sector. While the distinctions between them are decreasing, they are still significant. The first is investment banks (or securities firms), which locate funds for borrowers (securities underwriters), match up savers and borrowers (brokers), and buy and resell securities of borrowers (dealers). Only in their role as dealers do investment banks actually make investments themselves. Some of the largest or best-known investment banks are Merrill Lynch, Shearson Lehman American Express, and Donaldson Lufkin & Jenrette. Investment banks earn fees for issuing securities and by selling securities for more than they paid for them. The second type of financial institution is financial intermediaries, or intermediary banks. Commercial banks, savings banks, savings and loan associations, credit unions, loan funds, insurance companies, finance companies, mutual funds, and venture-capital funds are all financial intermediaries. In contrast to investment banks, these institutions are always investors. They first raise capital on their own behalf and then lend or invest the proceeds. Financial intermediaries generate revenues through the spread between what they pay their investors and what they earn on debt and equity investments. Depository institutions are a special subgroup of financial intermediaries that includes commercial banks, savings and loan associations, and credit unions. They are granted charters by public agencies that allow them to offer federally insured savings products. Depository institutions allocate two-thirds of the money managed by financial intermediaries.

When financial intermediaries reallocate money on its way from sector to sector, the funds end up on their balance sheets as investments (assets) and borrowings (liabilities). Not surprisingly, among private financial intermediaries commercial banks have by far the largest financial assets, holding more than $2.9 trillion at the end of 1988. The troubled savings and loan industry holds a very distant second place, with assets of about $1.4 trillion in 1988. Life-insurance companies, holding reserves for future policy payouts, had more than $1.1 trillion in assets in 1988, slightly exceeding the resources of private pension funds. The federal government is a much smaller source of lent capital (in contrast to spending) than any of these financial intermediaries, but with loans of $161.8 billion in 1988 it remains significant.

Households generally do not care how financial intermediaries use their money as long as they are offered investment products with attributes they want. For example, commercial-bank savings accounts offer deposit insurance, easy access, and relatively low minimums on the size of investment. Most savers are not concerned with choosing between commercial banks that invest in local businesses and those that invest in Treasury securities. A growing number of households choose to examine how their savings are invested, although these "social investors" still control a tiny share (probably less than 5 percent) of all investments in the United States. According to the Social Investment Forum, $600 billion are invested with some kind of social screen, the vast majority being controlled by pension-fund investors eschewing only investments in South Africa.[5]

Financial institutions create investment products, that is, financial instruments, to carry out their role of allocating capital. The most common of these are stock, U.S. Treasury securities (bills, notes, and bonds), home mortgages, and corporate bonds. There are hundreds of other instruments tailored to meet the needs of particular kinds of investors and borrowers. While stock and other equity interests in businesses are the single largest financial asset, there is still two times more capital in debt instruments than equity instruments. Furthermore, many debt instruments created to serve business markets are only available to very large firms. The volume of commercial paper has grown faster than any other financial instrument in the past decade. Commercial paper is now an important and relatively cheap source of short-term debt, but only to around eight hundred of the largest and strongest companies who have publicly rated debt of any kind. The single largest source of long-term debt is the public market for corporate bonds. This market is open only to large companies, both strong and weak. With the weak served in its junk-bond segment, most of the remaining tens of thousands of companies must rely on banks and the businesses from which they buy supplies and equipment for credit. Supplier, or trade, credit exceeds bank loans to corporate businesses. One reason is that trade credit has more flexible terms; a second is probably the greater willingness of trade creditors to accept risk. Both of these sources of capital are overwhelmingly short term in nature. Capital markets have generated few products to serve the long-term capital needs of new and expanding ventures.

Financial institutions concentrate their investments in what they decide are growth regions and growth markets. Most financial institutions make the same assessment of which regions and markets have the greatest potential to use capital profitably for investors. Thus, while the assessments are usually sound, it is not unusual for growth regions and markets to receive more capital than they can use effectively and for slower-growth and declining regions and markets to receive less than they can use well. Capital-market participants usually realize they have gone too far when losses on lending in the growth markets pile up. Loans to build luxury condominiums in the northeastern United States in the late 1980s are one example of the propensity of financial markets to excess.

Community economic development results from many investment decisions, but it is a factor in the choices of only a small share of financial institutions or households. Most households neither want nor are offered input into capital-allocation decisions. Accordingly, it is only possible to allocate large enough amounts of capital to achieve the development goals of communities nationwide by producing financial instruments that meet the needs of savers who do not have strong social goals (or who are motivated more by financial return than by social concerns in their investment decisions). It is left to proponents of economic development to produce financial innovations that will serve these savers and community development.

A Tool for Economic Development

The goal of development finance is to provide capital to viable economic-development projects that would otherwise not come into being. Development finance is not grantmaking, and it should not simply substitute for the activities of existing financial institutions. Because the financial institutions and markets of each community, state, or region differ from each other, capital needs vary in different locales. In one place, racial discrimination in housing lending may create a need for color-blind mortgage loans. In another place, inadequate competition among commercial banks may create a need for loans to smaller companies.

One approach to development finance is to convince regulators to encourage or require financial institutions to meet local capital needs. In the past two decades, consumer groups have been able to convince governments at various levels to barter new powers for community investment or otherwise encourage commercial banks to pay closer attention to economic development. For example, New York State has a community-reinvestment act that offers new real-estate-investment powers to commercial banks based upon their community-reinvestment performance. The commerce commissioner of Minnesota has proposed expanding community-reinvestment standards to include life-insurance and securities firms and making public ratings of financial institutions based upon their service to communities.[6] Under the Financial Institutions Reform, Recovery, and Enforcement Act of 1989, ratings of depository institutions' performance in serving their communities must be disclosed to the public. And because of lobbying by the Financial Democracy Campaign, there are provisions in the act directing each district Federal Home Loan Bank to provide advances to savings institutions to subsidize affordable housing. While these kinds of laws only modestly change the lending practices of banks and S&L associations, the cumulative amount of capital set aside for community development as a result may be significant at the local level.

Community groups around the country have also convinced individual financial institutions to make commitments to community development by exerting public pressure. The federal Community Reinvestment Act (CRA) was passed in 1977 to counteract the practice of "redlining," that is, arbitrary geographic discrimination in the granting of credit. The act requires depository institutions to prepare reports describing what products they offer and how these meet the credit needs of the area they serve. When a bank or savings and loan association applies to its regulators to buy or sell a bank or open or close a branch, the communities it serves are allowed to comment on the effect of the action on the local supply of credit, to request public hearings, or to file a protest challenging the approval of the application (which can delay approval) because local credit needs are not being met or would not be met under the proposed change.

Using the opportunities provided by the CRA, local groups have been able to negotiate some landmark community-reinvestment agreements. Between 1978 and 1987, 64 percent of protested applications to the Federal Reserve Board resulted in negotiations or settlements between the protestant and the applicant bank.[7] Many other settlements were reached without a protest being filed. One of the most extensive community-reinvestment agreements is the Neighborhood Lending Program negotiated between the Chicago Reinvestment Alliance and the First National Bank of Chicago, Harris Trust and Savings, and Northern Trust Company. By August 1989, after five years, the three lenders had made 572 loans totaling $117.5 million. According to Calvin Bradford, the Neighborhood Lending Program has served markets, especially multifamily and mixed-use properties, that were not being supported when the programs began in 1984. A strong indication that the program has been a financial success is that all three financial institutions have agreed to an additional five-year investment program at $200 million.[8] As of 1989, reinvestment agreements were estimated at between $6 billion and $10 billion, or about one-tenth of 1 percent of total bank deposits. By 1992 the amount had doubled. Many agreements also have provisions that do not involve dollar commitments, but that may eliminate lending practices that hamper reinvestment.[9] Most settlements have not

changed overall investment strategies, but they have encour-
aged development. The Community Reinvestment Act is
growing in impact and influencing more and more financial
institutions to respond in some measurable way.

Sometimes it is possible to change the practices of financial
institutions simply by showing them how they can earn competitive profits in new markets. The Mountain Association for
Community Economic Development (MACED) in Berea, Kentucky, helped form the Eastern Kentucky Banks Consortium
for Mortgage Lending to make long-term mortgages with low
down payments and fixed interest rates more available through
local banks. The association sought and obtained changes that
made secondary-market programs more usable in rural areas.
It then presented seminars for local banks on how to use the
programs. In addition, MACED obtained reforms in Federal
Housing Administration (FHA) processing procedures, which
made it easier for small rural banks to use the agency's mort-
gage-insurance programs.[10]

Convincing government organizations to create new financial institutions and programs is another approach for financing communities in need. Such efforts may range from revenue-
bond and tax-increment financing, to loan-guarantee programs,
to direct-loan funds. While government organizations have a
very important role to play in development finance, it is usually
not as direct lenders. Most federal and state loan programs
have not been effective development vehicles. Many have lacked
lending expertise, which usually must be found outside of public bureaucracies. Some have not been allowed by politicians to
take an objective view of investment decisions. A few have been
very good programs, but were changed or dismantled at the
whim of new public administrations. Because public financial
institutions have suffered from such handicaps, business-development lending within the public sector has generally failed
regardless of how it is evaluated. This is true of the Small Busi-

ness Administration, the Economic Development Administration, the Export-Import Bank, and a long list of other public attempts at development finance. Only in the rarest of circumstances should purely public development banks, at any level of government, be attempted.[11]

Public institutions can, however, play a very productive role in development finance by giving incentives to private financial institutions. The Michigan Strategic Fund, a state agency, has four programs that provide incentives for private financial institutions to accept more risk in business lending—the Capital Access Program, the Business and Industrial Development Company (BIDCO) Program, the Minority BIDCO Program, and the Seed Capital Program. Privately operated financial institutions, BIDCOs are designed to address the growth-capital needs of moderate-risk businesses that cannot be met by banks or venture-capital funds. As of fall 1992, the Michigan Strategic Fund had made commitments to provide up to one-third of the equity capital for ten BIDCOs. As the result of a $21.45 million investment by the state, companies in the state have already attracted more than $70 million in new capital, and the pace of investment is rapidly increasing.[12]

Some social entrepreneurs choose to create their own private financial institutions when there are no other local sources of funds. Community organizations and socially motivated entrepreneurs take this step most often in communities experiencing dramatic disinvestment or in rural areas served by few financial institutions. The Lower East Side Community Credit Union and the Mid-Bronx Community Development Federal Credit Union in New York City were both formed to serve residents after the closing of a commercial-bank branch. Southern Development Bancorporation in Arkansas was established to fill gaps in the availability of capital in rural communities.

Social entrepreneurs also form their own financial institutions when established private and public institutions will not meet a specific capital need. The Institute for Community Economics (ICE) loan fund in Springfield, Massachusetts, was formed to serve community land trusts because few other lenders would make loans to these organizations. According to Chuck Matthei, a founder of ICE, the capital pool established the group's professional capability and "gave it a place at the table" to demonstrate why land trusts should receive capital from mainstream financial institutions.[13]

New institutions have also been formed in a few cases because they can throw off revenue to support other economic activities. For this small minority of development programs, financial services are crucial to their survival. Northern Community Investment Corporation is a rural-community-development program located in St. Johnsbury, Vermont, that does business financing and real-estate development. Its business-loan fund generates revenue that supports staff who do housing development and community projects.[14] Although South Shore Bank in Chicago was not envisioned solely as a source of revenue to support more-costly development activities, this was one of its goals.

Financial institutions dedicated to community development represent a very small subset of financial intermediaries. The total capital they control is probably less than $5 billion.[15] However, the amount of capital under the control of these dedicated financial institutions is continuing to grow, and they are beginning to form a group identity as development banks.

Development Banks

Financial institutions created primarily to foster economic development are development banks. As financial institutions, they seek to conserve their capital; as development vehicles, they seek to contribute to economic development. Development banks must be both sustainable financial institutions and cost-effective development vehicles, and these roles sometimes conflict. Development banking does not imply a particular structure but, rather, a mission and a point of view about credit and communities.[16]

There are many kinds of development banks, including commercial banks, savings institutions, credit unions, business-loan funds, loan funds that invest in community- or cooperative-owned organizations (community-development loan funds), loan funds that invest in very small businesses (microenterprise loan funds), business- and industrial-development corporations (BIDCOs), small-business investment companies (SBICs), minority-enterprise small-business investment companies (MESBICs), and venture-capital funds. Each type of financial institution provides some of the kinds of capital needed for economic development. While none of these development banks can meet all of the capital needs of a region alone, in concert they can.

The discussion in the following chapters focuses on those models that we feel best illustrate the potential, problems, and strategies of private development banks: commercial banks, savings and loan associations, community-development credit unions, community-development loan funds, microenterprise loan funds, and a special category of venture-capital funds, namely, royalty-investment funds. Commercial banks are already important lenders to small businesses and, as depository institutions, they have a unique capacity to attract insured funds. Savings and loan associations and credit unions are also included because they are depository institutions. In addition, there is a subcategory of credit unions whose goal is to serve community development. The other three models represent the frontier in financial innovation for development finance. Community-development loan funds are essentially the first loan funds to attract private capital routinely and to act like financial institutions. Microenterprise loan funds use unusual methods to lower the costs and the risk of small-scale business lending. Royalty-investment funds offer an alternative to equity capital that is more appropriate for slower-growth companies and cooperative and nonprofit businesses. Innovative examples of each model have been used to broadly characterize these types of financial institutions.[17]

None of the models selected for intensive treatment is primarily an equity investor, although commercial banks can own small-business investment companies, and royalty-investment funds offer products that meet needs similar to those met by equity. We focus on debt and patient alternatives to equity because community ventures and entrepreneurs do not want to give up control in exchange for capital. Also, current tax laws favor debt and royalty financing by allowing interest, but not dividends, to be deducted from income in figuring tax liability.

Commercial Banks

A commercial bank is a for-profit corporation owned by private investors that provides insured deposit services to individuals and organizations and uses the proceeds to make personal, commercial, and real-estate loans. In return for access to federal deposit insurance, commercial banks' activities and ability to incur risk are limited and closely regulated. A commercial bank that is part of a bank holding company (a company that owns one or more commercial banks) can have affiliates and subsidiaries that engage in a much broader range of activities than the bank itself. While its primary goal ordinarily is to increase the value of its stockholders' investment, a commercial bank can alternatively attract investors who wish to reinvest in a community and promote economic development.

Shorebank Corporation, in Chicago, is the best-known of the development-oriented banks and bank holding companies. It has earned rates of return that compare well with those of its peers while participating in the rehabilitation of a large part of the housing stock in the South Shore neighborhood of Chicago. Newer commercial banking institutions include Southern Development Bancorporation in Arkansas (formed with the assistance of Shorebank Corporation), Blackfeet National Bank in Browning, Montana (formed by the Blackfeet Tribe), Ameritrust State Bank in Cleveland, Ohio (formed by Ameritrust Corporation, a bank holding company), Bank of America State Bank (formed by Bank of America, near San Francisco, California, in April 1990), and Community Capital Bank in Brooklyn, New York. A handful of union-owned commercial banks also pursue development goals, and several dozen minority-owned commercial banks operate in predominantly low-income neighborhoods.

Savings and Loan Associations

A savings and loan association is a for-profit corporation with many of the same general characteristics as a commercial bank, but only some savings and loan associations are owned by stockholders. Others, known as mutual savings and loan associations, are owned by their depositors and borrowers. The number of mutual savings and loan associations is falling rapidly because of conversions to stock ownership and mergers with stock-owned thrifts. Traditionally, savings and loan associations have been predominantly residential-mortgage lenders. Today, they are able to offer the same kinds of loans as commercial banks. Savings and loan holding companies have a broader range of powers than even bank holding companies.

There is no parallel example to Shorebank Corporation for a savings institution. However, there are many cases of small thrifts that have made home loans to buyers who were ignored by other thrifts due to discrimination. These small thrifts have served development purposes without being development banks. The National Cooperative Bank (NCB) purchased a thrift in Hillsboro, Ohio, to support NCB's lending to cooperative businesses and to members of housing co-ops. The labor-owned Union Savings Bank of Albuquerque, New Mexico, is another example. Finally, there are several dozen minority-owned savings institutions that operate in low-income neighborhoods.

Community-Development Credit Unions

A credit union is a nonprofit cooperative financial institution owned and controlled by members who have some common bond. Credit unions are regulated depository institutions that can offer deposit insurance. They are also exempt from federal income taxes. While credit unions can make consumer, housing, and business loans to members, most small ones focus on consumer loans. Federal credit unions (and some state-chartered ones) whose members have a residential or associational common bond and in which a majority of the members are low income, can be designated a community-development credit union. Only they (and student credit unions) are allowed to accept insured deposits from nonmembers. The goals of community-development credit unions are to provide loans to members, encourage savings, promote community reinvestment and neighborhood revitalization, and educate members about financial and community issues.

Such credit unions are becoming important providers of banking services in a growing number of low-income urban communities where commercial-bank branches have closed and in rural areas that have never had good access to banking services. Examples of the three hundred or so development-oriented credit unions include the Self-Help Credit Union in Durham, North Carolina, the Quitman County Federal Credit Union in Marks, Mississippi, the Northside Community Credit Union in Chicago, and the Santa Cruz Community Development Credit Union in Santa Cruz, California. All of them are committed to community development.

Community-Development Loan Funds

There are thousands of loan funds throughout the country. Some are small, informal capital pools available to help constituents of community organizations in emergencies. Others are multimillion-dollar independent organizations with very specific goals and rules. Most loan funds were originally funded with allocations of capital from government authorities and were organized by community-development corporations, rural organizations, and local-government agencies. As of April 1986, there were 211 revolving-loan funds sponsored by the Federal Economic Development Administration, each with an average amount of EDA funding of $850,000.[18] There are many more government-sponsored housing- and business-loan funds supported by Urban Development Action Grants (UDAGs), Community Development Block Grants (CDBGs), Farmers Home Administration grants and loans, and state funds. Examples of these loan funds include the Mountain Association for Community Economic Development Loan Fund in Berea, Kentucky, and the Northern Community Investment Corporation in St. Johnsbury, Vermont.

A far smaller number of loan funds are capitalized by grants and loans from private investors—foundations, churches, corporations, and individuals—to promote job creation and housing affordability for and by low- and moderate-income people. As of the end of 1990, there were forty such loan funds that were members of the National Association of Community Development Loan Funds (NACDLF), a trade association of community-oriented loan funds located in Philadelphia. Member funds had an average capitalization of $1.8 million.[19] There are a number of similarly structured loan funds that are not members of the NACDLF.

Unlike depository institutions, loan-fund activities are not regulated by a specific body of law. Thus, loan funds fit no common description; even the members of the NACDLF take many different forms. Nevertheless, loan funds can be categorized based upon who they serve and who invests in them. In this book, we focus on community-development loan funds (CDLFs), nonprofit organizations that: make loans to assist low- and moderate-income people, women, and minorities in obtaining housing and jobs; lend to businesses and other organizations rather than to individuals; are privately owned, not-for-profit corporations; and seek loans to their loan funds from individual and institutional investors who are sympathetic to the goals of the loan fund. Common borrowers from CDLFs include cooperatives, community land trusts, and nonprofit organizations. Some CDLFs make only housing and real-estate loans, others make housing and business loans, and a few make only business loans. The goals of community development loan funds are to mobilize capital for community development, to educate community organizations, investors, and financial institutions, and, in many cases, to expand community ownership of resources.

Community-development loan funds have demonstrated that they serve a need, but they have not yet been tested under the less-favorable conditions of real-estate markets in decline and funders whose attention has shifted elsewhere. They are supporting affordable housing that depository institutions cannot fund and demonstrating the creditworthiness of new kinds of affordable-housing arrangements. Examples of community-development loan funds include the Institute for Community Economics Loan Fund in Springfield, Massachusetts, the Delaware Valley Community Reinvestment Fund in Philadelphia, the Low Income Housing Fund in San Francisco, California, the Cooperative Fund of New England in Hartford, Connecticut, and the Industrial Cooperative Association Loan Fund in Boston.

Microenterprise Loan Funds

A microenterprise loan fund is a not-for-profit corporation that makes very small, short-term loans for working capital to "microentrepreneurs." Such persons work alone or with their families to provide basic goods and services for the poor and the middle class by using a low-capital, labor-intensive mode of production. Microenterprise loan funds lend to businesses that require very little capital to commence operations and are able to begin quickly to generate income to make loan payments. Their credit, training, and organizing activities each have aspects distinct from other loan funds. Microenterprise loan funds generally keep losses low without relying on traditional collateral or equity requirements, decentralize to keep operating costs low while serving many small borrowers, and charge borrowers close to market rates of interest.[20] Their goals are to increase the incomes, employment, and empowerment of poor people by organizing them and helping them build self-esteem and business skills.

Small-scale lending programs in developing countries (such as the Grameen Bank of Bangladesh and the Badan Kredit Kecamatan Program in Indonesia) have been credited with reducing or eliminating the huge loan defaults encountered by other development banks, effectively linking credit with savings, significantly increasing family incomes, and organizing low-income people.[21] With few exceptions, the microloan programs operating in the United States are too young for evaluation of their results. Micro Industry Credit Rural Organization (MICRO) in Tucson, Arizona, the Self-Employment Circle Fund at the Neighborhood Institute (a subsidiary of Shorebank Corporation) in Chicago, and the loan fund of the Women's Self-Employment Project in Chicago were all formed in 1986. The Lakota Fund was organized on Pine Ridge Reservation in Kyle, South Dakota, by First Nations Financial Project in 1987. The Good Faith Fund was formed in Pine Bluff, Arkansas, by

Southern Development Bancorporation in 1988. Somewhat older funds are the Women's Economic Development Corporation, formed in 1983 in St. Paul, Minnesota, and the loan fund of the Center for Southeast Asian Refugee Resettlement, formed in 1983 in San Francisco, California.

Most of the information on results of microenterprise loan programs applies to situations quite different from those in most communities in the United States. There are also barriers facing U.S. microenterprises that do not exist in developing countries. For example, home work is prohibited in some communities, licensing requirements for small businesses can be expensive, and people who are receiving public aid risk losing these benefits before their business income can replace them. There are fewer small-scale trading opportunities in the U.S. economy, which is dominated by mass marketers. And rural areas in the United States do not have the concentration of population necessary to achieve the scale of programs in developing countries. The microenterprise model is included because of its potential to reduce the operating costs and credit risk of very small business lending rather than its proven results in the United States.

Royalty-Investment Funds
A royalty-investment fund is a for-profit or not-for-profit limited partnership or corporation whose purpose is to advance capital to businesses in return for a royalty on specified sales. A firm enters into a contract with the royalty-investment fund (RIF) whereby the company receives a grant and, in return, promises to pay royalties. These are equal to some percent of sales for the number of years it takes for the fund to receive a negotiated multiple of its original investment. Royalty financing can be used to support the start-up of a new firm or the expansion of an existing firm adding a new product. The goal of for-profit RIFs is to earn high rates of return for investors

and to finance the growth and development of businesses and jobs.

Royalty-investment funds serve entrepreneurs who need more patient money than loans, but who either cannot meet the growth requirements of venture capitalists or who resist external equity investment because they want to retain control of their company. Thus, they can more effectively provide venture capital to smaller, slower-growth companies, cooperatives, and community organizations than can traditional venture funds. Royalty financing does not require a firm to make payments before a product achieves some success ("patient" money), does not place the firm in the position of being sold out against its interests to a competitor or larger firm, allows the investor to achieve high returns if the firm or product is successful to compensate for risk and inevitable losses elsewhere, and offers a means to achieve high returns other than capital gains dependent on selling the security—that is, the return is achievable even without the security being liquid.

There are very few venture capitalists who have used royalty financing, but the number is growing. Among public venture-capital pools, one well-known example is the state-funded Connecticut Product Development Corporation (CPDC), which funds new-product development by existing businesses in the state. The corporation provides about 60 percent of product-development costs, asks for about 5 percent royalties on sales, and terminates its agreement if royalties accumulate to five times the original investment. As of 1989, it had made more than eighty investments, ranging from $22,000 to $700,000. Other states that have enacted legislation to form product-development corporations include Illinois, Iowa, Louisiana, New Mexico, North Carolina, Ohio, and Utah.[22] Although not a primary financing vehicle, royalty agreements are also available from the Alaska Renewable Resources Corporation (ARRC) and the Massachusetts Technology Development Corporation (MTDC).

The only arenas in the private sector in which royalty financing has been relatively common are research and development (R&D) and marketing-investment partnerships. For example, Prudential-Bache has offered public limited partnerships designed to fund research-and-development projects where returns to investors are based primarily on royalties on resulting products. PruTech Research and Development Partnership I raised $74 million from 7,275 limited partners. Recent changes in tax law have diminished interest in research-and-development partnerships using royalty financing, but using it for product development is becoming more common.[23] For example, Innovative Ventures Inc., an East Lansing, Michigan, investment fund, has made royalty investments in small companies that are developing new products.

Because there are few examples of royalty-investment funds, this model is included based upon its potential to enhance access to patient capital for slower-growth companies rather than upon its proven results in financing new businesses.

The Importance of
Community-Development Banking

Development banks often are outstanding catalysts for changes in credit practices by mainstream financial institutions. They introduce such firms to creditworthy new markets and demonstrate to them how to use public subsidies to contribute to community economic development without sacrificing financial returns. The Santa Cruz Community Credit Union has found that local commercial banks are now interested in making loans to the alternative businesses for which it once was the only source of credit. The Institute for Community Economics Loan Fund has begun to find financial partners for its community-land-trust loans based upon its performance with them. The NCB Savings Association in Ohio is buying multifamily cooperative-mortgage loans from National Cooperative Bank in the hopes of demonstrating the safety and profitability of this market to other savings and loan associations.

Development banks are the most likely candidates to produce financial innovations that will serve both investors and community development. There is a growing cadre of development bankers who understand financial markets well, are experienced in community development, and have a strong personal desire to find ways to serve communities. The required innovations are much less likely to come from mainstream financial institutions because they have no special concern for community development and there is insufficient financial incentive for them to focus their research and development on small, local markets. A few development banks are advancing what may become immensely important structural innovations in financial markets. The Connecticut Product Development Corporation is addressing liquidity barriers that make it difficult for small businesses to attract equity capital by providing companies with patient capital that can be repaid without putting their independence at risk. The handful of U.S. microenterprise loan funds testing peer-group loans, in which a group of borrowers is held collectively responsible for loan repayment, is addressing concerns about credit risk and transaction costs for small-business lending.

Development banks also can provide more permanent solutions to capital problems than other tools of development finance, and they can enhance the credibility and impact of development activists. Development-bank lending programs can be safeguarded more effectively than special programs within mainstream financial institutions or government programs. If development-bank organizers pay sufficient attention to ownership issues, the banks' programs can be permanently safeguarded. When forced to retrench, private financial institutions are likely to cut "development" programs first, and government programs change with each change in administration. Managers of development banks that run successful financial programs can also become influential spokespeople for development finance and community development. Their ability to provide capital while preserving it demonstrates that they understand the essential business of financial intermediaries.

Development banks also can be very effective engines for economic development in declining or disadvantaged communities. An array of development banks have been created to promote comprehensive community development, addressing business, housing, and community needs. Some have made a big difference. Between January 1976 and December 1988, Shorebank Corporation subsidiaries and affiliates financed the rehabilitation of 25 percent of the 24,140 multifamily housing units in the South Shore neighborhood of Chicago, helping to change the outlook for the neighborhood.[24] Not many development banks have achieved a scale large enough to have such an impact, but many are moving in this direction.

Development banks deserve the attention of economic-development policymakers and strategists for what they currently accomplish and for what they can accomplish in the next decade. They are already acting as lenders of last resort in abandoned communities and as proving grounds for financial innovation. They are already demonstrating the viability of markets and borrowers that mainstream financial institutions have neglected. However, development banks are not achieving their potential as agents for economic development. Most are much smaller than average financial institutions, and many of the smallest ones are busy with their own survival. If they are going to matter, they need to grow in scale and in number. To challenge the status quo, strong development banks are needed in each major city and in many rural regions. This will not necessarily happen. Development banking is difficult to do well because of conflicts between impact and survival and insufficient funding

Table 1-1
The Flow of Funds among Real Sectors in 1978* (in $ billions)

Sector	Amount Saved	Amount Borrowed	Net
Households	251.9	168.3	+83.6
Nonfinancial business	98.1	171.3	−73.2
State and local government	20.1	22.7	− 2.6
Federal government	24.6	63.5	−38.9
Foreign	58.7	55.6	+ 3.1

*Theoretically, the figures in this table should balance. Because of problems in collecting the macroeconomic data, however, there are discrepancies.
Source: Federal Reserve Board Flow of Funds, Federal Reserve Board, Washington, D.C., 1981.

Table 1-2
The Flow of Funds among Real Sectors in 1988* (in $ billions)

Sector	Amount Saved	Amount Borrowed	Net
Households	440.3	295.6	+144.7
Nonfinancial business	124.7	136.2	−11.5
State and local government	14.7	32.0	−17.3
Federal government	.8	178.5	−177.7
Foreign	172.7	36.5	+136.2

Source: Federal Reserve Board Flow of Funds, Federal Reserve Board, Washington, D.C., 1989.

to support experimentation. With changes in policy and practice on the part of development banks, mainstream financial institutions, government organizations, and foundations, however, it is possible. This book covers the steps necessary to succeed. If these are followed, we are confident that an infant industry can become the basis for a new financial system.

Table 1-3
The Relative Size of Major Financial Intermediaries
(Outstanding Financial Assets, Current Dollars)

Financial Intermediary	1978 $ billions	1988 $ billions
Commercial banks	1,221.0	2,938.2
Savings and loan associations	506.3	1,359.9
Life-insurance companies	378.3	1,113.3
Private pension funds	326.2	1,139.9
Federally sponsored mortgage pools	70.4	810.9
State and local pension funds	153.9	610.1
Mutual funds	46.0	478.3
Finance companies	159.6	489.3
Other insurance companies	133.9	434.4
Federally sponsored credit agencies	134.6	423.6
Money-market funds	10.8	338.0
Mutual savings banks	158.2	280.0
Credit unions	58.4	196.2
Securities firms	32.9	140.5
Real-estate-investment trusts	3.5	13.6

Source: Flow of Funds Accounts, Financial Assets and Liabilities Year End, 1965–1988, Federal Reserve Board, Washington, D.C., 1989.

Table 1-4
Loans by the Federal Government in Current Dollars
(in $ Billions)

Recipient	1978	1988
Foreign borrowers	45.6	63.3
Nonfarm noncorporate business	7.0	46.2
State and local government	6.5	9.0
Farms	7.0	13.3
Households	7.4	20.1
Nonfinancial corporate business	5.7	9.9

Source: Flow of Funds Accounts, Financial Assets and Liabilities Year End, 1965–1988, Federal Reserve Board, Washington, D.C., 1989.

Table 1-5
The Relative Scale of Financial Instruments (Outstanding Financial Assets in $ Billions)

Financial Instrument	1978	1988
Corporate equities	982.5	3,130.0
Equity in noncorporate businesses	1,516.7	2,397.0
Treasury obligations	619.2	2,095.2
Home mortgages	727.7	2,138.8
Nonfinancial corporate bonds	320.6	885.0
Commercial mortgages	211.8	711.9
Consumer installment credit	264.7	671.4
State and local tax-exempt debt	253.5	564.5
Corporate trade credit	258.9	510.3
Bank loans to corporate business	175.1	501.9
Commercial paper	82.2	452.1
Multifamily mortgages	124.9	287.9
Finance company loans to business	74.4	236.5
Bank loans to noncorporate business	59.6	128.9
Industrial Revenue Bonds	25.0	116.3
S&L association loans to business	0.0	34.8

Source: Flow of Funds Accounts, Financial Assets and Liabilities Year End, 1965–1988, Federal Reserve Board, Washington, D.C., 1989.

Table 1-6
Outstanding Household Financial Assets in 1988

Instrument	$ billions
Equity in noncorporate business	2,397.0
Pension fund reserves (allocated)	2,592.8
Small time/savings accounts	2,131.4
Equity in corporate business	1,824.9
U.S. government securities	859.5
Checkable deposits/currency	488.8
Mutual-fund shares	418.0
Life-insurance reserves	313.6
Tax-exempt bonds	275.8
Money-market funds	287.0
Large time deposits	140.1
Mortgages	120.0
Corporate/foreign bonds	115.5
Open-market paper	125.1

Source: Flow of Funds Accounts, Financial Assets and Liabilities Year End, 1965–1988, Federal Reserve Board, Washington, D.C., 1989.

2
Capital-Market Failures

THERE IS broad discussion and great disagreement about whether capital markets—the marketplaces where funds are channeled from investors to borrowers—do a good job of allocating capital to projects that deserve financing. At one pole, some economists believe that capital markets are perfect allocators of capital. Others argue that capital markets have completely lost track of their purpose of facilitating real economic activity. The truth lies between these poles. Financial markets work pretty well in facilitating economic growth, but there are failures and missed opportunities. Examining how capital markets allocate capital reveals why some borrowers are denied capital and whether interventions to give these borrowers better access to capital are warranted.

How Financial Markets Price Capital

Most investors want financial instruments that provide high returns, safety, liquidity, and convenience. Since it is usually not possible to get everything they want, investors make trade-offs. An average investor told that her investment is at risk may be willing to accept that risk if she is compensated with a higher return. This might be a higher interest rate on a loan or a cheaper price at which to buy stock. If she is then told that her investment is illiquid and cannot be cashed in for a decade, she would want even higher returns as compensation. And, finally, if told that to buy the investment she has to fill in five forms, each notarized, and pay a lawyer to review them, the demanded return would rise yet again. It is not surprising that there are a limited number of deals that can offer high returns with low risk. After these are snapped up, investors are forced to make more difficult choices. Projects that present unappealing combinations of risk, return, liquidity, and simplicity find themselves without investors. At the same time, investors who demand excessive returns for relatively modest amounts of risk or illiquidity find themselves without investments.

Because it is very difficult to judge the attributes of an investment, investors frequently hire others to help make their choices. Something might be riskier (or less risky) than it appears. Inflation might rise and devalue the agreed-upon interest payments. Liquidity could disappear. Investors improve their chances of correctly assessing the attributes of an investment by hiring professional investment managers. Pension funds hire investment advisors. Small savers "hire" commercial banks. These financial intermediaries identify the attributes of investments for investors, seek ways to eliminate undesirable aspects of investments, and price the investments to compensate investors for those undesirable aspects that cannot be eliminated.

What investors charge borrowers for capital depends upon both the attributes of their deals and overall economic conditions. The price of capital is the total financial return to investors. Financial returns can take the form of interest, dividends, fees, appreciation in the value of investments, royalties, and even tax write-offs. Investors are usually flexible in the form of return they will accept.

Investors want the rate of return to take into account the

possibility that returns on an investment can be less than expected. A borrower may not pay back the money in full and on time. He may default on the loan. Individuals who supply capital are subject to this uncertainty, or risk, and usually demand compensation for it in the form of a higher return. The risk premium is smallest if the investor can bear the risk in an efficient manner. To do so, she needs to construct an investment portfolio that includes partial claims on a large number of investment projects. By holding a portfolio, she can increase the likelihood that some investments will experience sufficient growth to balance out losses on others. This risk-pooling benefit stems from the fact that some of the variability in returns depends on factors unique to a particular investment. These "nonsystematic" risks can cancel each other out in a portfolio that includes investments in businesses in unrelated industrial sectors.

Investors tend to require higher compensation when it is costly to buy or not easy to sell a security. Investors also want to be compensated for all of their transactions' costs, including obtaining information on a project, reviewing the proposal, negotiating investment terms, completing legal agreements, and monitoring the borrower. And they want to be compensated for tying up their money. An investor may unexpectedly need her money to pay off a creditor or to make a more attractive investment. If she cannot quickly liquidate an investment at a very modest cost, she will usually demand higher returns. The premium investors require for accepting illiquidity can be quite large. According to most studies of the performance of stocks listed on major stock exchanges, less-liquid stocks—those in which there is less trading activity—have to generate returns much higher than the average issue. The size of the liquidity premium depends upon how actively a security is traded, its level of standardization, the degree to which risk information about the instrument is publicly available, and whether there is an easy-to-use mechanism for buying and selling it.

Overall economic conditions affect the required rate of return on investments in the same way regardless of their individual characteristics. Rapid economic growth tends to bid up rates of return because the competition for capital increases. Conversely, recessions usually produce lower interest rates, since the demand for capital recedes as businesses cut back on production and consumers spend less. Rates of return are also higher when the expected rate of inflation is high. Investors require a premium as compensation for a potential reduction in the purchasing value of their investment dollars due to inflation. Because business cycles and inflation cannot be predicted, there is always uncertainty about what interest rates will be in the future. Because the uncertainty increases with time, investors generally require a premium for longer-term investments.

The market rate of return on an investment is what a project would have to pay if it raised money from among a large number of competing investors, each of whom understood the risks and costs of the investment and overall economic conditions. Market-rate returns on investments are higher if there is rapid economic growth, high expected inflation rates, a long term to maturity, high risk that returns will not be as expected, low liquidity, or high transaction costs. There is no single rate of return that constitutes the "market rate of return." It is not what the bank down the street charges; since it depends on the deal and the financial instrument used to finance it, the market rate of return will vary widely.

Projects that can offer market rates of return should be able to attract funding at a price no higher than that paid on other investments with similar attributes. Projects offering to pay less than a market return simply do not get financed unless they find an investor who drastically disagrees with the assessment of a project's risk or who finds something in it that no other investor does—such as a hidden profit potential, a way to meet an obligation to a relative, or a desire to accomplish some social good.

Market rates of return are relevant even to investors who choose investments based upon their potential social benefits. The market rate of return provides a benchmark for what investors should charge to manage their risk and recover their costs. If a social investor chooses to charge less, the benchmark helps him determine whether he will preserve or deplete his capital. Computing the gap between what he charges and market rates also helps him evaluate whether the social benefits anticipated are sufficient to make up for the loss of capital. There is no reason why social investors should not reserve big concessions for deals that offer large social benefits. Such investors also need to understand how the market prices capital to be able to identify what actions on their part are most likely to improve access to capital for worthy projects. They are likely to identify quite different interventions for projects able to pay market rates that cannot attract capital, below-market-rate projects that cannot attract capital, and projects that can attract capital, but at rates higher than they should be based upon their attributes.

The Reasons for Intervening in Capital Markets

Studies and experiences shared by development-finance professionals across the country indicate that gaps exist in the availability of capital for small-business development and for housing. The greatest evidence of gaps is for long-term and unsecured debt for small and moderately sized businesses, equity financing for new businesses and early stage businesses that are unlikely to go public and for small businesses that want to develop new products, loans for nontraditional organizations (such as cooperatives and nonprofits), loans of all types to businesses in low-income neighborhoods, and home-mortgage loans to minorities.[1] A survey of capital markets reveals why these gaps may exist.

Risky projects sometimes are not able to attract investors because of lack of competition between investors or regulations that limit risk taking by prominent financial institutions. In regions or capital-market segments where there are few financial institutions, these institutions sometimes act as monopolists. They overprice credit on very-low-risk investments, which makes it unnecessary to seek higher returns by taking on small amounts of additional risk. Monopolistic behavior on a geographical basis is now largely confined to rural areas. Legal limits on risk taking also prevent financial institutions from making certain investments that could compensate them for risk. Regulations govern what assets commercial banks, savings institutions, life-insurance companies, and pension funds may hold and to whom and for what purpose they may supply funds. While intended to ensure the security of liabilities, these regulations also have the effect of cutting off funds entirely to some risky enterprises, even those with a very high expected rate of return. In particular, small and new firms that are not excellent credit risks are denied credit because they must rely for it on commercial banks, which by law cannot incur much risk.

In some cases, capital is available to high-risk projects, but only with a higher risk premium than efficient financial markets should require. This is often due to insufficient risk pooling. Private financial intermediaries, such as mutual funds, routinely provide risk pooling for the securities of large firms already traded in public capital markets. There are, however, very few financial institutions that serve viable new ventures with moderate growth potential. These ventures must seek a few large investors. Because risk cannot be pooled efficiently, investors require substantial risk premiums above what would otherwise be required.

Small and unfamiliar deals are sometimes unnecessarily denied funding because they have high transaction costs. It takes at least the same amount of time to gather information and prepare investment documents for a small loan as for a large one. Banks interviewed for the Interagency Task Force on Small Business Finance indicated that one reason new businesses and those with revenues of less than $2 million are not desirable customers to banks is the costs of handling their loans. Even though borrowers frequently can bear the cost, some investors do not bother with these loans, preferring to seek out larger deals. The bias of investors against small deals also means that they are not willing to expend much effort to find innovative ways to pass through the higher proportional costs to borrowers. Investors generally approach unfamiliar kinds of borrowers in the same way. Loan review is easier and less expensive in the short run for familiar deals, even if such deals may be relatively less profitable in the long run.

Financial institutions sometimes minimize the up-front costs of evaluating investments by resorting to unfair means of screening potential borrowers. If some individuals of a particular class have been bad risks, they assume that membership in the class is a good (and cheap) screen for risk. Class can be defined by size or age of firm, type of technology, form of organization, location, sex, or race. In the past decade, outright discrimination has diminished, and many community developers now believe that well-constructed proposals for profitable business ventures do not have problems attracting some kinds of capital. Nonetheless, a number of financial institutions still have market definitions and credit policies that lead them to screen out potentially good business and personal loans. Several new studies have found that it is still much harder for blacks to obtain home loans than it is for whites. A Pulitzer Prize–winning story appearing on 22 January 1989 in the *Atlanta Journal and Constitution* included a study of ten million applications for mortgages across the United States and found that there is a pervasive lending gap. The Federal Reserve Bank of Boston also released a report which found that commercial banks and savings and loans had failed to meet their obligations to serve the credit needs of black neighborhoods in Boston.[2]

It is also probably the case that transaction costs on business loans are higher than they need to be. Financial institutions have radically reduced the transaction costs of making car loans and single-family housing loans by making large volumes of loans and standardizing documentation and review, but they are just beginning to investigate ways to standardize business loans. Specialized financial institutions—or even units within financial institutions—reduce transaction costs for small-business loans by creating a cadre of lenders with relevant experience and spreading fixed costs over a lot of activity. There are few of these small-business specialists (other than the Money Store, which is the largest producer of SBA-guaranteed loans to small businesses) operating in the United States.

The lack of liquidity mechanisms for business loans also cuts off access to capital. While studies have found that short-term credit is relatively easy for smaller businesses to obtain, intermediate- and long-term unsecured credit still is not.[3] Smaller businesses find that there are no investors willing to make them long-term loans or to invest in their stock since exit from these investments can be difficult. All but the largest companies are excluded from public markets that provide liquidity for long-term debt. Some medium-sized firms are able to place long-term debt with insurance companies or pension funds, but only for amounts in excess of $1 million. Others must depend on banks that do not make long-term loans unless they can find ways to obtain liquidity, such as through the use of SBA-guaranteed loans that are marketable. Equity is even more difficult to find than long-term debt unless a business has the potential to achieve sales of $100 million or more in five years. Venture capitalists want to be able to exit from their investments in a few years, usually by selling their stock in a public stock offering. This is possible only for a very small minority of new and young businesses.

These capital-market failures have the greatest adverse effect on young, independent enterprises and minorities. Risk aversion, high transaction costs, illiquidity, market concentration, and public regulations make it difficult for small firms to acquire long-term debt and equity. Discrimination, frequently embedded in loan-review criteria, hinders women and minorities who seek to purchase assets. The number of firms and individuals denied capital at market rates or charged more for it than should be necessary is unknown. We only know that it is more than argued by finance professors who preach completely efficient markets and less than asserted by community groups who equate need with creditworthiness. The Industrial Cooperative Association is a technical-assistance organization in Somerville, Massachusetts, which has helped worker cooperatives for more than a decade. According to Steve Dawson, a member of its board, "it is a myth that many low-income businesses exist, or at least are straining to be born, but are held back by a lack of capital, training, and other resources. The reality is that business ownership is substantially outside the experience of most low-income people."[4] The reality is also that job-producing businesses are thwarted for lack of capital or the right kinds of capital.

While the failure of capital markets to provide market-rate capital to projects should be of the gravest concern to society, we also should be concerned if we miss opportunities to improve social welfare by offering capital to projects that compensate for below-market rates of return with social benefits. Since capital markets define productive value through private financial returns, external benefits or costs rarely influence investment decisions. The creation of new jobs by a firm that results in lower unemployment and reduced costs for social services, welfare, law enforcement, and health care is a social consideration rather than a financial one. It can make sense for society to capture these social benefits by carefully intervening in capital markets to improve the attractiveness of investments by providing external subsidies. *Careful* is the watchword here because there is a danger of wasting subsidies on efforts that do not need them or cannot justify them.

Capital-market failures create an important role for development banks in the U.S. financial system. We need a strong response to the failure of capital markets to allocate capital to all investments offering market-rate returns. We also could make much more effective use of capital markets as a means to promote social welfare. Financial institutions dedicated to these tasks—that is, development banks—are most likely to succeed at them. To articulate how development banks should carry out their role requires more knowledge about the markets in which they must compete and survive.

The Current State of Capital Markets

During the past two decades, the United States has seen some of the most profound financial changes in its history. Underlying many of them have been the effects of inflation and disinflation and of large fiscal and trade deficits. At the same time, there has been a wave of deregulation comparable only to the wave of regulation that followed the collapse of the stock market and the banking industry just before and during the Great Depression. A few decades ago, the boundary lines were clear in the nation's financial markets. The bulk of the banking business consisted of checking accounts and relatively simple business and consumer loans. Today, Merrill Lynch offers more checking accounts than all but one commercial bank; General Electric Credit is one of the nation's five largest business lenders; and General Motors is the country's biggest automobile lender.

Faced with increased competition in their home territories, the largest commercial banks and savings and loan associations have sought to offset lowered profits by charging higher fees for services and moving to new loan markets. In the late 1970s, many large commercial banks flocked to Third World debt and oil-drilling loans. In the early 1980s, high-priced condominiums and high-rise developments were the vogue. From the mid-1980s to the end of the decade, the fashion was leveraged buyouts and hostile takeovers. Only in the case of leveraged employee stock ownership plans (ESOPs) has there been anything remotely "developmental" in the new loan markets.[5]

The dramatic increase in the volatility of bank deposits has affected the kinds of loans banks make. In 1933, Congress placed strict curbs on the ability of commercial banks and savings and loan associations to pay interest (particularly unlimited interest) on accounts. Depository institutions persuaded Congress to phase out interest-rate ceilings in the 1980s after they lost several hundred billion dollars to money-market funds when inflation pushed short-term interest rates sky high. While depository institutions today can pay more to attract funds, they also charge more to their customers—banking fees have exploded. In addition, depository institutions are relying more on money brokers and less on loyal core depositors. Money brokers provide "hot" money, that is, funds that can change hands rapidly to get just a bit more yield or flee if their safety is in question. Because their funds are less stable, the banks prefer to make loans with shorter and shorter terms. The most frequent term to maturity of business loans made by commercial banks in 1989 was less than one week.[6]

Interstate banking is another contributor to the financial revolution that has profoundly affected lending activity. Twenty years ago, a business lender—typically a commercial bank—

raised most of its funds through local deposits and made most of its loans to local borrowers. The money was local, it was loaned locally, and the commercial bank evaluated its loan opportunities relative to other local borrowers. If none of them were of sufficient quality or return, the commercial bank bought tax-exempt bonds or Treasury bonds while waiting for better local-loan opportunities. The McFadden Act of 1927 placed the power to regulate the location of banking activities squarely on the doorstep of state governments. They could choose to limit where a commercial bank conducted its business in almost any way desired. And, for decades, states wanted to limit what has come to be known as interstate banking—the collecting of deposits or the making of loans in states other than the headquarters state of the commercial bank. Typically, such restrictions were advocated on the basis of keeping local deposits at home or reducing competition for local bankers from out-of-town commercial banks who might provide more service or make loans on better terms.

In the last decade, many interstate banking restrictions vanished, and those that remained were increasingly avoided through complicated legal maneuvers. Some local commercial banks, recognizing that geographical restrictions were coming to an end, convinced their own legislatures and those of neighboring states to allow mergers between commercial banks in selected regions, particularly in the Southeast, New England, and the upper Midwest. And where not allowed into such regional compacts, some major commercial banks reached special deals with state legislatures that allowed them to locate in a state in return for increasing jobs or lending activities. Most states now have laws allowing, in some fashion, commercial banks from anywhere in the country to operate freely as long as their home state grants reciprocal privileges. Interstate banking has almost arrived. Local areas will be increasingly financed, or not financed, by distant lenders who have no stake in lending in one community over another. While this change will improve the overall flow of capital—it should increase capital availability to growing communities that have not been adequately served by existing financial institutions—it may also lead to a more rapid flight of capital from declining communities and to less room for judgment about borrowers in lending decisions.

The changes in capital markets have reinforced market pricing of assets. The commercial banks' best customers—whether businesses or home buyers or car buyers—have alternative sources of funds, and banks must compete on price. Of even more importance, many loans—both business and consumer—are being made by one financial intermediary and then packaged to be sold to other individual and institutional investors, such as mutual funds, insurance companies, and pension funds. These investors compare the yields and risks on the loans to every other investment choice facing them. Every year, fewer and fewer financial assets are priced independently of what a disinterested investor would pay for them. No financial intermediary that wants to sell its loans is immune to market pricing; even those that do not sell loans are affected. If a financial intermediary charges more than market rates for loans, it will lose its loan customers. If it charges less than market rates for loans, it will earn less than its peers and be unable to raise capital (except possibly from social investors).

Because most loan assets are now priced from the perspective of a disinterested investor, there is less possibility for long-term borrowing relationships, negotiation of terms, or unique deal structuring. Commercial banks at every level are doing more complicated deals, but even these are extremely standardized across a spectrum of borrowers. There is also less leeway to consider local or nonfinancial factors in lending. Assets are priced on a fairly uniform basis across the country.

Another important aspect of the financial revolution is the emergence of indexing. Where once institutional investors carefully sought to pick stocks, increasingly they simply buy a small piece of every stock without regard to its individual merit. This practice, known as indexing, described more than $200 billion of investment by the beginning of 1990. At that time, the two hundred largest pension funds in the United States had already tied 30 percent of their assets to an index.[7] In contrast to those investors who seek out undervalued companies or companies with superior management and products, these passive investors buy stocks indiscriminately. Because they do not need to maintain expensive analysts, purchase expensive research publications, or keep track of the companies, they can offer their services very inexpensively, and they usually deliver better results than most investment managers. The message conveyed by the success of indexing is that judgment may not improve financial results.[8] There is also less opportunity in indexing to consider the social benefits produced by a business.

Many of the transformations in financial markets described above occurred because of the inflation of the 1970s. There had never before been a period when inflation was so unpredictable and volatile. It was the inflation of the 1970s that dealt the first blow to the savings and loan industry. Thrifts could no longer get away with funding long-term mortgage loans with short-term deposits. Hedging interest-rate risk is now a key consideration for most sophisticated investors. Because this cannot always be done, the volatile inflation of the 1970s has also caused a flight to liquidity. Investors are less willing to make long-term investments unless they can be hedged. Thus, along with many of the changes in financial regulation, the other legacies of inflation are the high premium placed upon liquidity in financial markets and the strong desire to avoid the risk of unanticipated volatile movements in the rate of inflation.

The financial revolution has had a very real impact on whether a small business gets a loan to finance its growing sales or a family with modest savings obtains a mortgage. Today, the great majority of business lending is done by financial intermediaries that have formal methods to compare the local business loan to finance inventory with a loan to finance the latest megamerger, or a loan to finance construction of a power plant in Brazil, or a loan to finance the purchase of mortgages made in a distant state. Increasingly, every investment is compared to every other investment on the basis of risk, return, and liquidity and priced accordingly. Using their armies of analysts, the securities firms are checking to see if the banks are making the most profitable decisions. If the stock of a bank does not perform well because it made the wrong kind of loans, the securities firms are eager to raise capital for raiders to take it over. Similarly, the pension funds are watching the securities firms to see that the stocks they selected perform well. If they are not profitable in the short run, the pension fund is likely to fire the investment firm and hire someone, not to pick stocks, but simply to buy them all.

The linkage between all investment decisions is not new, but it has penetrated more deeply into the financial system than was once thought possible. What has changed in capital markets is the margin for judgment, patience, and carefully tailored deals. Prices and money move ever more rapidly. There is more information and more herd behavior. What has become the norm in the world of finance is a desire for large investments, liquid investments, diversification, the ability to hedge risk, the ability to adjust to constant price or interest-rate changes, standard terms, short-term results, and, consequently, the ability to react quickly if short-term results are not pleasing.

Development banks are frequently called upon to make investments that have radically different characteristics. Their investments are small, unfamiliar, illiquid, undiversified, offer risks not easily hedged, need unique terms, and require patient investors. Thus, they must move against the very strong currents in financial markets—away from integration with international markets, expectations of short-term returns, transaction (rather than relationship) banking, and quick decision making.

For development banks to fulfill their economic-development role, they must insulate themselves from many of these changes in the financial markets. A development bank must seek out those investors who are willing to invest with a long time horizon and who are in a position to accept substantial illiquidity. It would hardly be wise for a development bank to sell its common stock to investors who closely monitor quarterly returns and who sell and buy at the earliest indication of troubles or windfall gains. As a result of the changes in financial markets, patience characterizes a declining proportion of today's investors. Unless development bankers create new funding mechanisms that broaden the pool of investors, they will have to place excessive constraints on their own investments. Development banks must also find competitive alternatives to the standard packages offered to borrowers in mainstream financial markets. They must develop products for which they can be adequately compensated and find ways to deliver them more cheaply, manage their risk, and increase their liquidity. Finally, development banks need to deal with the tension between social impact and financial solvency that is inherent in development banking. A growing number of development banks are successfully addressing these issues.

3
Effective Development Banks

To ASSESS whether development banks are performing their important roles in the financial system, we need a standard for effectiveness. Our standard is that an effective development bank produces net economic-development benefits at the lowest possible cost and performs well enough financially to attract and retain capital. Unfortunately, there is not much empirical research on the effectiveness of the existing array of development banks based upon this or any other standard. Some have generated figures on the jobs they have helped create, the number of housing units they have renovated, and the capital they have mobilized; the numbers are impressive. Nevertheless, most development banks have not found the time to review thoroughly their impact relative to the resources they use or to articulate the reasons they have achieved this impact. This makes it difficult to talk about what attributes determine development-bank effectiveness, but not impossible. In our experience, development banks that survive for more than five years and continue to attract capital have certain common "success" characteristics. These same qualities usually were missing from failed development banks.

Fit into an Overall Economic-Development Strategy

A development bank is more likely to be effective if its services are offered as part of a comprehensive development strategy. Greater Richmond Community Development Corporation's loan fund in Richmond, California, had difficulty achieving its goal of reducing poverty and unemployment and promoting commercial revitalization because its minority-business-financing efforts were not accompanied by a strong commercial-redevelopment program and management assistance to minority entrepreneurs.[1] Shorebank Corporation in Chicago had a very similar experience to that of Greater Richmond Community Development Corporation when its commercial-bank subsidiary, South Shore Bank, began to lend to individual minority businesses on the commercial strip in its South Shore neighborhood. In response, Shorebank took on the task of coordinating an overall redevelopment strategy for the strip. A variety of other development banks also have become involved in designing and implementing economic-development strategies, including Kentucky Highlands Investment Corporation in London, Kentucky, Coastal Enterprises in Wiscasset, Maine, and Mountain Association for Community Economic Development (MACED) in Berea, Kentucky.

Cooperative efforts and pooled resources seem also to enhance development impact. Northern Community Investment Corporation (NCIC) in Vermont leverages its resources by working with local financial institutions, the state government, and the business community to promote business development. Northeast Community Federal Credit Union in San Francisco, California, has a much broader scope of activity than would be possible if it did not participate in joint ventures with the Southeast Asia Refugee Resettlement Center, Asian Foundation for Community Development, and the Refugee Business Service Center.[2] A critical element of Shorebank Corporation's housing strategy is the ability of the Neighborhood Institute to piece together dozens of different kinds of financing.[3]

Select Markets Carefully

Development banks that survive tend to pay close attention to the task of targeting services for greatest impact. Perhaps the most important choice faced by the organizers of a development bank is deciding what customers and markets to serve and what products to offer. There are relatively few examples of financial institutions that excel in all markets, and such successes usually involve extremely large firms, such as Citibank. Since most development banks are quite small, it is particularly important that they recognize their limits. When the Austin/West Garfield Federal Credit Union in Chicago decided on its initial mix of services, it knew it would not be able to serve immediately all the needs it had identified and so concentrated on only a few activities.[4]

There is a broad range of markets from which development banks can choose, depending upon local needs and opportunities. Among for-profit businesses, potential users of development-bank capital include new companies not funded by venture-capital funds that need seed capital and subordinated debt. Existing small companies may need what mainstream financial institutions would consider small loans to finance trade-show expenses, subordinated debt to finance expansions, long-term fixed-rate debt, or conventional or government-guaranteed loans not provided by other local lenders. Companies owned by women or racial minorities are also potential markets. Cooperative businesses may have difficulty obtaining capital simply because their organizational structure is unfamiliar and, thus, presents additional transaction costs to all but an experienced development bank. Two markets that straddle the business and consumer market are loans to individuals seeking to become self-employed in a very small business and loans to individuals seeking to join a producer cooperative where each employee must purchase stock in the enterprise. Of course, businesses usually need services in addition to capital, such as night depositories for receipts, payroll services, and business-trust services.

Such nonprofit organizations as community-service groups, churches, hospitals, and educational institutions may need bridge loans or lines of credit to meet the gap between the time funders approve contracts and actually release funds or to tide them over seasonal operating deficits. In these cases, loans can be secured by the funding source that will repay the loan. Nonprofit organizations may also want term loans to purchase fixtures and equipment or property. Those nonprofits that are developers may be interested in the full spectrum of housing and business loans.

Land trusts are a specific type of nonprofit "developer" with unique financial needs. A community land trust (CLT) is a nonprofit corporation whose purpose is to remove land permanently from the speculative market. The trusts acquire land and buildings through gifts and purchase. Some also construct housing on their land. They retain permanent possession of all land, but may sell buildings on it. The trusts make the land available for long-term private use by leasing it under agreements that give substantial security to building owners. If leaseholders wish to move away from the CLT, they may terminate their lease and sell the buildings to the trust under a formula that allows them to recoup their original and subsequent investments in the building, but not earn speculative gains. Community land trusts need loans to finance the purchase and development of land and leaseholder improvements and they need mortgage financing. Many commercial banks are unwilling to make mortgage loans for houses located on leased lands because they do not want restrictions on their rights to resell property.[5] Conservancy trusts, which acquire lands with the express intent of preserving them, may also be a loan market. These trusts have structures similar to community land trusts, but stress environmentally sensitive development. Conservancy trusts (such as the Nature Conservancy and the Trust for Public Lands) and other nonprofit organizations (such as the Girl Scouts of America) acquire or receive land for which they require financing for development and mortgages.

Housing is another target market to be assessed. Single-family mortgage lending in communities where there is redlining (or to specific groups who are discriminated against) clearly fills a capital-market gap. The same can be said for home-improvement loans. Even if mortgage loans are available, a development bank might be able to increase the affordability of housing with new mortgage products, such as graduated-payment mortgages. Development banks can supply home-mortgage products for individual low- and moderate-income families, particularly in conjunction with external programs that provide subsidies to increase mortgage affordability.

Funding the acquisition and rehabilitation of multifamily rental housing fosters community development by improving the physical condition of neighborhoods. Funding local housing developers and managers can also provide housing-related jobs, help build a base of local entrepreneurs who may foster commercial and industrial development, and create wealth for minority residents.[6] Predevelopment, construction, and permanent financing of moderate- and low-income housing projects of for-profit and nonprofit developers—whether co-ops, condominiums, for-profit or nonprofit rental development, SROs (buildings with apartments designed for "single-resident occupancy"), or shelters—may be a viable market for a development bank. However, these banks rarely serve all the needs of housing developers, who must look elsewhere for gap or subsidy financing, such as grants, contributions of land, and long-term rent subsidies.

Another potential market for development banks involves making loans to finance conversions to housing cooperatives and purchases of cooperative units. Because many financial institutions are unfamiliar with housing cooperatives, they do not make loans to them. There are both market-rate and limited-equity cooperatives. In the former, the tenant–shareholders have a share interest in the cooperative and a proprietary lease that entitles them to occupy a particular living unit. Shares can be sold at full market value either by individual unit owners or through the co-op corporation. In a limited-equity housing co-operative, the organization bylaws limit the amount of dividends that can be paid on funds invested in the co-op and the amount of return allowed when shares are sold. The co-op retains the right to repurchase and resell the shares of resident members either at the original value or with only modest appreciation. The bulk of equity accumulated by the co-op is maintained as reserves for its expenditures. Cooperatives need both blanket loans (which finance the acquisition of land and buildings and improvements on entire co-op projects) and loans for the purchase of individual co-op units. Clients for such loans include building-tenant associations, nonprofit corporations that develop or rehabilitate housing, and tenants of mobile-home parks.

Low-income consumers frequently have unmet credit demands. Consumer financial needs that might interest development lenders include education loans, investment services, and depository services. An education or student-loan program serves an important community need and can be profitable for the lender as well. A development bank may offer depository services to residents if such services are not already available at a reasonable cost. People need a safe and accessible place to keep money, a way to obtain cash, and a way to make payments to third parties. The combined effect of branch closings in many urban areas and higher fees and minimum balances on transaction accounts led to a sharp increase in the proportion of consumers without any checking account at all during the 1980s. Even many of the "no-frills" accounts offered by banks are not affordable for low-income people. Consumers may also seek personal loans for a variety of purposes. It is less clear what contribution these loans make to economic development. It is true that reducing the exorbitant cost of consumer loans in most low-income communities will reduce the income drain from these communities and increase local wealth. Whether this is a sufficient basis for including personal loans under the rubric of economic-development lending is debatable.

Development banks can also supply credit and financial or technical services to other financial institutions trying to assist community economic development. They can provide deposits in or loans to these institutions, buy or participate in their loans, or offer them depository or cash-management services. A development bank can also act as a loan packager for other depository institutions, provide check-clearing and data-processing services, or train employees of other institutions. Once a development bank has gained sufficient expertise, it may become the low-cost provider of services to traditional lenders as a means of encouraging them to serve developmental markets. For example, South Shore Bank has in the past acted as a clearinghouse for SBA loans for other commercial banks in exchange for a fee.

Serve Unmet Capital Needs

Development banks must take care to avoid displacing other sources of capital. Mortgages to minorities or small-business loans do not have a net economic-development impact if these kinds of projects can attract funding from mainstream financial institutions. The socially screened mutual funds offer investors the ability to support companies that operate consistently with their values, but they generally do not make a net contribution to economic development. When they buy a publicly traded stock, they simply displace other investors who would be willing to buy the securities at the same price. Mutual funds can invest a small share of their assets in illiquid, high-impact investments, as Calvert Social Investment Fund does. Business-loan funds started by community organizations to provide loans to small businesses have often displaced other investors because they made only secured loans to profitable manufacturing concerns. Charging borrowers market rates of return ensures that a development bank will not attract borrowers who could obtain funds elsewhere, but would certainly accept interest-rate subsidies if they were available.

Development banks can avoid displacing other sources of capital by continually testing the willingness of other investors to serve their markets. A development bank must be willing to move on to new clients when earlier customers gain access to traditional sources of financing. Otherwise, as borrowers mature, a development bank can begin to resemble a mainstream institution. The Institute for Community Economics Loan Fund in Springfield, Massachusetts, helps its borrowers to build up sufficient equity in their real-estate projects so that they can successfully approach mainstream investors. While the fund serves some seasoned borrowers by providing larger loans, it continually seeks new groups for whom its assistance is crucial. When South Shore Bank in Chicago first became a development bank, it offered single-family home mortgages because no other lender was providing these loans to residents of the South Shore neighborhood. Over time, other financial institutions began to offer these loans, and South Shore Bank cut back on this activity.

Avoiding displacement maximizes the development impact of a development bank, but it can undermine it as a financial institution. To ensure its survival, such a bank may need to make some low-risk loans that mainstream financial institutions would approve. This is one of the many areas in which development effectiveness may have to be balanced with sustainability.

Seek Out Development Opportunities

Development banks usually need to play an active role in generating good development opportunities, particularly in communities that have previously not had access to capital from any source. To generate good opportunities, they often must engage in activities that most mainstream financial institutions would consider as outside of their function, such as technical assistance, project development, and advocacy. Kentucky Highlands Investment Corporation, a venture capitalist in London, Kentucky, makes loans and equity investments, teaches business planning at local colleges, helps run a local small-business incubator, provides consulting services, does industrial recruiting, and prepares industrial sites for use.[7] Successful development banks are proactive, but not at the expense of their constituency. They make sure that borrowers are not dependent on them and resist the lure of cultivating new markets at the expense of old ones.[8]

Development banks often create bankable deals by offering technical assistance to prospective borrowers. A technical-assistance program in business planning, market analysis, and investment structuring can attract new customers and enhance the creditworthiness of existing customers. Sometimes one organization provides both technical assistance and capital. For example, the Institute for Community Economics (ICE) Loan Fund is a separate program of ICE, the technical-assistance organization. The institute feels that its technical-assistance capability allows it to make better loan decisions. The downside of this dual role is that it can blur the objectivity of loan decisions and create liabilities for the financial institution. Lenders who have provided extensive assistance to borrowers may be reluctant to turn them down for loans. Borrowers may claim that poor advice contributed to their loan defaults. This is probably a very small risk for housing lenders such as the ICE Loan Fund, but it is a larger risk for business lenders.

A less expensive and more objective alternative is for development banks to rely on external technical-assistance organizations. National Rural Development and Finance Corporation, a technical-assistance and financing group in Washington, D.C., identifies community-based organizations to provide technical assistance. Northern Community Investment Corporation in Vermont and Coastal Enterprises in Maine use publicly supported small-business-development centers. The main disadvantage of this approach is that there is no way to ensure that appropriate technical assistance will be available.

Finally, development banks can create separate technical-assistance organizations. Shorebank Corporation in Chicago has a nonprofit subsidiary, the Neighborhood Institute, which is a developer and social-service organization. The Self-Help Credit Union in Durham, North Carolina, has an affiliate, the Center for Community Self-Help, which provides assistance to worker cooperatives. An independent technical-assistance group can obtain charitable status and accept tax-deductible grants, even if the development bank is a for-profit institution. It can be endowed as part of the initial capitalization drive for the development bank. The technical-assistance organization rather than the development bank can bear the costs of technical assistance, enhancing the viability of the bank. In addition, the potential liability for "poor advice" should be smaller.

Where technical assistance has not been enough to spark the

deal flow, development banks have become developers and started businesses to meet basic community needs. Shorebank Corporation's real-estate-development subsidiary initiated the flow of multifamily rehabilitation projects in the South Shore community in Chicago by undertaking several projects of its own. The success of its development activities attracted private developers. Staff from Kentucky Highlands Investment Corporation (KHIC) in London, Kentucky, have moved on to run business ventures financed by KHIC. Quitman County Development Organization in the north Mississippi Delta started Quitman County Federal Credit Union. It operates in one of the poorest areas in the United States to organize the black community, create institutions responsive to this community, and mobilize local capital. It not only operates a credit union but also has created a laundromat and a thrift store.[9]

Most of the development banks that have attracted substantial assets to their institutions or their clients have also been advocates for their constituencies with investors, financial institutions, and government organizations. Through education, groups like the Institute for Community Economics feel they can convince people to invest more in community development and to accept lower financial returns. By using their credibility as financiers, some older development banks have been able to encourage the federal and state governments to support their activities in community development. For example, the Self-Help Credit Union successfully advocated changes in business-lending rules proposed by the National Credit Union Administration and convinced the government of North Carolina to authorize credit unions to issue what is equivalent to nonvoting capital shares and to provide $2 million in capital to the credit union.

Husband Economic-Development Resources Carefully

Development bankers that have thrived generally have the capacity to assess whether a venture will succeed and the will to turn down loans when ventures are not viable. Publicly funded loan programs, such as the SBA minority-loan program, that have financed marginal service businesses in low-income communities where there is an insufficient market for their products have not helped those communities. Project failures deplete the resources of the development bank and the confidence in a community or a set of borrowers. If development banks have a technical-assistance function, they can choose to work with weak projects to make them fundable; if not, the banks must turn them away.

Development banks are also more likely to survive if they reserve subsidies for cases where they make a big difference. Subsidies not needed to make a housing project affordable or to turn around the economics of a business reduce the funds available to other borrowers and the viability of the bank. Assuming that subsidies are necessary also discourages development lenders from aggressively seeking out socially desirable projects that have the highest possible financial returns.

Housing frequently requires interest-rate subsidies to be affordable for low-income borrowers, but there are projects serving low- and moderate-income families that do not need low-interest debt. The impact of loan price on affordability depends on the size of a loan and its term to maturity. Loan fees to cover transaction costs on small loans can have very little impact on affordability. Higher interest rates on short, bridge loans can also have very little impact on affordability.[10] In addition, it is possible to enhance affordability by properly structuring loan payments, such as through graduated-payment mortgages. Many multifamily mortgages and rehabilitation loans made on properties housing moderate-income residents pay their way at

South Shore Bank. Market rates are charged on the loans, and borrowers are also charged a service fee that covers direct costs of the program.[11]

Interest-rate subsidies on loans to business borrowers are much more difficult to justify than housing subsidies. Mt. Auburn Associates, a development-finance consulting firm based in Somerville, Massachusetts, produced a study of loan funds supported by the U.S. Economic Development Administration (EDA) that found little or no correlation between the interest rate charged to business borrowers and the level of job creation or retention.[12] It is quite likely that interest subsidies have been provided to business ventures because subsidies have been an important element of housing deals and many development lenders started out in housing. However, the economics of typical housing deals is radically different from that of typical business deals. For low-income housing projects, 50 to 80 percent of the venture's expenses might be for interest. In contrast, businesses usually spend far less than 10 percent of revenues on interest.[13] Table 3-1 shows examples of financial statements for a typical housing project and a business. As the table indicates, a 1 percent change in interest rates has a devastating impact on the housing project, but only a marginal effect on the business venture.[14] The impact is smaller because the business has a much lower share of debt on its balance sheet. Businesses that have extraordinarily low sales as a share of assets, high ratios of debt to assets, and small operating margins are affected more by changes in interest costs. Nevertheless, these costs are unlikely to be the deciding factor in the success of most business ventures.

The structure of a loan is much more likely to matter to a business than the loan's cost. If a principal payment is due soon after a loan is made, even at very low interest rates, a company will not be able to use the additional capital for expansion. The most appropriate use of development-bank capital in support

Table 3-1
The Impact of Capital Cost on Project Viability

Housing Deal		*Manufacturing Business*	
ASSETS			
Building	59,000	Cash and securities	500,000
Rehabilitation cost	207,000	Accounts receivable	1,143,000
		Inventory	1,241,000
		Property, plant, and equipment	1,482,490
		Other expenses	633,510
TOTAL	266,000	TOTAL	5,000,000
LIABILITIES AND EQUITY			
Assumed loan (6%, 30y)	29,000	Accounts payable	609,870
		Taxes payable	55,800
2d mortgage (15%, 15y)	93,000	Short-term debt	272,950
City loan (5%, 15y)	82,000	Long-term debt due	
Interest-free, deferred city loan	32,000	In one year	127,090
		Long-term debt	986,630
Equity	30,000	Other debt	650,470
		Capital stock and other stock	876,470
		Retained earnings	1,420,720
TOTAL	266,000	TOTAL	5,000,000
OPERATING STATEMENT			
Gross income	58,320	Net sales	8,207,040
Less vacancy	4,082	Nonoperating income	88,120
Effective gross income	54,238	Less operating expense	7,708,280
Less:		Less interest	159,320
Real-estate taxes	1,700	Income before taxes	427,560
Operations and maintenance	21,600	Plus depreciation	216,566

Table 3-1 (*continued*)

Housing Deal		*Manufacturing Business*	
Net operating income	30,938		
Less:			
Assumed loan	5,756		
Private-sector mortgage	15,620		
City loan	7,781		
Before-tax cash flow	1,781	Before-tax cash flow	644,126

	Effect of 1% Increase in Interest Costs	
	Housing Deal	*Manufacturing Business*
Before-tax cash flow	(1,772)	630,260
Percent change	(200%)	(2%)

Sources: For housing project: adapted from development costs for 1514 Cumberland Road, p. 16 of Michael A. Stegman, *Housing Finance and Public Policy: Case and Supplementary Readings* (New York: Van Nostrand Reinhold, 1986). For business: adapted from U.S. Department of Commerce, Bureau of the Census, *Quarterly Financial Report for Manufacturing, Mining, and Trade Corporations*, Second Quarter 1986, by annualizing and scaling the data for small manufacturing businesses.

of business growth is to maintain market rates of interest while carefully matching the structure of repayments to the growth of the business.

There are development banks that have had a substantial development impact while charging close to market rates to business customers. The Center for Community Self-Help in

Durham, North Carolina, suggests that "an enterprise which is marginal without a deep capital subsidy will be marginal even after the interest subsidy."[15] Many of the microenterprise loan programs initiated in the United States are following the lead of the Grameen Bank of Bangladesh, which has made loans to thousands of businesses while maintaining very low loss rates. The Grameen Bank charges rates that it expects will cover most of its costs on the small loans that it makes to low-income entrepreneurs. The results of the microenterprise loan programs are leading others to reject the use of low interest rates as an incentive for development, but only very slowly.

A development bank that is a depository institution must also pay attention to subsidies it offers to potential depositors. Deposit accounts with no restrictions on size or usage and no fees can be very costly products. According to the Federal Reserve Bank functional cost data for commercial banks with assets between $50 million and $200 million, banks lost $34 per year on each savings account with a balance of less than $200 in 1986. Thus, for every thousand accounts under $200, a commercial bank would lose $34,000. To recover the loss on this product, a development bank might have to charge borrowers higher rates of interest or reduce its lending. Savings from not offering small-saver services of $34,000 annually would cover the cost of a loan officer who could originate twenty-five to fifty development loans each year. There is a trade-off between offering subsidized deposit services and making development loans.

Attract Capable Management Professionals

To have any chance of success, development banks need to have managers who govern professionally and without regard to political pressure. The failure of many government programs has resulted from political decisions on the distribution of funds. The scandal involving the Reagan administration's Department of Housing and Urban Development is a prime example of fraud, but much better intentions can have the same result. Some early loans made by the EDA-funded Southern Mississippi Planning and Development District in Gulfport were made because board members who were elected officials showed great enthusiasm for applicants from their counties.[16] Development banks run by community organizations can be equally susceptible to such considerations.

Managers of successful development banks also have a vision for the bank, a commitment to social change, experience relevant to the deals they intend to make, and credibility in the eyes of potential investors. According to Chuck Matthei, a founder of the Institute for Community Economics in Springfield, Massachusetts, development bankers must be missionaries to attract the capital they need to succeed.

Survive

A viable development bank is one that is able to generate reliably sufficient revenues to cover its costs. A development bank's financial viability demonstrates that it is a sound place for investors to put their capital and that its borrowers and community are creditworthy. If the commercial bank down the street fails, outsiders question the quality of management. However, if the ICE Loan Fund, a key lender to land trusts, failed, outsiders would question the viability of land trusts. Shorebank Corporation bought South Shore Bank from owners who wanted to leave what they viewed as a Chicago community in a spiral of decline. If Shorebank Corporation had failed to restore the bank to profitability, that view would have been confirmed for residents of the community.

Development lenders require significant time to become experienced and effective. When development banks fail, this energy is lost. Also lost are the grants and low-cost capital development banks attract. These grants are not easy to come by, and funders who have financed failed development banks are often reluctant to try again. Community development is a long-term effort best supported by development lenders who plan to be around for the long haul.

Effective development banks are successful at balancing their roles as economic developer and financial institution. The characteristics of effective development banks described in this chapter address both functions. The first four apply more to being an effective development agent; the last three apply more to performing well enough to attract and retain capital. However, all are intertwined, as are the two development-bank roles.

4
Planning and Evaluation

THERE IS a great deal of variety among development banks in goals, objectives, and criteria for evaluating performance. Planning for a development bank is a dynamic process, beginning with an assessment of needs and followed by the establishment of initial goals and objectives that address the needs in a way that fits with the organizers' development philosophy. The process continues with evaluation and revision of goals to reflect changes in needs and in the financial environment.

Development banks that are most clear about what they want to accomplish have the easiest time balancing their community-development and banking roles. Clear goals give a development bank direction and define it for investors and users. Well-articulated objectives guide its organizational strategy and operating plan.[1] Program evaluations provide a means for it to determine whether it is on track and whether its contribution to development justifies the resources it absorbs. The Community Development Finance Corporation (CDFC) in Boston, formed to serve the financing needs of community-development corporations (CDCs), was one of the early experiments with development banking. CDFC's early years were filled with crises that were at least partially the result of confusion about the needs it was designed to meet, its mission, and its goals, including its priorities for financial versus fiscal returns.[2] Resolving this confusion helped CDFC to adopt a more effective development strategy.

Capital-Market Assessments

Development bankers can only establish goals and objectives for economic-development impact if they understand local capital markets well enough to articulate the needs they will meet. Organizers of effective development banks are usually driven by real credit needs with which they are familiar. The Industrial Cooperative Association (ICA) of Somerville, Massachusetts, sought to create a source of funding for the cooperatives to which it already was providing technical assistance. The organizers of the Lower East Side Community Credit Union in New York City sought to replace the services of another financial institution. Because decisions about how to intervene in capital markets are so important, both of these financial institutions used their experience only as a starting point for broader capital-market assessments. Most development banks have produced such assessments. While each one is quite different in scope and detail, the common questions are captured in the following discussion.

Impressions about a community's capital needs are corroborated and augmented through a community survey. The survey helps describe the community's economic base, establish to what degree this base currently supports stable housing and business growth, and suggest what general opportunities or needs are perceived by members of the community. A profile of residents provides a preliminary assessment of the likelihood that mainstream financial institutions are serving local banking needs (by comparing their likely savings levels to bank account minimums and their incomes to housing costs), the likelihood of residents providing deposits or loan funds and feasible amounts, and the income available to community members to repay loans. A housing profile is used to make the preliminary assessment of the affordability of home ownership and rent payments and of the conceivable need for loans based upon both the number of units of various types of housing and home values. A business profile is used to assess crudely the viability of various kinds of business activity in the community, the kinds of firms that may have credit needs, and the likelihood that these businesses can repay any loans they receive. A community-development-organization profile is used to identify local activity in business and housing development, the number and quality of organizations that could work with a development lender in addressing problems, and general impressions (and any studies that have been completed) on capital needs in housing finance, business finance, and consumer-banking services. A financial-institution profile can begin to identify why local financial institutions may not be meeting capital needs. Guided by the findings of the community survey, organizers of development banks are usually able to establish a general goal for the bank, whether it is to provide capital to save or create jobs, improve housing access, or provide savings opportunities for disadvantaged people. Once this decision is made, organizers target a smaller number of markets for further research (usually through surveys and focus groups) on potential customers, the specific characteristics of demand, and the kinds of financial products that can serve the demand.

A capital-market assessment must differentiate between need and demand. While most development-finance professionals agree that there is a great need for capital in communities around the country, they do not agree about whether there is the capacity to use this capital productively. According to Tom Miller of the Ford Foundation, there is a disappointingly low volume of business investments in urban low-income communities of sufficient value to merit the allocation of credit resources. According to South Shore Bank, while there is demand for credit from retail-store owners, financing them has often not been successful. At least for business loans, perceived need and capacity to use credit resources are not always the same. This is why community surveys usually include information on ability to repay loans.

Another important piece of the capital-market assessment is verification that existing financial institutions are unable or unwilling to fill the identified capital gaps. If financial institutions are able (even if unwilling), it may cost less and attract more capital to persuade them to fill capital gaps than to create new organizations. This approach was used successfully by the Mountain Association for Community Economic Development (MACED) in Berea, Kentucky, to expand access to long-term mortgages. It has also worked in a variety of negotiations between community groups and financial institutions. To identify the potential supply of capital to a community from existing sources, development-bank organizers collect information on the powers and capabilities of area financial institutions and their specific programs. Information about individual financial institutions can be found in Community Reinvestment Act statements, Home Mortgage Disclosure Act data bases, pamphlets describing their fees and services, and surveys of particular institutions and customers.

Organizers also have to decide if there is sufficient potential demand to support a development bank. Estimating demand where there has previously been no supply is very difficult. There is most likely to be sufficient demand if estimates of the number of potential customers are many times larger than what a development bank needs. The Connecticut Product Development Corporation (CPDC) dismisses 200 of the 400 inquiries it receives each year immediately, dismisses another 150 after additional time on the phone, looks at 50 or 60 in detail, and invests in 12 to 15 deals. Thus, its projected demand must be at least thirty times greater than its required volume of deals. Sometimes development banks move ahead with substantially less certainty than they would like about the presence of sufficient markets. As Ron Grzywinski of Shorebank Corporation noted in an interview in 1990, "Had we conducted a market survey in 1973 to get a sense of how many potential entrepreneurs we had in the community to buy, rehab, and then manage apartment buildings as small businesses, the answer would have been 'none.' In fact, they were all around us." Access to credit can unleash demand.

Goal Setting: Vision and Compromise

The goals of effective development banks are heavily affected by their assessments of capital needs, but there are other important factors. One is the bank's philosophy of economic development, especially its founders' beliefs about who should benefit from community development and who should own assets produced through these efforts. Strong philosophical stands can shape a development bank's goals more than any other consideration. For example, the Institute for Community Economics Loan Fund in Springfield, Massachusetts, will only provide capital to projects owned by community organizations or cooperatives representing or owned by low-income people. In contrast, Coastal Enterprises in Maine will finance any business enterprise committed to employing and training low-income people.[3]

Development banks frequently have adopted a more inclusive philosophy of economic development than they would ideally prefer to ensure that they have sufficient markets to serve. When the Industrial Cooperative Association in Massachusetts found that assisting completely worker-owned, low-income businesses with strategic local-development impacts set too fine a screen, it added to its market firms with the potential to move toward worker ownership. Northern Community Investment Corporation (NCIC) in St. Johnsbury, Vermont, originally targeted manufacturing businesses. While this is still its primary emphasis (at 45 percent of loans to date), it has expanded its focus to include the service, retail, and tourism sectors. The Center for Community Self-Help in Durham, North Carolina, also resolved this dilemma by establishing primary and secondary financing targets, as did the Santa Cruz Community Development Credit Union of California, whose targets are 60 percent community-development loans and 40 percent personal loans.

Compromises in philosophy are sometimes also necessary to ensure the viability of a development bank. Because emphasizing low-income populations can involve higher costs and higher delinquencies, some development banks decide to serve a mix of income levels, where the lower costs of serving moderate-income customers balance the higher ones of serving their low-income counterparts. The experience of the community-development credit union movement is that credit unions flourish best and demonstrate greatest growth in areas with some middle-income residents.[4] Diverse communities can provide more capital and can afford to pay for more services. According to Hubert Price of Citizens' Coalition Federal Credit Union in Pontiac, Michigan, which failed in 1989, the credit union would have done better to have marketed more to middle-class people to balance the small share accounts of low-income customers.[5]

The goals of development banks usually address a whole set of issues that are independent of capital-market assessments. Common goals of this sort include encouraging other entities to respond to identified capital gaps, serving as laboratories for testing (and then disseminating) development-finance strategies, advocating institutional and policy changes in financial markets that can affect a large number of disadvantaged communities or borrowers, using development resources efficiently, maintaining the viability of the development bank as a financial institution, and being a well-run business where people like to work.

Outcomes and Impacts

Evaluation provides a means for judging whether a development bank is meeting its goals, reveals deficiencies in its objectives, and helps it to keep abreast of changes in financial markets. Development banks also use program evaluations to raise capital and generate support for their constituencies. However, few development banks have undertaken in-depth evaluations. In a survey of twenty business-loan funds, Richard Schramm found that most conduct regular financial audits of operations and loans, but only a few perform evaluations of social impact.[6] Development banks are frequently understaffed, and they cannot raise money to pay for outside evaluations of their impact.

There are some development banks that have dedicated significant resources to evaluation. The Industrial Cooperative Association hired a consultant to develop a detailed evaluation plan and perform the evaluation. The association continues to prepare an annual impact evaluation internally, but it is hard to find the time, energy, or money to hire an outside evaluator.[7] Northern Community Investment Corporation in Vermont makes a yearly assessment of the number of jobs created or preserved, total annual payroll generated, real-estate taxes generated, and impact on county unemployment levels. This level of evaluation is not common.

The issues an evaluation ideally should address include appropriateness of goals, effectiveness in attaining them (outputs and impacts), and efficiency in using resources.[8] *Output* is the quantity of services provided; *impact* is the effect of these activities on community economic development. Output measures include dollars loaned, number of loans, number and dollar amount of loans leveraged from other sources, number of businesses assisted in other ways, and types of assistance. Measures of the efficiency with which outputs are produced include cost per loan, loans as a share of assets, loan turnover, rate of loan repayment, income from loans as a share of total costs, and profitability. Loans as a share of assets and loan turnover indicate how fully a development bank has been able to invest its capital. The rate of repayment indicates whether borrowers were able to use funds lent them. Profitability measures a development bank's success in covering its costs and whether the institution will be able to respond to long-term economic-development needs.[9]

For a development bank whose goal is job creation, impacts include number of businesses started or expanded, number of jobs created, viability of the businesses, type and quality of jobs, race, gender, and income level of employees, job training offered, multiplier effects (i.e., jobs indirectly created at other businesses), and the wage level of jobs created. Measures of efficiency in producing these impacts include the total cost per job created (including all transaction costs, loan losses, and interest subsidies) and the jobs created per loan.[10] For a development bank whose goal is housing, impacts include number of units of housing created or renovated, number of bedrooms per unit, the cost of units to residents, and the income level, race, and gender of tenants. The cost per unit of housing provided is the measure of efficiency in producing these impacts. For a development bank whose goal is enhancing the economic access of disadvantaged people, impact might be measured by changes in the rate or level of their savings.

Some outputs and impacts are not readily quantifiable. One example is the innovativeness of the bank in creating new products and in finding new markets. Other examples are increasing local control or self-reliance, development of new leadership, and changing perceptions of community lenders and borrowers. As pointed out in a 1990 interview by Katherine Gross of the Industrial Cooperative Association Loan Fund, "How do you judge the impact of a woman never employed not only getting a job, but also being active on the board of her own company?" These are impacts of primary importance to advocates of community ownership.

Without more and better program evaluation, it will continue to be difficult to determine the impact of development banking, and this will limit the amount of capital that development banks collectively can attract. There will not be much more program evaluation until funders demand it and pay for it.

5
Models That Serve Development

DEVELOPMENT BANKERS have chosen from a wide array of financial-institution models. Commercial banks, savings and loan associations, community-development credit unions, community-development loan funds, microenterprise loan funds, and royalty-investment funds all have advantages and limitations. Two of the best-known development banks (Shorebank Corporation in Chicago and the Self-Help Credit Union in Durham, North Carolina) have carefully examined the different alternatives. However, in most cases, development-bank organizers have selected a model because of one consideration, usually its familiarity or accessibility. Accessibility (including the cost of starting up) is a very important factor to consider, but it cannot be the only one. Many of the business-loan funds supported by the Economic Development Administration failed in the 1970s because they chose to provide high-risk, venture-capital-like investments through the structure of a low-interest loan fund. While these loan funds were relatively easy to create, they were not suited to serving the target credit needs. What credit activities a model permits is a factor that must be considered, as are access to subsidies, access to and cost of capital, the feasibility of compensating organizers for their time, and community orientation. One other important factor—the volume of activity required to attain self-sufficiency—is not discussed here because it is the subject of its own chapter.

Permitted Activities

A type of financial institution can only be effective as a development bank if its powers and capabilities match community needs. For example, if one of a development bank's goals is providing checking and savings accounts to low-income people, then commercial banks, savings and loan associations, and credit unions all can be powerful models. These depository institutions all have the capability to provide such accounts and can insure depositors against loss of principal and interest. If the primary goal of the development bank is providing these services to low-income people, then a community-development credit union (CDCU) may be the best choice among the depository institutions. Sustainable at a much smaller scale of activity than the other depository institutions, CDCUs generally have lower overhead and can afford to service more small accounts, and they are particularly well suited to do the necessary community outreach to encourage low-income members to increase their savings.

If offering savings services is only one of several goals, then the choice between the three depository institutions should be based upon their ability to provide the kinds of capital needed. Commercial banks have the broadest lending powers among the depository institutions. They can make any kind of loan and, in some states, they can also invest in real estate, underwrite securities, and sell insurance.[1] Many financial services that commercial banks themselves cannot provide can be obtained from bank subsidiaries or affiliates. Nonbanking activities permissible for subsidiaries of banks and bank holding companies (firms that own banks) include direct real-estate investment, funding community-development corporations and small-business-investment companies, some other equity investments (so long as they result in control of no more than 5 percent of the voting stock of the company receiving the money), consulting services to depository institutions, and consumer financial counseling.[2]

While savings and loan associations have essentially the same kinds of lending powers as commercial banks, they are subject to numerical limitations that make them less flexible models. For example, commercial and industrial loans for national savings and loan associations can be no more than 10 percent of assets, and mortgage loans for nonresidential property can be no more than four times their total capital. In addition, under the Financial Institutions Reform, Recovery, and Enforcement Act of 1989, savings institutions must meet a qualified-thrift test by investing 70 percent of their assets in loans related to real estate (although this basket can include some consumer, education, small-business, and nonprofit-institution-construction loans) or lose their branching rights, thrift powers, thrift tax benefits, and access to loans from the Federal Home Loan Bank.[3] While some state S&Ls had much wider powers in the past, they are now essentially limited to the activities permitted for federal associations. All S&Ls can invest 3 percent of their assets in service corporations that engage in activities reasonably related to savings and loan association business, as long as one-half of the excess over 1 percent of assets is invested for community-development purposes.[4]

S&L holding companies have broader powers than commercial-bank holding companies, and some of these powers can be quite useful for development banking. Savings and loan holding companies that own only one savings and loan association (and so long as that S&L itself is a qualified thrift lender) are almost free of restrictions on activities of their nonbank subsidiaries.[5] Multithrift holding companies (those that own more than one savings and loan association) can acquire, develop, or manage real estate, underwrite credit insurance, and prepare tax returns. They can undertake any nonbank activity permissible for bank holding companies. In addition, because S&L holding companies are excluded from the federal Glass-Steagall Act, which separates banking and securities activities, they can even form separate securities subsidiaries. However, the thrift regulators have from time to time placed limits on securities activities. While these powers of savings and loan holding companies could be useful, they must be weighed against the disadvantages of the poor reputation of the savings and loan industry, as well as the likelihood of continuing changes in regulatory structure as the savings and loan crisis continues.

Most community-development credit unions are small and, therefore, concentrate on small, straightforward personal loans. However, if their assets grow sufficiently, CDCUs can also offer education loans, first-lien mortgage loans (for up to 25 percent of assets), second-mortgage loans, home-improvement loans, first-lien mobile-home loans, loans for the purchase of housing co-op shares, loans for business purposes, and federal or state insured or guaranteed loans.[6] With some exceptions, federally insured state credit unions have lending and investment powers similar to those of federal credit unions.

Business and organizational lending is more restricted for credit unions than for other depository institutions. A federally insured credit union's aggregate construction or development lending cannot exceed 15 percent of its reserves, and no one borrower may receive member business loans exceeding 15 percent of a credit union's reserves or $75,000, whichever is higher.[7] For federal credit unions, if the borrower is a corporation, a loan can only exceed the shareholdings of the borrower in the credit union if the loan is made jointly to the business and to one or more individual members in the credit union who own a majority interest in the business. If the borrower is an association, the loan must be made jointly to the association and a majority of the members of the association. Limits on loans that exceed shareholdings of the borrower vary for state-chartered credit unions.[8]

In addition to being drastically more limited in their business-lending capabilities, credit unions can form fewer affiliates or subsidiaries to complement their services. What they can do, with National Credit Union Administration (NCUA) approval, is form, alone or with other credit unions, credit-union-service organizations (CUSOs) to provide members with credit cards, check cashing, ATM services, consumer mortgage loans, data and loan processing, financial planning and counseling, securities and real-estate brokerage, travel-agency programs, insurance, and personal-property leasing.[9]

While credit unions may be at a disadvantage relative to other depository institutions in their range of activities, they are usually better suited to make very small loans. The fixed costs related to producing one loan at a credit union are generally smaller than they are at the other depository institutions. Commercial banks and savings and loan associations balk at making $25,000 business loans. Many bankers believe that a loan of less than $100,000 guaranteed by the Small Business Administration is not cost effective. Almost all of the other models are better suited than commercial banks and savings and loan associations to make predominantly small loans.

None of the depository institutions may be appropriate models if a development bank wants to provide what the market judges to be relatively high-risk or illiquid capital, or to lend a large share of its capital to a few borrowers. Regulatory considerations make it quite difficult to combine insured depository services with high-risk lending. Regulators expect depository institutions to incur annual losses of less than 1 percent of total loans. Since they cannot participate in the profits of borrowers, they cannot offset losses on some loans with large gains on others.[10] Depository institutions are also limited in the amount of their capital that they can lend to any one borrower. While they can make long-term loans, they usually limit such lending to markets where they can sell the loans because they are required to maintain a high level of liquidity in their loan portfolios. Credit unions have perhaps more regulatory baggage than other kinds of depository institutions. When credit-union insurance was instituted in 1972, the National Credit Union Administration quickly shut down almost one hundred low-income credit unions because they had insufficient reserves to be eligible for insurance.[11] In 1984, NCUA capped loans at $1,000 at Mississippi's Quitman County Federal Credit Union to reduce risk. Shortly thereafter Quitman's loan-to-asset ratio fell to 23 percent. In 1989, NCUA decided to limit nonmember deposits in credit unions to 20 percent of total deposits because of its concern about risk taking and fraud at credit unions. The restriction applied to every credit union, including Quitman County Federal Credit Union, even though it had just received high ratings from NCUA for safety and soundness.[12]

The development banks that do not offer insured deposits—community-development loan funds (CDLFs), microenterprise loan funds (MLFs), and venture funds, such as royalty-investment funds (RIFs)—have much more discretion to accept credit and liquidity risk. If they can find a way to manage the risk, these "development funds" can base their terms of investment on their understanding of the economics of a project, its fit within their own portfolio, and its contribution to meeting the financial needs of their own investors. They can be more flexible about terms (e.g., interest only, balloons, subordinated loans, varying royalty rates, etc.). Several of the loans made by the Delaware Valley Community Reinvestment Fund in Philadelphia are for five years, with fifteen-year amortization schedules.[13] These loans would not be considered prudent for a commercial bank, even if they made economic sense given local conditions. The development funds can be more liberal than depository institutions in the kinds of collateral they accept. They also have no regulatory limits on amounts that can be lent to one borrower, and they use this flexibility to make very large investments relative to the size of their total portfolio if the benefits are clear and the risk is reasonable.

While the development funds are free to accept more risk, some of them are restricted in how they can manage it. Community-development loan funds, microenterprise loan funds, and royalty-investment funds that obtain 501(c)(3) tax exemptions from the Internal Revenue Service are restricted from making loans that the private sector would deem profitable. While the terminology in the IRS regulations is ambiguous, it makes it hard for 501(c)(3) loan funds to make market-rate, bankable loans in order to subsidize the costs or offset the risk of developmental lending.

Even without external regulation of risk, all development banks are ultimately subject to the implicit direction that accompanies having outside investors. To maintain the confidence of social investors, CDLFs must either carefully avoid loan defaults, attract large grant reserves to absorb any losses, or charge borrowers rates of interest high enough to cover losses. The Institute for Community Economics (ICE) Loan Fund in Springfield, Massachusetts, which is mainly a housing lender, seeks to sustain small losses. The Industrial Cooperative Association (ICA) Loan Fund in Somerville, Massachusetts, which is a business lender, holds large grant reserves. There are no loan funds that deal with this constraint by charging borrowers rates of interest that fully compensate for very large anticipated losses. Microenterprise loan funds also try to keep loan losses low, generally between 2 and 5 percent of loans outstanding. The Grameen Bank of Bangladesh, a very successful microenterprise lender, has losses of about 2 percent of total loans. Programs in the United States have made too few loans to judge results; because they are highly experimental, loan losses may be as high as 10 percent in the early years. If the model is to prove broadly useful, loss rates must eventually reach 2 to 5 percent. Royalty-investment funds, as with most venture funds, can sustain relatively large losses and make up for them with gains on other investments in their portfolios. It would not be unusual for one-fourth to one-third of the projects of a RIF to produce no revenues at all.

There are market niches that each of the development funds serves by choice. Royalty-investment funds and CDLFs generally try to meet wholesale rather than retail needs (that is, they make loans to organizations, not individuals). Community-development loan funds most often finance housing, including up-front project costs, construction, rehabilitation, bridge loans, and "permanent" financing in the form of medium-term loans with balloons. Some also provide worker-equity loans and business loans for working capital and equipment purchase. A few focus on a single market. The Institute for Community Economics Loan Fund favors loans to community land trusts. The New Hampshire Community Loan Fund, in Concord, commonly finances renters' acquisition of mobile-home parks. The Industrial Cooperative Association Loan Fund helps producer cooperatives and employee-owned businesses contemplating cooperative ownership. Loans usually are in the range of $5,000 to $50,000, but some are $100,000 or more. The loans tend to be for relatively short terms (one to five years) because loan maturities are matched to the maturity of funds raised. However, many loans are amortized over longer periods.

Such royalty-investment funds as the Connecticut Product Development Corporation, in Hartford, serve the needs of new and growing businesses for patient capital. While there are no limitations on who can receive a royalty grant from RIF, client businesses usually must have the potential to achieve growth in sales equal to ten or twenty times the royalty investment within ten years. Royalty-investment funds make high-risk investments (in the range of $100,000 to $500,000) and usually do not require collateral; investments sometimes extend beyond ten years.

Microenterprise loan funds only lend to individuals or members of small solidarity groups made up of individual microentrepreneurs. By design, MLFs make loans for purchases that will greatly increase the productivity of a business in a short time. They generally make short-term loans (less than one year) with frequent payments (weekly or monthly); loans tend to be from $1,000 to $10,000. Microenterprise loan funds make a large number of small loans.

Access to External Support

External programs that help manage risk, transaction costs, and liquidity can substantially enhance a development bank's impact. The most appropriate model is the one with the best access to required external support. Development banks with the goal of redressing deep-seated social ills need a model that has maximum access to direct subsidies and cost-savings programs. Development banks that aim to provide market-rate capital where it has not previously been available should be able to operate without direct subsidies. They can still improve their effectiveness by choosing a model that has access to external programs that reduce their cost and risk of doing business.

The ease of access to subsidies is mainly determined by whether a development bank is a nonprofit 501(c)(3) organization. This status provides both a clear statement of social purpose and access to tax-deductible contributions. Community-development loan funds and microenterprise loan funds are usually formed as 501(c)(3) charitable organizations. They frequently obtain program-related investments (PRIs) from foundations and grants from governments, foundations, religious organizations, and individuals. Electing to be this kind of tax-exempt organization also increases the income retained by the development bank, which would otherwise be paid in taxes (of course, there must be a surplus or profit for this to be relevant). Even though they are not 501(c)(3) organizations, credit unions also are exempt from federal and state corporate-income taxes. Not surprisingly, this is a source of ongoing controversy with banks and savings and loan associations, which have watched credit unions expand rapidly during the past decade.

While they cannot be 501(c)(3) organizations, depository institutions can have an affiliated 501(c)(3) organization that accepts tax-deductible grants to fund development activities related to the depository institution. For example, Shorebank Corporation in Chicago formed the Neighborhood Institute, which, among other activities, trains entrepreneurs and runs a business incubator. The Self-Help Credit Union in Durham, North Carolina, is affiliated with the Self-Help Venture Fund, another 501(c)(3) organization, which accepts grants specifically to provide reserves for higher-risk lending by the credit union.

Depository institutions also can attract subsidies in the form of below-market capital and donations of time and equipment. Those that focus on community development frequently have programs through which investors are offered savings accounts that pay below-market rates, where the concession is passed on to borrowers or retained to cover the costs of development activities. These are known as "linked deposit" programs. New CDCUs often receive donations of staff time, space, and furniture and fixtures from sponsoring community organizations and local businesses. Although it is rare, financial institutions sometimes donate technical assistance, employee training, and correspondent-bank services to CDCUs. As a result of tough negotiations, a handful of commercial banks that have closed branches in low-income communities have given CDCU organizers grants to pay for feasibility studies, donated branch buildings, and provided seed deposits at low or no interest.

Depository institutions have much better access than development funds to government programs that can lower the costs of financing development. They can use loan-guarantee and insurance programs offered by the Small Business Administration (SBA), Federal Housing Administration (FHA), Veterans Administration (VA), Economic Development Administration (EDA), and state student-loan authorities. They have access to state and local loan-guarantee programs. They are eligible to use secondary markets administered by the Federal National Mortgage Association (Fannie Mae), the Federal Home Loan Mortgage Corporation (Freddie Mac), the Student Loan Marketing Association (Sallie Mae), and private securities firms that make markets in SBA-guaranteed loans and FHA-insured loans. Credit Union National Administration (CUNA), the national trade association for credit unions, also has a mortgage corporation that pools credit-union mortgages and sells them in the secondary markets.

In reality, these programs are seldom used by community-development credit unions, and they constrain those commercial banks and savings institutions that do employ them. Community-development credit unions usually do not make large enough loans—or a sufficient number—to meet the requirements of the guarantee or secondary-market programs. Commercial banks and savings institutions can only use these programs if they produce standardized loans with designated underwriting criteria. Thus, the programs are only appropriate for that portion of the development bank's portfolio that most closely resembles traditional banking services.

Even though development funds generally cannot use these programs at all, they have access to an array of smaller and less visible programs in some states. There are community-development and housing programs at all levels of government in which loan funds may participate. The National Association of Community Development Loan Funds (NACDLF), in Philadelphia, is attempting to create some form of secondary market for the loans of its members. The Community Reinvestment Fund, in Minneapolis, has already created a secondary-market mechanism for loan funds in Minnesota, and is expanding to Wisconsin, Michigan, and other states. In the long run, the Good Faith Fund, a microenterprise loan fund in Pine Bluff, Arkansas, hopes to sell its loans to Elkhorn Bank, a fellow affiliate of Southern Development Bancorporation. Other loan funds have also found individual buyers for their loans.

Access to and Cost of Capital

There needs to be a match between the kinds of capital required to serve a market and the access a bank has to capital. The amount and type of capital a development bank needs depends upon the size of the markets it will serve and its goals and objectives for serving them. Development banks intending to tap a market that requires a large amount of funds need to choose a model that can attract significant capital. Those intending to provide venture capital need to be able to attract equity. Development banks that need heavily subsidized capital must choose a model that can attract grant funds. Because the models do not all offer the same access to capital, the choice matters.

The most significant difference in ability to attract capital is between the depository institutions and the development funds. Commercial banks, savings and loan associations, and credit unions have access to virtually unlimited debt funds because of federal deposit insurance. With careful attention to the rules limiting insurance to $100,000 per account, depository institutions can offer customers essentially risk-free deposits and investments at the same time that they are making loans that have credit risk. Relative to their value in attracting funds, insurance rates are a bargain. Greater access to debt capital does not necessarily translate into greater development impact. Depository institutions cannot lend out as large a proportion of their capital as can development funds because of reserve and liquidity requirements. A depositor cannot expect a commercial bank to lend out much more than 70 percent of its deposits. Community-development loan funds, and certainly mature venture funds, can lend out or invest 90 percent or more of their funds. Depository institutions are also less well suited to serve what are perceived by the market to be high-risk development markets.

Access to insured deposits is more limited for community-development credit unions whose entire community of membership is low income. These credit unions find it difficult to attract deposits, and nearly two-thirds of their share balances are less than $500. The members with the lowest balances are among the heaviest users of CDCU services.[14] However, CDCUs are allowed to solicit, and need, insured deposits from nonmembers for up to 20 percent of their total deposits. In addition, CDCUs can choose to serve communities with a more diverse resident base and attract deposits from their middle-class members.

For commercial banks and savings and loan associations owned by stockholders, there is a cost of unlimited access to insured deposits. These financial institutions are required by regulators to attract several millions of dollars of equity capital. These illiquid, long-term investments are difficult to attract even for mainstream financial institutions. Credit unions and mutual savings and loan associations do not have initial equity requirements. However, they are required to retain a set share of earnings each year to slowly build up equity, and they must restrain their loan activity until equity does grow. New and small credit unions and mutual savings institutions face a dilemma—they need equity to grow, and they need to grow to generate equity.

Community-development loan funds and microloan funds have a more difficult time raising debt capital and an equally difficult time for equity capital. For debt capital, they must rely on loans from investors that are not insured by any agency and that are not secured by collateral. What protection exists derives from the underlying collateral on the loan fund's loans, the existence of loan-loss reserves, and the competence of management. The Institute for Community Economics Loan Fund, one of the best known, had assets of $11 million in its twelfth year of operation. In contrast, the Vermont National Bank, with its insured Socially Responsible Lending Fund, attracted more than $30 million in deposits in its first year of activity. The nonprofit loan funds meet their initial equity needs by attracting deductible contributions. They have been successful in attracting grants for reserves or loans at very low or no interest from which income earned could be allocated to reserves, but many operate with less equity than they would like. The most severe problems in attracting appropriate capital are faced by the loan funds serving low-income businesses. To make their high-risk, low-return loans, they should be funded mainly with equity or grants. Because funders are more willing to provide short-term loans, these loan funds struggle with a continuing mismatch between their sources and uses of funds.

Most capital for microenterprise loan funds has come from grants and very-low-interest loans from government agencies and foundations. Both the Women's Self-Employment Project and the Self-Employment Circle Fund in Chicago have received Job Training Partnership Act (JTPA) funds; the former also received funding from the Chicago Department of Economic Development. Several state governments, including those of North Carolina and Arkansas, have also funded such loan funds. As long as self-employment continues to appeal to foundations and local governments, microenterprise loan funds will be able to attract capital. This leaves them with a very uncertain future, unless they become more like community-development loan funds in their capacity to use loans from social investors. In fact, in 1988 Acción International started a successful program to attract funds from individual investors for an International Loan Guarantee Fund. The investments of $10,000 or more have terms of 2.5 years or longer and earn 5 percent.

Because of the kinds of funding they provide, capital raised by royalty-investment funds must be in the form of equity. For-profit RIFs compete with other venture funds for investors by offering the potential for comparable after-tax rates of return and by demonstrating past performance of their management in venture investing. Several small venture funds with social screens have been able to sell limited-partnership interests to private investors. Not-for-profit funds might seek support similar to that given to the Connecticut Product Development Corporation, that is, grants based upon their anticipated job-creation benefits and loans with open repayment terms (really another form of equity investment). There are few nonprofit venture funds because there are few funders willing to make commitments of millions of dollars.

Development bankers must also consider the cost of capital. Because of federal insurance, depository institutions do not pay much more than the federal government for their debt. However, the market rate for insured deposits is still higher than the rate paid by many community-development loan funds and most microenterprise loan funds. Frequently, CDLFs pay less for long-term loans than the rate for short-term insured deposits at depository institutions. This is a tribute to their performance and marketing efforts. If their performance worsens, or if one loan fund has significant loan losses, funding costs are likely to rise for all CDLFs. Their low interest rates have limited their pool of investors to far below that of commercial banks, but the current economics of CDLFs and microenterprise loan funds requires that they continue to attract below-market sources of capital to survive.

Equity investors in for-profit development banks expect much higher rates of return. Commercial banks and S&L investors expect rates of return on their stock higher than 15 percent. However, some development-oriented commercial banks have been able to attract investors who are willing to accept much lower returns or to have earnings contributed to support specific development activities and not paid out to investors. For-profit royalty-investment funds should be able to offer rates of return similar to those of venture-capital funds that do deals at the same level of risk. They offer investors potential returns on investment of at least 20 percent.

What It Takes to Start Up
There is a great deal of difference among the models in the cost and difficulty of starting up. The amount of capital that development-bank organizers think they can attract to cover these costs commonly determines which model they choose. Commercial banks and savings and loan associations require the most start-up capital. The out-of-pocket organizational and preoperating expenses of creating or purchasing a commercial bank—charter and incorporation fees, legal and professional fees, printing, and salaries—generally range from $85,000 to $190,000. Costs are generally lower for state charters, experienced organizers who do not need as much legal help or ones who get it pro bono, and stock offerings that attract a few large investors. For example, Community Capital Bank, a development-oriented commercial bank in New York City, received pro bono legal and investment-banking services. Other assist-

ance was obtained at fees below what is usually charged. The organizational costs of buying a commercial bank or savings institution are likely to be of much the same magnitude as for a start-up. Organizational fees will be lower, but search and negotiating expenses will be higher.

Start-up costs for credit unions are substantially lower than for other depository institutions because less legal work, market research, and detailed financial projections are required. The main preopening costs for CDCUs are organizing volunteers, conducting a pledge drive, and preparing a feasibility study. Newly chartered federal credit unions pay no chartering fee to regulators and no operating fee until the year following the first full calendar year after the date they are chartered.[15] If volunteers prepare and carry out the member surveys, get commitments for participation on the board and committees, and prepare the business plan, out-of-pocket chartering and organizing expenses can be as low as $1,500 (to pay for printing, meeting, telephone, and filing costs). While many credit unions have started without these expenditures, computer systems and leasehold improvements are desirable; including these costs raises total preopening costs to at least $5,000. If staff is hired to coordinate the start-up, the cost could rise to $10,000 or more. This is the amount raised by Austin/West Garfield Credit Union to fund its start-up. If technical-assistance providers are hired to coordinate organizing the credit union, the cost (which may be funded by a grant) could be as much as $20,000. The time donated by volunteers is likely to have an equal or greater value since starting a credit union requires a great deal of volunteer effort.

For loan funds, start-up costs are also dominated by organizer time (and, on occasion, legal fees). Organizers of loan funds are frequently able to arrange for a donated staff person. If they cannot, the cost might be $10,000 to $20,000 for a half-time person for six months. Community-development loan funds also form volunteer committees to do staff work; the value of the volunteers' time is probably $30,000 or more. Legal services to determine local registration requirements are unavoidable unless another loan fund has already conducted such a review. If they are not secured pro bono, such services can cost $20,000. If a loan fund needs to register its securities, legal expenses can exceed $50,000. Other small costs include space, telephone, postage, printing, and filing fees for incorporation and for establishing tax-exempt status (which can cost as little as $200); with donated time and services, out-of-pocket costs are often less than $1,000.

If organizers take a very active role (e.g., preparing the business plan and offering memorandum) in organizing a venture fund, such as RIF, start-up costs can be kept to about $30,000 for professional fees, marketing costs, and a limited number of state registrations for the securities of the fund. A nonprofit fund that receives legal services pro bono and avoids registration requirements might have out-of-pocket costs below $10,000. The costs of organizers' foregone income might be $50,000 to $200,000, depending on the speed and efficiency with which business planning occurs.

While it seems to take all development-bank organizers one to two years to open their doors, quite different activities absorb their time during this period. The most significant differences in start-up requirements are between the depository institutions and the development funds. All three kinds of depository institutions must obtain charters from public agencies. It is fairly common for applicants to be turned down by regulators or by the federal agency that insures their deposits. For example, after a multiyear organizing drive, the Community Capital Bank in New York City was initially turned down by the Federal Deposit Insurance Corporation (FDIC) because its proposed senior officials did not have sufficient banking experience.

In contrast, loan funds and venture funds, like royalty-investment funds, only need incorporate under the laws of their state (or, if a RIF chose to be structured as a limited partnership, it would have to file partnership documents). Many funds also apply for exemption from federal taxes under section 501(c)(3). Funds that take this approach are likely to be exempt from Securities and Exchange Commission (SEC) securities-registration requirements for the time being, but they may still need to register securities at the state level and comply with regulations that apply to individuals, such as truth- and fairness-in-lending laws. In California, for example, charitable organizations that borrow money from individuals to achieve their purpose are not exempt from state securities laws.[16] The Northern California Community Loan Fund required more than $100,000 worth of pro bono legal services to comply with the state securities-registration requirement.

Commercial banks and savings and loan associations face an extra hurdle because they must meet an initial equity-capital requirement within a set number of months or lose the chance to proceed. The minimum required equity capitalization for new commercial banks depends on their location, population, experience of organizers, and regulator. However, it is rarely less than $1 million plus start-up expenses. This was the amount of capital raised by Blackfeet National Bank on the Blackfeet Reservation in Browning, Montana. In metropolitan areas, the Office of the Comptroller of the Currency (OCC) prefers that national-bank applicants have initial capitalization greater than $3 million. The majority of initial capital must consist of common stock and preferred stock. New national S&Ls and state thrifts insured by the Savings Association Insurance Fund (SAIF) must have minimum capital stock of $2 million if the population of their area is less than 50,000 and capital of $3 million otherwise. New mutual S&Ls must have pledged savings of the same amounts. Generally, initial capital is required to consist of common stock and perpetual preferred stock.

Credit unions must make a quite different showing of commitment of "equity capital" before they receive a charter. Members are considered shareholders, and credit-union organizers are required to show that they have sufficient member interest to sustain the credit union. Organizers must also demonstrate that a minimum number of members will subscribe soon after the issuance of a charter by gathering nonbinding pledges of support from prospective members. Most applications prepared with the assistance of the National Federation of Community Development Credit Unions (NFCDCU) in New York City have 300 to 500 pledges. Regulators unofficially prefer membership pledges of closer to 1,000 people.[17]

Credit unions, CDLFs, and microenterprise loan funds do not have initial equity requirements, but they still need some initial equity to cover operating costs until they begin to generate income. The Austin/West Garfield Federal Credit Union formed to serve several low- and moderate-income neighborhoods in Chicago decided it would need grants of $50,000 per year for several years. In fact, these financial institutions are likely to need grants equal to their operating costs for at least their first two years of operations, plus the amount they must set aside for loan-loss reserves. Initial capital grants (or donated services) for a community-development loan fund should probably be at least $200,000. Most CDLFs grow more organically and begin with only enough capital to see them through their first year, perhaps $100,000.

There are also no legal requirements for minimum-equity capitalization for royalty-investment funds, but they are unlikely to be profitable if they are capitalized for less than $7 million.

The Feasibility of Compensating Organizers for Their Time

Even entrepreneurs with social goals may need to be compensated for the large block of time that it takes to form a development bank. The degree to which organizers can be compensated for their time and out-of-pocket costs varies dramatically among the financial-institution models. For community-development loan funds, microenterprise loan funds, and credit unions, the means are very limited. For commercial banks, savings and loan associations, and royalty-investment funds, they are quite extensive. The differences between these two groups are mainly due to differences in how they are owned and their tax status.

Loan funds can only compensate organizers if they raise funds for this purpose up front. Predevelopment grants for loan funds are very hard to find, and loan-fund organizers are reluctant to approach people who they will need to ask for far larger sums later on. Nonprofit loan funds are not permitted to compensate organizers by promising to share future earnings with them, and most funders would not allow them to use initial capital to reimburse organizer costs. This is one reason that loan funds rely on donated time and money to cover organizing expenses. Organizers are compensated for their time with the satisfaction of their contribution. Outside funders who finance out-of-pocket costs also cannot expect a financial return.

The situation is not substantially different for credit unions. If its charter is approved, members who pay for out-of-pocket organizing costs can be reimbursed by the credit union for reasonable expenses.[18] However, a credit union that expects to grow slowly would not want, or be able, to incur this expense. The time of organizers must either be donated or funded by a third party that expects no financial compensation. For employee credit unions, employers absorb these costs; for associational credit unions, affiliated large organizations absorb these costs. For low-income credit unions, however, there is usually no such obvious benefactor.

Commercial banks can provide market-rate compensation to organizers and investors who finance organizing expenses, even though regulators prefer that organizers have the financial wherewithal to fund organizing costs and donate their time. The Office of the Comptroller of the Currency allows national banks to compensate organizers for their time so long as the terms of the compensation are revealed to other investors. Organizers can be paid for their time, after the bank opens, with stock on the same terms as other investors or with cash equal to their salary costs. They can also be included in a stock-option plan that rewards them for work performed during the organizing phase. And, as long as the terms are revealed, they can be sold shares of a class of stock that is not made available to other equity investors.

Organizers of commercial banks can obtain a loan to finance organizing expenses so long as they do not pledge the future stock of the bank. The rate of interest cannot exceed what the OCC considers to be market rates. As long as the proposed payment is disclosed in offering documents, the loan plus interest can be repaid from proceeds of the bank's sale of stock. If organizers plan to create a bank holding company, they can compensate early investors for their higher risk with a separate class of stock in the bank holding company made available to them at a preferential price.[19]

Thrift regulators make it more difficult to finance organizing expenses, but it is possible to compensate organizers for their time. They are required to bear all costs of organization, and expenses for applications that are not approved are the sole responsibility of the organizing group.[20] If a charter application is approved, organizers can be reimbursed from the proceeds of the institution's stock sale. If they become employees or directors of the thrift, organizers can be awarded stock options as compensation for time spent during the organizing phase. If they plan to create a thrift holding company, organizers probably can raise funds to finance the process and compensate investors for the higher risk they take by issuing one class of stock to initial investors and another class to later investors.[21]

Organizers of a for-profit royalty-investment fund can be compensated for time spent creating the fund with stock or partnership interests at preferential terms. Out-of-pocket costs can be financed by organizers (who can be repaid if and when the fund is established) or financed by an initial sale of equity in a corporation that will either become the fund or its general partner.

Degree of Community Control

A critical consideration for activists who are committed to community control of their financial institution is ownership. All development banks reach out to community organizations and residents. However, the degree to which local input dictates priorities is determined by the choice of model.

Investors in commercial banks, stock-owned savings and loan associations, and for-profit royalty-investment funds elect the board of directors (which selects management and sets priorities). Development-bank investors can choose to require strong community representation on the board of directors, but they need not. Commercial banks and savings institutions generally retain the discretion to go in directions other than those advocated by community organizations.

If members are active, community input is likely to be greater at mutual savings and loan associations, whose objective is to serve members rather than to maximize profit. There are no shareholders, and assets are owned by depositors and credited to their accounts after provision for current expenses and additions to surplus. Unfortunately, the members at most mutual associations do not actively participate as owners.

Community involvement at credit unions has the potential to be, and ideally should be, much greater. Because they are member-owned cooperatives, members elect the board of directors. If the membership is active (and does not simply sign the ballot provided by management), then it can set the priorities of the credit union. Even when members are not active, community-development credit unions tend to seek close contacts with local groups and residents and to maintain close ties with their sponsoring organizations, which tend to be based in the community.

Because of their public charter, initial community input is also likely to be significant for the nonprofit loan funds. Even in this case, however, organizers define who can be a member of the nonprofit and, therefore, elect its board of directors. Since the membership can be as narrow as the organizing group, community involvement is not necessarily greater than at for-profit development banks. There are some good reasons to limit membership. It simplifies governance and reassures investors that loan-fund policies will not abruptly change. And, if the original board of directors represents diverse interests, it minimizes the chances that one constituency will come to dominate the CDLF's board of directors. Limiting membership also has disadvantages, however. It can insulate the board of directors so that it does not respond to changes in the needs of its constituencies. A large membership increases accountability and also can broaden access to funders, investors, and volunteers. A compromise between the two extremes is to allow the board of directors and members to each elect some of the directors. Another alternative is to adopt several classes of membership, with each class electing a portion of the directors.

What Are the Most Suitable Models for Development Banks?

Any of the six models described in this chapter can be effective development banks. However, under the right conditions, we favor commercial banks. If a community can support a development bank with assets of $20 million or more, if it needs the variety of services one can offer, and if organizers can attract the necessary banking experience and capital, then they should form or buy a commercial bank.

These banks are generally viewed as credible and solid financial institutions. As in the case of South Shore Bank, their presence in a community can inspire confidence. Because of deposit insurance, they can attract virtually unlimited low-cost funds. Commercial banks holding 10 percent or more of their assets in residential-mortgage loans now have the same access as savings and loan associations to Federal Home Loan Bank loans for their housing activities. Commercial banks can produce sufficient income to attract mainstream equity investors with market returns or to fund affiliates serving other economic-development needs. Although they are not tax exempt, commercial banks can avoid paying taxes if they are part of a holding company that has other development subsidiaries—the earnings of the bank can be offset by the losses of the other development subsidiaries. In essence, profits that would have gone to pay taxes can be used to pursue development activities. They, along with savings and loan associations, come closer to full-service financial institutions than any of the other options. In addition, there are thousands of commercial banks in the United States providing a large proportion of all business loans. If a development-oriented commercial bank can demonstrate the profitability of unfamiliar kinds of loans or borrowers, the same strategy may be adopted by many other financial institutions around the country. The large organizing costs, substantial initial capitalization, and level of experience required by regulators are major hurdles, but with hidden benefits. The experience and large capitalization necessary improve the chances for long-term survival.

Commercial banking is far from a perfect model for development banks. All of its aspects are heavily regulated, and development bankers find themselves constantly trying to stretch rules that will not give way to their social goals. The restrictions on risk taking and losses mean that commercial banks are best suited to serve the needs of persons of moderate income rather than very-low-income people. A development bank that is a commercial bank can easily adopt slightly more flexible underwriting criteria, provide more technical assistance, be a proactive catalyst for development loans, and make more SBA loans, multifamily rehabilitation loans, student loans, or loans to community organizations. A portion of its funds can be directed to low-income people if below-market-rate deposits are attracted and the interest savings are used to subsidize loans. Organizers also can use bank or bank-holding-company subsidiaries or affiliates creatively to engage in development activities that the commercial bank cannot undertake, such as direct real-estate investment and providing venture capital.

Savings and loan associations also have significant potential as community-development banks. However, their few advantages over commercial banks are canceled out by the relatively poor health of the thrift industry. At least for now, carrying the savings and loan emblem inspires less confidence, and it can raise the cost of bringing in deposits. What is most attractive about such institutions is the broader powers of thrift holding companies to make direct investments in equity and real estate and to underwrite securities.[22] These powers could greatly expand development capabilities. It is also easier for thrifts to establish interstate branches.

If one of the powers only thrifts have is important to a proposed development bank's strategy, forming a new savings and loan association is a justifiable choice. Even if thrifts do not have powers that are important, it still may make sense to buy an existing S&L if one is found that fits well with goals. When the National Cooperative Bank in Washington, D.C., decided to buy a depository institution, it purchased a savings and loan association partially because the price was more reasonable. Thrifts often sell at a smaller premium over book value than banks. Including S&Ls expands the pool of potential institutions that can be acquired in areas where there are few commercial banks available or for sale. In addition, thrift regulators in a particular state or region may be more approachable than those overseeing commercial banks.

Where forming a commercial bank is not appropriate (that is, where few financial services are needed in small amounts, or where all of the needs require substantial subsidies or are of high risk), other models may be able to fit the need very well. For example, individuals who have little experience in banking, have little initial capital, and who expect to achieve a much smaller asset size than is required to sustain a commercial bank can still start CDCUs, CDLFs, and microenterprise loan funds.

A community-development credit union is dramatically less expensive to form than a commercial bank and can cover its costs at a smaller size than a commercial bank. A CDCU with assets of $5 million or less can adequately serve as the primary financial institution in a low-income community where access to depository services and credit is otherwise nonexistent. However, most CDCUs have asset sizes (many of less than $500,000) much smaller than they need to play this role. These credit unions cannot hire sufficient staff to serve their community or to market the credit union, and they earn too little to pay competitive dividends to members. Because most community-development credit unions cannot sell stock to raise equity capital, they are frequently trapped in a continuous struggle for survival. Only CDCUs that achieve a much larger size than the average can be effective development banks. Even much smaller CDCUs can play a valuable community role by organizing volunteers and fostering self-confidence and community cooperation.

Community-development loan funds also can survive at a smaller scale than commercial banks and can be formed by people with little banking experience. Such loan funds hold a very conspicuous advantage over all of the depository institutions, since they have significantly more leeway in the kinds, sizes, and terms of loans they make. They are free to structure loan terms to fit the economics of the project, as long as they can repay their investors. The community-development loan fund may be the best model to provide capital for housing deals that are of moderately more risk than commercial banks can accept, but it is as yet unclear that the model can sustain the risk of lending to low-income businesses without much more massive subsidies than are now available. Of the thirty members of the National Association of Community Development Loan Funds (NACDLF) at mid-1988, thirteen financed only housing development. Another ten financed both housing and business development. Only seven financed purely business development. This may be because the organizers were more familiar with housing lending or because there was a more evident need for housing capital, but it is a distribution that seems to play to the strengths of community-development loan funds. Such funds have not yet figured out a way to provide high-risk loans with low-risk capital. The Interfaith Loan Fund closed because it could not resolve this issue of how to absorb losses in its loan portfolio when the portfolio was funded by loans from social investors. The Industrial Cooperative Association Loan Fund continues to struggle with the same problem. As long as CDLFs rely on loan capital from investors who expect their loans to be repaid (and who cannot be compensated for taking higher risks), they may be better suited to finance housing, or at least a mix of housing and business loans.

The community-development loan fund is still a new and evolving model. These loan funds have been successful in attracting investors, but the total investment in all of them is still smaller than the liabilities of most commercial banks. Most CDLFs are not yet at a sustainable scale. If such loan funds continue to proliferate, competition for capital may make it even more difficult for many of them to achieve an effective scale of operations. They have been growing rapidly because few investors in a loan fund that is a member of NACDLF have lost their investment. A significant loss by a few funds could lead to a flight of loan capital from all funds. Community-development loan funds also may in the future be subject to greater regulatory scrutiny, at an enormous cost. According to attorneys consulted by the Institute for Community Economics (ICE) in Springfield, Massachusetts, and the National Association of Community Development Loan Funds in Philadelphia, loan funds based upon the model described in *The Community Loan Fund Manual* prepared by ICE are not subject to federal banking law and are not required to register with the Securities and Exchange Commission as securities issuers. Furthermore, 501(c)(3) charitable organizations also appear to be exempt from SEC securities-registration requirements.[23] However, the SEC federal charitable institution exemption probably did not anticipate the proliferation of community-development loan funds and could be modified at any time.

A microenterprise loan fund is the obvious, but not the only, choice for a development bank that intends to serve microenterprise borrowers. Commercial banks can make small-business loans through their consumer-loan window, and several have developed viable products to provide businesses with very small lines of credit. Credit unions also make many loans to very small businesses, some as consumer loans and some as business loans. With the cooperation of regulators, the credit approaches pioneered by microenterprise loan funds, such as peer-group lending, could be used by a credit union or even a commercial bank. Microenterprise loan funds are a particularly attractive option because of the innovations they offer in risk and operating-cost management for small-business lending. However, it is still only in developing countries that microenterprise loan funds have been entirely successful in implementing these innovations and raising the standard of living for large numbers of very-low-income people. Since there is insufficient experience to indicate whether the techniques applied by microenterprise loan funds can achieve the same results in urban and rural communities in the United States, these loan funds must be viewed as an experimental model.

The royalty-investment fund is the only one of the six financial institutions included in this book that offers something close to equity financing. We believe that there is no better model for providing venture capital to slower-growth companies and to cooperative and nonprofit businesses. In the United States, small businesses are overburdened with debt financing. Increasing the availability of small-scale venture capital—which will also lower its cost—will make the greatest contribution to growth of any economic-development strategy. The venture-capital industry (and informal venture investing by family, friends, and associations) is as close to development banking as mainstream financial markets get. In this regard, royalty-investment funds deserve special attention as development banks because they can make start-up capital available to the companies most likely to be part of a community-development strategy: firms that do not have sufficient growth potential to attract venture capitalists and those that do not want to sell out, such as cooperatives and nonprofit businesses. Royalty financing has not been broadly tested, but the number of examples is increasing. In a few years, it will be much easier to assess the real potential of this model.

Making the Most Effective Use of Each Model

For those who contemplate creating a development bank, we would like to share some additional thoughts about how to improve the chances of success. For example, buying an existing commercial bank can save time and money. The advantages of this course are that organizers acquire existing assets, deposits, operating systems, facilities, and staff for an investment of less than 10 percent of assets. They also acquire a stream of earnings, unless the existing bank is doing poorly or the organizers need to revamp the bank's portfolio radically to meet their goals. Buying a bank can save a couple of years that would otherwise be dedicated to building the depositor base in order to cover costs. It can be worth it even if the existing portfolio and staff of the candidates for purchase do not fit perfectly with the needs of organizers. Even though South Shore Bank never succeeded in converting the old loan officers, it still made sense for its organizers to buy an ongoing institution. Buying a commercial bank only makes sense if a modest premium—up to 1.5 times book value—is paid for a stable bank that has had few bad loans in the past. Where likely buy-out candidates cannot be found, it still may make sense to purchase a branch office of a commercial bank. Buying a branch can provide the physical facility, some deposits, and some support staff.

Commercial banks that are part of bank holding companies (BHCs) can be more flexible and responsive development lenders. These holding companies are corporations that own one or more commercial banks. Almost half of all commercial banks are owned by bank holding companies, and they control a much larger share of banking assets. The reason many small banks are part of holding companies is that this arrangement enhances a bank's access to capital. Another reason is that bank holding companies are allowed to form subsidiaries and affiliated corporations to undertake activities that may not be allowed for the bank itself. The development corporations formed by South Shore Bank's holding company five years after it purchased the bank were a real-estate property development company for residential and commercial property, a minority-enterprise small-business investment company to invest equity capital, and a nonprofit social-development organization.[24] The real-estate-development corporation and the social-development organization are authorized as community-development corporations and must operate primarily for the benefit of low- and moderate-income persons. While a bank cannot be capitalized with debt, a holding company can raise debt capital to capitalize a bank through equity.[25] As long as the bank holding company owns at least 80 percent of the voting stock of a subsidiary bank, the holding company can file a consolidated tax return. As a result, the subsidiary bank may pass dividends to the parent "tax free" (i.e., the transactions of paying dividends and receiving them cancel each other out). If the BHC financed its equity investment in the bank with debt, it can deduct its interest payments. The dividends paid by the bank are effectively converted to deductible interest expenses. Since bank holding companies and the banks they own can file consolidated tax returns, interest on BHC debt, and losses of other subsidiaries, can offset bank earnings.[26] By reducing the bank's tax liability, funds are freed up for development purposes. For example, Shorebank Corporation has an agreement whereby South Shore Bank makes payments to the holding company equal to what its tax liability would have been if it were not a member of the consolidated group. The difference between taxes paid and the tax payments is available for development uses.

Even if organizers of a commercial bank decide not to create a bank holding company, they are likely to form a subsidiary community-development corporation (CDC) unless there are other development lenders and organizations in the community. A bank CDC can create deals for the bank and do deals that the bank cannot (such as equity investments). Community-development corporations can be created to serve low- and moderate-income areas or to serve small businesses. They can acquire property, make equity investments, and provide grants, loans with flexible terms, and technical assistance. Investments in any one CDC are limited to 2 percent of a bank's capital and surplus, and aggregate investments in such projects are limited to 5 percent of a bank's capital and surplus.[27] Bank holding companies may also establish CDCs under quite similar guidelines; however, the Federal Reserve Board has not set any specific requirement on the level of investment a holding company can make in a community-development corporation. The amount must be adequate to fund the CDC's operations and still maintain the integrity of the holding company. Bank CDCs can be for-profit or not-for-profit corporations. If a CDC will undertake functions that cannot generate much revenue—such as the work on the social and planning needs of the South Shore community undertaken by the Neighborhood Institute—then it probably makes more sense to form a nonprofit CDC.[28]

Whether to start fresh or take over an existing institution is also an increasingly important decision for credit unions. More stringent chartering requirements and economic retrenchment are cutting back on the number of new credit unions being formed. Federal and state regulators seem to prefer to match new groups with established credit unions over granting new charters.[29] Rather than forming a new community-development credit union, organizers may need to consider "buying out" an existing credit union and building new programs on its foundation.

Organizers of new CDCUs that have their charters approved face the task of reaching a scale where they can survive. Greater competition among financial institutions has diminished their chances, particularly as consolidation produces fewer, larger credit unions.[30] Regulators are putting more restrictions on all such institutions, especially CDCUs, and closing more of them down. Between thirty and fifty low-income credit unions were liquidated or merged from 1980 through 1984.[31] More have failed since then. Accordingly, CDCUs need to secure more capital and achieve larger asset sizes than they have in the past. Of the three hundred or so low-income, limited-income, or community-development credit unions, only 18 percent had assets of more than $1 million in 1985, with the majority having assets of less than $250,000.[32] To achieve their potential as development banks, the average must move much closer to the range of $3 million to $5 million. Some CDCUs, including Santa Cruz Community Credit Union in Santa Cruz, California, and Community Self-Help Credit Union in Durham, North Carolina, have attained a scale that allows them to be sustainable and offer a large variety of products and services. It is possible for most community-development credit unions to achieve a sustainable scale with some help.

When necessary, CDCUs can increase their potential asset base by selecting fields of membership that include middle-income people, so long as they demonstrate that a majority of members are low income.[33] Community-development credit unions with a mix of low- and middle-income members are more likely to thrive because receipts from the latter members balance the high cost of low-income accounts. For example, Northside Community Credit Union in Chicago serves a population with diverse income levels; under a new marketing strategy, it hopes to pull in social investments from middle-income residents.[34] Organizers should consider the feasibility of expanding their credit union's field of membership and scope by merging with other credit unions (especially those that are inactive).

Community-development credit unions need to find sponsors who will actively support them financially until they achieve a scale where they can cover their own costs and who will promote them to the community. Sponsoring groups must have credibility (and a broad membership base) to help attract deposits. Sponsorship by an already existing organization is virtually a prerequisite for obtaining a credit-union charter, but not all sponsors add the value that can enhance a credit union's chances of survival. Even with strong community support, the credit union will need a variety of donated services when it first opens; it is easiest if the sponsor can provide them. Likewise, if the credit union has unforeseen operating costs, it is certainly helpful to have a sponsor who can step in with assistance.

Frequently, CDCUs must find grants to help them cover the costs of reaching the break-even point and of funding special programs the sponsor cannot cover. To attract sufficient grants and donations, CDCUs need a nonprofit affiliate that can receive tax-deductible contributions, or they must be able to funnel such funds through a 501(c)(3) sponsor.

To the full extent allowed by law and regulation, CDCUs need to attract nonmember deposits. With the exception of deposits by organizational members in the field of membership of a credit union, nonmember deposits tend to be larger than those of members. Nonmember deposits are essential if CDCUs are to expand sufficiently to break even on their fixed costs and meet the credit needs of their community. The odds of reaching a break-even volume of assets without nonmember deposits (or large deposits from organizational members) are slim. The Quitman County Federal Credit Union, located in a very-low-income community in the north Mississippi Delta, built its assets to $100,000 between 1981 and 1987. Because it depended on its very-low-income members for deposits, it could grow no faster. However, in 1987 the credit union discovered the National Federation of Community Development Credit Unions (NFCDCU); with its assistance in attracting nonmember deposits, it was able to boost its assets to $500,000 by the end of 1988.[35] In recent years, CDCUs have been able to increase their access to nonmember deposits. For example, the John D. and Catherine T. MacArthur Foundation has purchased certificates of deposit ranging from $25,000 to $100,000 in ten community-development credit unions through the NFCDCU. The Bank of Austin in Chicago deposited $100,000 in the Austin/ West Garfield Federal Credit Union as part of a Community Reinvestment Act agreement. South Shore Bank in Chicago deposited $100,000 in the same credit union in support of an allied development bank. While federal law now limits nonmember deposits to 20 percent of total deposits, it is possible to gain limited waivers from this limit. For example, the Mid-Bronx Community Development Federal Credit Union in New York City was granted a limited waiver to accept an interest-free deposit from Chemical Bank.[36] Credit unions also should work with the National Federation of Community Development Credit Unions and other groups that are trying to remove the limit on nonmember deposits.

In addition, CDCUs must take full advantage of the services available to them from their state credit-union leagues, ranging from technical assistance, to loan packaging, to secondary markets for loans. In the past, credit-union leagues have been reluctant to work with low-income credit unions that generate few dues while potentially using many services. However, today, the leagues see helping low-income credit unions as a means to demonstrate their community involvement and to fend off the assault by commercial banks and savings institutions on their tax-exempt status. State credit-union leagues can help CDCUs to achieve the professionalism they need to survive.

Because loan funds are not regulated, they must grapple with some issues that commercial banks and credit unions have had taken out of their hands. One question facing all community-development loan funds is how to manage each other's risk taking. Investor confidence in CDLFs is very high because there have been few losses by investors, but it could be shaken by losses at a few loan funds. It is hard to protect against this outcome because loan policies are established independently by each loan fund. To safeguard the reputation of them all, it may be necessary to have peer-group review of loan policies and practices. The National Association of Community Development Loan Funds in Philadelphia is trying to create a peer-review system.

Another issue is how to manage the proliferation of loan funds so that it does not become self-defeating. Many groups wish to create loan funds (sometimes several groups in the same city or region). Because the volume of loans necessary to break even on costs is in the millions, it can make more sense for groups to work together to form one regional loan fund. The National Association of Community Development Loan Funds is addressing this concern also by providing technical assistance to CDLFs and by bringing together community groups interested in forming a loan fund, as it did with the New Hampshire Community Loan Fund.

Community-development and microenterprise loan funds may be most effective as adjuncts to a technical-assistance organization skilled in serving and well known by the clients of the loan fund. There are few cases where either of these kinds of development funds has reached a scale sufficient to cover its costs. The scale required is much lower if a separate technical-assistance organization absorbs the expenses of finding deals and of assisting borrowers to improve their projects and uses the loan fund to service its customers. This arrangement is fairly common. The Institute for Community Economics Loan Fund (Springfield, Massachusetts) and the Industrial Cooperative Loan Fund (Boston) are community-development loan funds affiliated with technical-assistance organizations. The Good Faith Fund (Pine Bluff, Arkansas) and MICRO (Tucson, Arizona) are microenterprise loan funds with similar affiliations.

6
Sustainability

Economic-development impact and survival are inseparable goals for development banks. Ensuring their survival enables such banks to achieve their development goals. They need time to develop staff, create a local information base, increase their deal volume, fine-tune their programs, and build confidence in their institution. They need to be able to count on being around next year, and five years from now, to formulate strategies to attack complex economic-development problems that will only respond to long-term efforts. Communities also count on their permanence. Businesses want to know that their funder will still be there when they need a second round of capital.[1] If a development bank fails, its borrowers and community may be blamed and cut off from capital again.

Mainstream financial institutions and development banks frequently use different measures of their capacity to survive. The former almost universally strive for self-sufficiency. A self-sufficient financial program generates revenues from investments and loans at least equal to its loan losses, operating costs, and the cost of funds from its investors. On the other hand, most development banks accept sustainability as a more realistic goal. A sustainable financial program may earn revenues lower than costs, but it has reliable sources of external subsidies that make up the difference.

Development banks serving borrowers who can pay market rates can become self-sufficient. Some venture funds and business- and industrial-development corporations (BIDCOs) have started up and operate without any subsidies. These development banks provide high-risk capital not available from other financial institutions, and they charge borrowers for the risk. Sand County Ventures, an investment bank and venture-fund manager in San Francisco, started up without any capital subsidies. Self-sufficiency is also attainable for development banks that find innovative ways to reduce the costs of lending below the norm. Some community-development credit unions and commercial banks have become self-sufficient in their core operations by being better bankers, but most of them still undertake activities that rely on external subsidies. For example, some of the profits earned by South Shore Bank in Chicago support the activities of other development entities owned by Shorebank Corporation; these entities, in turn, seek additional external subsidies. Self-sufficient development banks can concentrate on long-term economic development, rather than short-term survival.

Self-sufficiency in development banking, however, is the exception rather than the rule. Development banks whose goal it is to redistribute wealth or to address problems in very-low-income communities have generally relied on large and ongoing subsidies to continue. According to Steve Dawson, a past president of the Industrial Cooperative Association in Somerville, Massachusetts, "low-income enterprise development is too costly, too littered with barriers and risk, to place the burden of self-sufficiency on intermediary development organizations. . . . Development funds will always require some form of grant support—unless fully endowed."[2] However, low-income enterprise loan funds believe they can be sustainable institutions if they can attract limited ongoing subsidies to cover their extraordinary costs. There is some evidence (presented later in this chapter) that, at a much larger scale of activity than the norm, all of the development-bank models covered in the book are capable of self-sufficiency.

Even where self-sufficiency is not immediately attainable, development banks generally have as a goal steady progress toward it. To improve their chances of survival, they strive to reduce their reliance on ongoing subsidies. One of the goals of the Good Faith Fund in Pine Bluff, Arkansas, is to show a steady trend toward self-funding. Likewise, the Industrial Cooperative Association Loan Fund is working toward at least covering its operating costs from interest revenue.

Evaluating Sustainability

To be sustainable, a development bank's revenues must be as great as its costs from loan losses, operations, and compensating investors. All the better if revenues exceed costs, since the excess can be used to start up new programs and weather setbacks. Financial statements reveal a great deal about whether a development bank is sustainable. The following tables use the example of an average small commercial bank (with $25 million in assets) and an average small credit union (with $5 million in assets) to define the terms in the balance sheet and income statement and then describe what the financial statements tell us about sustainability.[3] The main assets of commercial banks and credit unions according to their balance sheets in Table 6-1 are loans and investments. The other significant asset is fixed assets, which includes buildings and furnishings. Their liabilities consist of loans, notes, debentures, deposits, and the share accounts of credit unions.[4] The proportions for assets and liabilities are quite similar for commercial banks and credit unions because they are both depository institutions.

Table 6-1
The Composition of the Balance Sheet (as a Share of Assets)

	Commercial Bank	*Credit Union*
Loans	.51	.59
Investments	.45	.39
Fixed assets	.02	.02
Other assets	.02	—
	equals	equals
Deposits (or credit-union shares)	.90	.92
Other liabilities	.02	.01
Stock	.045	—
Undivided profits and reserves	.035	.07

Source: Federal Deposit Insurance Corporation, Commercial Bank Financial Statements (with adjustments to scale to $25 million from a range of $25–100 million), 1986; NCUA, 1986 Yearend Statistics for Federally Insured Credit Unions (with adjustments to scale to $3 million from a range of $2–5 million).

Equity for financial intermediaries is usually a much smaller share of assets than for nonfinancial companies. Equity can be common or preferred stock, retained earnings, grants, and, sometimes, loan-loss reserves. Only the commercial-bank balance sheet shows stock because credit unions are cooperatives owned solely by the members who purchase share accounts. Credit unions build equity by retaining earnings and setting aside general and special reserves (in addition to loan-loss reserves). Loan-loss reserves are an accounting convention created by deducting from revenues estimates of future losses and accruing the balance on the balance sheet until losses are actually incurred (when the reserve is reduced by the amount of the loss). The purpose of the loan-loss reserve is to adjust downward the value of loan assets to reflect their true worth

Table 6-2
The Composition of Income (as a Share of Assets)

	Commercial Bank	Credit Union
REVENUE		
Loan and lease interest	5.8	7.22
Securities interest	2.6	2.50
Noninterest income	.7	—
Other income	.7	.34
Total revenue	9.8	10.06
EXPENSES		
Interest on debt	5.1	5.68
Noninterest expense	3.2	3.18
Provision for loan losses	.9	.40
Total expenses	9.2	9.26
NET INCOME	.64	.80

Source: Federal Deposit Insurance Corporation, Commercial Bank Financial Statements (with adjustments to scale to $25 million from a range of $25–100 million), 1986; NCUA, 1986 Yearend Statistics for Federally Insured Credit Unions (with adjustments to scale to $3 million from a range of $2–5 million).

after taking into account anticipated loan losses. These reserves are included in equity by some financial intermediaries because, although they are segregated in the balance sheet, they are essentially retained earnings until the losses are incurred. However, the reserves are always separate from retained earning because it is anticipated that they will have to be used to cover losses.

The composition of revenues and expenses for both financial institutions is summarized in Table 6-2. Most of the revenue of each is generated by interest earned on loans and investments. In addition, the commercial bank receives interest on money it deposits in (or lends to) other depository institutions. Fee income is small, as it is for most development banks. Non-interest expenses, namely, operating costs, consist of employee compensation, office occupancy and operations, travel, dues, education and promotion, professional services, and insurance. For both of the financial institutions examined, operations account for about one-third of all costs. This is a usual share for development banks.

Losses are taken into account in Table 6-2 through a "provision for loan losses." Unlike actual losses, which only take into account loans charged off as uncollectible in the current period, the provision for loan losses is a charge against loan revenues to capture the amount of all projected loan losses for which there are not already reserves. In each financial period, the loan-loss reserve is reduced by the amount of loans actually charged off and increased by the amount added to provision for loan losses, plus any amount of loan charge-offs that are recovered. Provisions for loan losses vary in size with the risk of the bank's loan portfolio.

The largest expense for most financial institutions is the cost of funds that are invested in it or that it borrows. Since the two financial institutions illustrated here are depository institutions, most of their funding costs are interest payments to depositors and, for credit unions, dividends paid to holders of their shares. These costs are comparable for the two financial institutions because they pay similar rates on deposits.

Net income is simply the difference between revenues and expenses. In Table 6-2, net income as a share of assets in 1986 was somewhat higher for the credit union (.80 percent) than for the commercial bank (.64 percent). One reason is that its provision for loan losses was less than half the size of the provision for the commercial bank. In 1986, commercial banks made larger-than-average additions to their loan-loss reserves because their loss experience worsened. Using the provisions for loan loss for 1988, the commercial bank would have earned a return on assets of 1.09 percent and the credit union would have earned .96 percent.[5] Other reasons the credit union's performance stands up so well to that of the commercial bank may be that it charged higher rates or received subsidies of time and space unavailable to commercial banks.

Positive net income is an easy proxy for sustainability, but it has several limitations. First, the provision for loan losses is not the same as anticipated annual loan losses. It is only a good proxy for anticipated annual loan losses if past additions to the loan-loss reserve were accurate and neither the volume of new loans, the kinds of loans, nor loan policies has changed. Second, net income excludes the cost of equity and, therefore, understates the costs of the financial institution. In the case of stock-owned financial institutions, equity investors have a residual claim on earnings after all expenses are paid. People generally invest because they anticipate earnings on their equity investment equal to what they could earn elsewhere. For example, commercial-bank investors generally seek a return on equity of 15 percent or more. What a financial institution actually earns on its equity is simply net income from the income statement divided by total equity from the balance sheet. If the result is less than what investors expected, then they are unlikely to invest again. Providing a return on equity high enough to attract investors is one of the costs of business. Credit unions also have required rates of return on equity, even though they do not have stock investors. Their required return on equity is what management or regulators feel is necessary for the credit union to preserve its integrity as a financial institution.

In Table 6-2, revenues are greater than the cost of operations, losses (as indicated by the provision for loan losses), and cost of debt for both financial institutions. Their net income, and therefore their return on equity, may or may not be sufficient to sustain them in the long run. If the required return on equity (either to attract new stockholders for commercial banks or to meet requirements to set aside reserves for credit unions) is less than 8 percent, then they have both reached their respective break-even points. Otherwise, they have not.

The Importance of Scale

The break-even analysis in Table 6-2 ignores the crucial effect of asset size or volume of activity on sustainability. Operating costs have a fixed and a variable component. Fixed costs—such as buildings, computers, fixtures, and the salaries of some staff—must be incurred no matter how little activity there is and show little growth no matter how much activity there is. Variable costs—such as salaries for employees who are added to serve expanding demand, data processing, postage, and forms—grow at the same rate as lending activity. As the volume of activity grows, the fixed costs are spread over a larger and larger base, and operating costs per unit of activity decline, an outcome illustrated in Table 6-3. A minimum volume of activity must be attained before a financial institution can reach the break-even point (generate revenue greater than its costs). In the example in Table 6-3, the break-even level of operations is achieved when there are 15,000 accounts. After this point, the financial institution earns a profit on every account.

The volume of activity or asset size a development bank needs to break even depends upon the kind of financial intermediary it is and how well it manages pricing and costs. We can estimate the break-even asset size for most development banks if we assume that they hold on to most of their loans and equity investments. Development banks that sell their loans have a higher level of activity than is captured on their balance sheet, and they may break even at a lower level of assets. Develop-

Table 6-3
The Effect of Volume on Cost and Profit per Account

Number of Accounts	Fixed Costs	Variable Cost per Account	Variable Costs	Total Cost	Total Cost per Account	Number of Accounts	Revenue per Account	Total Revenue	Total Profit
10,000	$30,000	$2.00	$20,000	$50,000	$5.00	10,000	$4.00	$40,000	($10,000)
15,000	$30,000	$2.00	$30,000	$60,000	$4.00	15,000	$4.00	$60,000	$0
20,000	$30,000	$2.00	$40,000	$70,000	$3.50	20,000	$4.00	$80,000	$10,000

Source: G. Michael Moebs and Eva Moebs, *Pricing Financial Services* (Homewood, Ill.: Dow Jones–Irwin, 1986).

ment banks that receive higher-than-average donations of facilities, staff, or services, or that find ways to cut other costs to below those of their peers, will have lower break-even levels.

For a new commercial bank, the break-even point for assets is probably close to $25 million. The minimum number of employees is likely to be at least two officers and five other employees.[6] Based upon minimum staffing needs and costs for space, furniture, marketing, stationery, telephone, FDIC and other insurance, travel, fees for legal work, accounting, and exams, and other expenses, minimum operating costs are likely to be at least $650,000 per year. Average net-interest income after interest expenses for commercial banks has been 4 percent of assets, with average loan losses at .7 percent of assets. Based upon these figures, breaking even requires assets of no less than $20 million. With more standard operating costs, the break-even level is closer to $25 million (approximately what Booz-Allen and Hamilton, management consultants, found for retail branches in 1987).[7] Today's savings and loan associations are likely to have break-even operating levels quite similar to those of commercial banks.

A professionally staffed credit union offering a diverse set of products that only receives subsidies of space cost and board and committee volunteers probably requires total assets of at least $5 million to cover its costs.[8] According to the National Federation of Community Development Credit Unions in New York City, the break-even point for a credit union with a limited product mix could be as low as $3 million. Most credit unions with less than $5 million in assets that do not receive substantial sponsor subsidies acutely need capital. While the average credit union has about $10 million in assets, the average community-development credit union has about $500,000 in assets.[9] A credit union of this size that operates under the wing of a sponsoring organization that is able to absorb its operating costs and to provide it with loan-loss reserves might be sustainable. However, it is unusual for a sponsor of a low-income credit union to have sufficient resources to play such a role.

Credit unions break even at lower asset levels than commercial banks because they use volunteers, small amounts of donated space, donated goods and services, and fewer professional resources, such as lawyers. The average credit union with less than $2 million in assets has only one equivalent full-time employee.[10] A commercial bank would not even be allowed to operate with a staff of one. Beyond a small core of employees, credit unions depend upon committed volunteers. According to a survey of credit unions by *Credit Union Magazine,* volunteers for small credit unions usually include a board of five to nine volunteers who together donate fifty hours per month, a supervisory committee of three to five volunteers who together donate twenty hours per month, and a credit committee of four volunteers who together donate fifty hours per month. The treasurers in the survey donated as much as forty hours per month.[11] The credit union cannot survive without these volunteers; commercial banks, in contrast, do not use volunteers and often compensate their directors.

Because few if any loan funds have attained self-sufficiency, the asset level at which it is achievable can only be estimated, based upon the operating costs, loss rates, and costs of funds common for these development banks. The summary report of a 1988 loan-fund workshop states, "Given the conditions they face currently, $10 million is a minimum base to even approach self-sufficiency."[12] Even at this asset level, community-development loan funds must attract low-interest loans, keep down overhead, obtain pro bono services, offer modest salaries, use volunteers, have very low loan losses (or externally supported reserves for them), and fund technical assistance separately.

The break-even operating level for a CDLF is so much lower than for a commercial bank because of subsidies. The minimum effective scale is probably larger than for credit unions because target spreads between interest earned and charged are smaller, provisions for loan losses must be higher, and there are fewer cost-saving services provided by trade associations to CDLFs than to credit unions. Community-development loan funds may also have higher costs than credit unions because, as tax-exempt 501(c) (3) organizations, they are not allowed to serve conventional loan markets. This restriction limits their ability to lower loan costs and increase revenues by doing a mix of conventional and development loans.

The vast majority of CDLFs have assets of far less than $10 million. Most are able to sustain themselves at lower asset levels because they receive operating grants, are closely associated with an organization that covers some of their costs, or pay interest far below bank savings-account rates to their investors. The Northern Community Investment Corporation in St. Johnsbury, Vermont, was able to cover its costs without external subsidies by the time it had assets of $6 million because it had a very low cost of funds (most of its capital was in the form of grants), had very small loan losses, and targeted creating jobs for low-income people rather than enabling them to own businesses.[13]

A microloan fund (with operating costs based upon those originally projected for the Good Faith Fund in Pine Bluff, Arkansas) that charges borrowers 16 percent, pays, on average, 5.5 percent for its loan capital (which is 90 percent of total capital), and sets aside reserves for losses equal to 7 percent of loans, would break even when its assets reached $8 million.[14] The number of borrowers required to reach this point is much larger than most microenterprise loan funds will ever serve. If the average loan size is $2,000, there must be 4,000 borrowers. Unless a microenterprise loan fund operates in an area where both population and self-employment are very high, it cannot break even on its costs without substantial subsidies.

Microenterprise loan funds are still relying only on very-low-cost foundation capital, which allows them to cover their costs at a much lower level. They have much lower debt than 90 percent of their capital, and they pay much less than 5.5 percent for that debt. Micro, a joint project of PPEP (Portable Practical Educational Preparation) and Acción International in Tucson, Arizona, anticipated that it would cover its costs when it reached $1.75 million in assets, assuming that losses stay below 5 percent of loans outstanding, field staff continue to be paid in the range of $6.43 per hour, other organizations provide meeting space, independent experts volunteer their time to lead seminars, and the average cost of funds remains at 1 percent.

Some microenterprise loan programs that do not expect to make more than a couple of hundred loans a year should be able to continue to operate as programs of technical-assistance or community-service organizations. The Women's Self-Employment Project Loan Fund and the Self-Employment Circle Fund, both in Chicago, are supported by organizations of which they are a part. They also receive operating grants.

The break-even point for a royalty-investment fund (RIF) depends on investee performance, royalty rate, and management fees. Using the royalty terms, royalty rate (5 percent), operating expenses, and performance of the Connecticut Product Development Corporation (where the performance of the portfolio can be fairly characterized by dividing it into three outcomes: no returns, a return of initial capital, and a return of five times investment), a royalty-investment partnership that intended to pay market rates of return to investors probably is not feasible.[15] At higher royalty rates, it would be possible to create a self-sufficient royalty-investment fund. Assuming a royalty rate of 8 percent, the amount required by a PruTech publicly offered partnership, the minimum scale that generates a return to investors of 20 percent is $7 million. Some venture funds operate at a much smaller scale than this. Sand County

Venture Fund is a $1.25 million venture-capital fund in San Francisco whose general partner, an investment-banking firm, bears the costs of identifying, reviewing, and underwriting the deals in which the venture fund invests.

It can take a long time for a development bank to attain an asset level or volume of activity that allows it to cover its costs. Many mainstream financial institutions lose money for several years until they can expand their volume of activity sufficiently to absorb their fixed costs and to break even on all costs. For an average commercial bank, organizers expect to reach the break-even point by the second or third year of conservative operations. Recently formed commercial banks in quickly growing markets have broken even in their first or second year.[16] Development banks cannot be expected to do any better, and they do not. South Shore Bank managers expected it would take at least a year before people in the Austin neighborhood of Chicago, where the bank had located a branch, would begin to seek loans.[17] In its early years, the Connecticut Product Development Corporation received approximately sixty inquiries per year; it now receives four hundred.[18]

In the first few years following start-up of a development bank, there is often a sense of urgency to expand quickly. While rapid growth can result in lower costs as a share of rising assets, losses can pile up on poorly structured loans. Growth sometimes occurs at the cost of excessive risk. Planning with and sticking to reasonable growth assumptions helps ensure that a development bank will survive. Union Savings Bank of Albuquerque, a labor-capitalized bank in New Mexico, decided to grow slowly because the local economy was troubled. It did not want more deposits than it could prudently lend out.[19] When funds grow faster than funding capacity, development banks can invest in certificates of deposit and Treasury bills or buy loan participations from more experienced development lenders. The latter approach can allow a new development bank to expand its portfolio of loans quickly, while it builds up its internal lending capacity more slowly. It is also a valuable way to begin developing relationships with other financial institutions. For example, early in its life the Northwest Bronx Credit Union approached other New York community-development credit unions to join in a $55,000 participation loan that would otherwise have exceeded its capabilities.[20]

The Role of Subsidies

Most of today's development banks operate with varying levels of external subsidies from investors, members, donors, or volunteers. We know less than we should about whether these subsidies are well spent. In some cases, they would probably be better devoted to creating development entrepreneurs who could approach the private financial system for capital. In other cases, the expenditures are probably more than justified, based upon the development benefits they produce. However, we know a great deal about what these subsidies imply for the long-term sustainability of development banks.

Initial capital subsidies in the form of below-market stock or low-interest loans are completely consistent with sustainable development-bank operations. A development bank that requires a single infusion of below-market-rate capital becomes self-sufficient once it receives this capital. Most successful development banks in the United States, including South Shore Bank, have received some portion of their initial capital at little or no cost.

Because the pool of below-market capital is limited, development banks that rely on capital subsidies after the start-up period are somewhat more at risk. However, many development banks continue to attract capital from what seems to be a reliable pool of socially motivated investors willing to accept returns at least slightly below market. The financial position of a development bank will be stronger—and it will use capital resources more efficiently—if it can create investment products that offer sufficient returns to pay market-rate investors for at least a part of their capital. Development banks that are depository institutions commonly use a mix of subsidized capital and market-rate deposits to expand their capital pool.

While capital subsidies should be sought over those for operating expenses, short-term subsidies of operating costs are the only thing that will allow some development banks to achieve long-term sustainability. This is the case for all development banks unable to sell stock, which need grants and donations until they can cover their own costs. As already described, it is standard for very small credit unions to receive subsidies, such as volunteer staff and donations of space and services. These subsidies tend to decline as a credit union grows, as should the need for them. Most community-development loan funds also rely on operating grants until they reach a scale where they can break even.

Because financial institutions can take three years or longer to reach their break-even point, they need capital to cover costs during this period. If a development bank can expect to generate revenues greater than its unsubsidized costs after a fixed period, relying on short-term operating subsidies is consistent with sustainability.[21] Even in this case, however, endowments or multiyear operating grants should be sought over annual operating grants. It is to be hoped that funders will become more willing to make multiyear commitments where funds are released based upon performance targets. In a relatively rare occurrence, California's Santa Cruz Community Development Credit Union was able to attract a three-year operating grant from a regional foundation. It covered three staff positions in the first year, two positions in the second year, and one position in the third year. By the end of the third year, the credit union was self-supporting.[22]

Planning to use large operating subsidies to keep afloat for the long term is not a desirable approach for a development bank. Operating subsidies are difficult to attract, and multi-year commitments are rare. An institution that does not know whether it will cover its costs by year's end cannot be effective. Development banks need to know that they have a decent chance of repaying investors when they accept their investments, and they must be able to plan more than one year ahead to play a responsible role in community economic development. The withdrawal of sponsor subsidies from the Lower East Side Federal Credit Union in New York was one reason that it failed. Between 1969 and 1975, the credit union did not grow enough to be able to absorb its costs without these subsidies.[23]

There are exceptions to the assertion that development banks should avoid long-term operating subsidies. If the bank must provide extensive technical assistance to clients, then subsidies are essential. Technical assistance is expensive to provide and frequently too costly for borrowers to bear the full cost. Development banks can create an entity to accept tax-deductible grants for education and technical assistance. In 1989, Santa Cruz Community Development Credit Union began the process of creating a 501 (c) (3) technical-assistance organization to subsidize the development work required for start-up business loans and for loans to minority businesses.[24] Operating subsidies also make sense for a development bank that has covered its essential costs and wants to expand into new development activities that cannot pay their way. These subsidies allow a development bank to maximize its development impact without jeopardizing its existence. Operating grants can also make sense to fund loan-loss reserves. A few funders have been willing to make grants to development banks that allow them to make higher-risk loans using debt. Rather than compensating for loan losses with higher returns on other investments, these development banks dip into dedicated reserves for losses. For example, the Industrial Cooperative Association Loan Fund in Somerville, Massachusetts, tries to maintain a loan-loss reserve funded by various donors equal to 30 percent of its loans. As long as a development bank can find funding for such a reserve, this approach is consistent with sustainability.

As this still-young industry gains experience and more development banks reach a sustainable scale, fewer subsidies will be required. Innovations in operating procedures and creative financial-product development should result in lower costs and greater efficiency for all development banks. In the meantime, it is critical that external support for thoughtful experiments continues to be available.

7
Managing the Risk

MANAGING RISK is an integral part of how development banks achieve sustainability. Risk is uncertainty about what level of investment returns will be achieved at some future time. A borrower may or may not repay a loan as planned; it may cost more or less than expected to attract funds to finance an existing loan portfolio; loans may need to be sold for less or more than their face value. The uncertainty in development banking can be greater than for conventional lending, but the losses are not necessarily higher. Even mainstream financial institutions are confirming that losses from community-development lending need not be high. Wells Fargo Bank says it has not had any defaults on $137 million in Community Reinvestment Act housing loans made between 1986 and 1990. Union National Bank of Pittsburgh's $65 million community-development portfolio has a lower default rate than the bank's overall portfolio in every category, including loans for single and multiple families, commercial real estate, and small business.[1] Nevertheless, development banks must be particularly proficient in evaluating and managing credit risk, interest-rate risk, and liquidity risk.

Credit Risk

It would be hard to justify the existence of banks, let alone development banks, if there were not uncertainty about whether a borrower will repay a loan. Investors "hire" financial intermediaries to help them eliminate unnecessary risk taking and to identify those risks for which financial compensation is adequate. If a financial intermediary misjudges this credit risk, it will eventually fail. Credit-risk management is particularly important for development banks because they often undertake projects that mainstream lenders would not. It is also important because losses represent lost opportunities, reducing the amount of capital available for additional deals and taking up substantial staff time.

Judging the repayment prospects for a particular loan or investment is not difficult for experienced lenders. There are very few cases that do not bear some resemblance to a loan or investment that someone has made in the past, perhaps hundreds or even thousands of times. Categorizing credit risk involves evaluating both expected losses and the variability in losses, that is, unexpected losses. The expected-loss component reflects the kind of average, long-term risk assessment that a good lending officer might make: "This loan should have about a 1 percent chance of loss." In the long run, a development bank should obtain the expected (or average) loss rate; an estimate can be produced simply by examining past loss rates for the type of loan being considered. The actual loss rates for that type of loan for the last five to ten years can be averaged to provide a working estimate, which may be modified to take into account personal judgment about changes likely to occur in the future in loss rates. The same historical loss rates are needed to make a working assumption about unexpected loss rates. However, in this case, it is necessary to measure the size of the annual variations, ignoring the average. It is not the average loss that will kill a development bank, but the unexpectedly high loss in a particular year. The size of these year-to-year variations can be measured using the statistical value called the "standard deviation," adding and subtracting it from the average loss rate to give a range that captures both expected and unexpected losses. The odds are about two out of three that the actual loan loss in a particular year will fall within this range.

A development bank can increase the chances that its loss experience on loans will be close to the loss rate it predicts by holding a portfolio of many loans. It is possible for a bank to fail if one of the two loans it makes (each with a chance of default of only 1 percent) actually defaults. The smaller the number of loans, the greater the chance that in any one year a single loan default will lead to a high actual loss rate. The adage that it is possible to drown crossing a river with an average depth of one foot applies to banking with a vengeance. Since losses tend to bunch up in particular years, a critical problem for a development bank is to survive long enough to experience the expected loss rate. If it has the bad luck to suffer from unexpected losses early in its life when it has only a few loans in its portfolio, it could fail.

Each kind of credit activity has a unique level of credit risk. Table 7-1 illustrates how loan losses vary across types of loans by presenting the average loss experience of small and medium-sized commercial banks. In the table, the measure of loan losses is annual loans charged off as lost as a share of loans outstanding. Charge-offs in one year is not the best measure of loss experience, given the tendency of loan losses to bunch up in certain years. However, it is commonly calculated, and comparisons with the experience of similar financial institutions can be revealing.[2]

The loss experience of small and medium-sized commercial banks indicates that real estate (which for them is dominated by home mortgages) is the least risky area of lending, with com-

Table 7-1
Net Loan Charge-offs as a Share of Loans for Commercial Banks in 1988

Assets (Millions)	Real Esate (%)	Commercial (%)	Individual (%)
$300–500	.37	.64	1.05
$100–300	.26	.93	.81
$50–100	.15	.97	.79
$25–50	.23	1.47	.84
Under $25	1.67	2.89	2.11

Source: Robert Morris Associates, Statistical Supplement: A Semiannual Supplement to RMA's Commercial Lending Newsletter (Philadelphia, July 1989).

mercial loans (including those to business and agriculture) generally being the most risky. Housing projects can be easier to evaluate than businesses, and they often offer better collateral to protect against losses. While the vast majority of the loan portfolio of the Local Initiative Support Corporation (LISC), a national organization started by the Ford Foundation to finance housing and economic development, was in real-estate loans, 80 percent of LISC's defaults as of 1988 were in its business portfolio.[3] The single most important factor in explaining why certain black-owned commercial banks are less profitable than their peers is probably that a larger share of their loan portfolio is in commercial loans. The more profitable black banks concentrate on real-estate lending.[4] Of course, residential real-estate lending in declining economies has a higher risk profile than lending where there is vigorous economic growth; commercial real-estate lending generally has a higher risk profile than residential real-estate lending; and some real-estate loans are more risky than commercial loans. The higher loss rates for commercial lending for the smaller banks may be explained by the size of the businesses to which they lend. Smaller banks are more likely to make loans to smaller businesses, and the market perceives small-business lending to be more risky than lending to large commercial firms. Large businesses often have assets that can be more easily used as collateral, better financial records, and are already seasoned borrowers.

Financial institutions, even those of the same type, accept quite different levels of credit risk because of the activities they choose. Table 7-2 reports the loan losses experienced by an array of mainstream financial institutions and development banks in one year; they range from the minuscule .19 percent experienced by Chicago's Shorebank Corporation in 1988 to minority-owned banks' 2 percent in 1985. Perhaps not surprisingly, J. P. Morgan, the money-center bank whose balance sheet has been described as "strong as a fortress," had losses of only .42 percent in 1986, while the Bank of America in San Francisco, in the same year, had losses of 1.79 percent.

Loss rates vary in Table 7-2 because of different mixes of lending activity, different kinds of borrowers within individual loan markets, and year-to-year variations in losses. South Shore Bank in Chicago stresses real-estate lending, while Northern Community Investment Corporation (NCIC) in St. Johnsbury, Vermont, mainly does business lending. J. P. Morgan Bank, within the general category of business lending, simply does not make loans to many of the borrowers in the portfolio of the Bank of America, let alone the portfolio of NCIC, which makes loans to smaller, younger businesses, using less strict underwriting criteria. Furthermore, part of the difference is simply the result of the year picked. A second look at Table 7-2 reveals that Shorebank had losses of only .19 percent in 1988, but 1987's figure, at .62 percent, was more than three times higher. It is less likely that the bank's underlying loans or loan philosophy changed so much in one year than that defaults bunched up in 1987.

Table 7-2
Historical Rates of Loan Losses for Various Financial Institutions (Ratio of New Losses/Loans Outstanding)

Program	Purpose	Loss Rate (%)
Shorebank Corporation, 1988[a]	Mixed	.19
J. P. Morgan, 1986[b]	Business	.42
Credit unions, 1987[c]	Mixed	.6
Shorebank Corporation, 1987[d]	Mixed	.62
Santa Cruz Community Development Credit Union, 1988[e]	Mixed	.64
Commercial banks, 1988[f]	Mixed	.78
Community-development credit unions[g]	Mixed	.75–1
Quitman County Federal Credit Union, 1988[h]	Mixed	.99
Small-business-investment companies[i]	Business	1.0
Shorebank's peer group of commercial banks, 1988[j]	Mixed	1.05
Citicorp, 1986[k]	Mixed	1.05
Bank of America, 1986[l]	Mixed	1.79
Northern Community Investment Corporation[m]	Business	2.0
Minority-owned commercial banks, 1985[n]	Mixed	2.0

[a]*Annual Report, 1988.*

[b]*Annual Report, 1986.*

[c]National Credit Union Administration, *Annual Report, 1987*, p. 33.

[d]*Annual Report, 1987.*

[e]Figures provided by Karen Zelin, Santa Cruz Community Development Credit Union, December 1989.

[f]Robert Morris Associates, *Statistical Supplement: A Semiannual Supplement to RMA's Commercial Lending Newsletter*, July 1989.

[g]Rough estimate provided by Cliff Rosenthal, National Federation of Community Development Credit Unions.

[h]Figures provided by Robert Jackson, Quitman County Federal Credit Union, December 1989.

[i]Neal Nathanson, "The Sustainability of Economic Development Investment Funds," National Rural Development and Finance Corporation, unpublished paper, March 1988.

[j]*Annual Report, 1988.*

[k]*Annual Report, 1986.*

[l]*Annual Report, 1986.*

[m]Figures provided by Stephen McConnell, Northern Community Investment Corporation, November 1989.

[n]Federal Reserve Bank of Richmond, *Black Banks: Highlights and Profile* (1985 data), December 1986.

Although the level of risk that a development bank chooses to accept should be solely determined by its chosen markets, in reality there are other factors. Development banks are sometimes severely constrained in serving high-risk customers or those who need long-term capital by the limited supply of patient investors willing to accept high risk. A banker who commits to repay a loan tomorrow cannot ethically or prudently invest the proceeds in penny stocks today. Development banks are also sometimes constrained by how they price their financial services. It is difficult for a development bank to serve high-risk markets if it is unwilling to charge borrowers for the risk or if borrowers cannot afford to compensate it. If a development bank expects one-fourth of its deals to fail, it must recoup the losses from the other three-fourths or it will deplete its capital.

Development banks have accepted risk levels all across the spectrum. Table 7-3 illustrates the result for some development-finance programs that do only business lending or do a mix of business and housing loans. The measure of loss experience used is cumulative loan losses as a share of cumulative loans made. This measure describes the total dollars lost from lending rather than the proportion of loans that go sour in any single year. Although it has several limitations, it is the measure commonly prepared by development banks.[5]

Development banks that make loans to moderate-sized businesses generally expect and incur higher losses. The Mountain Association for Community Economic Development (MACED) Loan Fund in Berea, Kentucky, found that most of its losses occurred on very small loans. Vermont's Northern Community Investment Corporation found that its delinquencies on loans to very small businesses were two to three times higher than on its other business loans. In contrast, microenterprise loan funds that lend to the smallest businesses generally expect that within a few years they will achieve loss rates of 2 to 5 percent. The Women's Self-Employment Project has achieved losses within

Table 7-3
Rates of Loan Loss for Development Banks (Ratio of
Cumulative Losses/Cumulative Loans Made)

Program	Purpose		Loss Rate (%)
A religious/foundation eco-nomic-development loan fund[a]	Business	1979–86	44.0
A religious/foundation eco-nomic-development loan fund[a]	Business	1981–86	27.0
Job Loan and Urban Venture Corp.[b]	Business	1968–70	41.4
Rural Enterprise RLF[c]	Business	1982–84 as of 1985	39.2
SBA Minority Loan Portfolio[d]	Business	1968 as of 1976	33.0
Southern Mississippi Planning and Development District[c]	Business	1982–84 as of 1985	29.9
Industrial Cooperative Asso-ciation[i]	Business	as of 1989	26.0
Philadelphia Commercial De-velopment Corporation[f]	Business	1981–85	19.0
SBA Minority Loan Portfolio[d]	Business	1967–76	18.3
Massachusetts Technology De-velopment Corporation[c]	Business	1982–84 as of 1985	13.6
U.S. EDA–sponsored Revolv-ing Loan Funds[c]	Business	1982–84 as of 1985	12.2
A sample of low-income busi-ness loan funds[g]	Business	as of 1988	12.0
City-based Working Capital Revolving Loan Funds[f]	Business		6.85
SBA Nonminority Loan Port-folio[d]	Business	1967–76	6.0
SBA Nonminority Loan Port-folio[d]	Business	1968 as of 1976	5.44
Women's Self-Employment Project Microloans[i]	Business	as of 1991	4
Santa Cruz Community Devel-opment Credit Union[h]	Mixed	1978–89	.8

Program	Purpose		Loss Rate (%)
Cooperative Fund of New England[j]	Business	1975–87	.63
Delaware Valley Community Reinvestment Fund[k]	Mixed	1986–89	0
Women's Self-Employment Project Peer Group Loans[i]	Business	as of 1991	0

[a]Richard Schramm, Massachusetts Institute of Technology (for 44 loans totaling $2,127,730 to 40 community, cooperative, and Native American businesses serving low-income populations between 1976 and 1986).

[b]Robert H. Edelstein, "Improving the Selection of Credit Risks: An Analysis of a Commercial Bank Minority Lending Program," *Journal of Finance* 30, no. 1 (March 1975): p. 39.

[c]Mt. Auburn Associates, *Factors Influencing the Performance of U.S. EDA–Sponsored Revolving Loan Funds*, vol. 2, *Case Studies* (Somerville, Mass.: Mt. Auburn Associates, 1987).

[d]Richard Klein, "Financial Results of the Small Business Administration's Minority Business Loan Portfolio," *University of Michigan Business Review* (January 1978): p. 22.

[e]Figures provided by Katherine Gross, Industrial Cooperative Association, November 1989.

[f]Interface, *Where Credit Is Due: A Study of Small Business Access to Capital* (New York: Interface, 1988), Appendix C, pp. 2–3.

[g]Laura Henze, Nancy Nye, and Richard Schramm, *Roundtable Workshop for Business-Development and Self-Employment Loan Funds Serving Low-Income People: Summary Report*, Tufts University, Medford, Mass., 1 October 1988.

[h]Figures provided by Karen Zelin, Santa Cruz Community Development Credit Union, December 1989.

[i]Figures provided by Connie Evans, Women's Self-Employment Project, November 1991.

[j]Cooperative Fund of New England, *Information for Social Investors* (31 December 1987).

[k]Delaware Valley Community Reinvestment Fund, *Prospectus* (Philadelphia, 1989).

this range and, on its peer-group loans, has had 100 percent repayment. The techniques that microenterprise loan funds use to manage losses are very different from those of other small-business lenders.

Development banks that lend to businesses with no operating history by which to judge future performance or market demand anticipate higher losses. Most of the business-loan losses of the Center for Community Self-Help in Durham, North Carolina, have involved new companies with inadequate management.[6] New-business lending is also one of the factors that explains the high loss rate experienced by the Industrial Cooperative Association (ICA) Loan Fund in Somerville, Massachusetts; it is essentially making venture-capital investments, and experiencing anticipated loss rates for venture capital.

Development banks that lend to low-income people operating businesses in low-income communities also generally expect to experience higher losses. Where businesspeople have fewer resources to fall back on and more uncertain markets for their products, the risk of default is greater. The Good Faith Fund in Pine Bluff, Arkansas, has found that borrowers are repaying their loans, but many cannot pay on time because they have nothing to fall back on when something unexpected, like a theft, occurs.[7] Lending to businesses in poor communities does not have to be high risk if the companies have strong prospects. Northern Community Investment Corporation in Vermont focuses on new and young firms that, although perhaps undercapitalized, have strong prospects for growth and managements with the skill and experience to achieve it.

Higher loss rates are also anticipated by new development banks. They often experiment with new products or try proven methods in new settings. Their losses tend to decline over time as programs gain experience in development lending, refine products, and fine-tune their loan mix and structures. The Philadelphia Commercial Development Corporation's working-capital business-loan fund was able to reduce its loss rate from 19 percent to 5.5 percent by changing its loan policies.[8] Quitman County Federal Credit Union, in the north Mississippi Delta, had delinquencies of 18 to 20 percent in its early years. Over time, it was able to reduce them and its losses dramatically by tightening its loan procedures, requirements, and collection efforts.[9] Many of the new microenterprise loan funds anticipate loss rates of 10 percent in the first few years, but much lower rates in the long run. Lack of experience has been a factor explaining high losses for some minority-small-business loan funds and for some supported by the Economic Development Administration (EDA). Rural Enterprises, an EDA–backed loan fund in Durant, Oaklahoma, initially tried to make product-development investments for which it lacked financial expertise. As a result, loans were made with overly generous terms and with little regard for financial soundness.[10] Performance does not always improve with age. Some programs that are poorly conceived are not revamped and they eventually fade away. It is generally agreed that this is the case for the Job Loan and Urban Venture Corporation, a banking program, and the Small Business Administration Minority Loan Program. The majority of privately financed loan funds launched in the 1960s were also abandoned because they were ill-conceived and poorly managed.[11]

Development banks have taken a variety of effective steps to minimize the risk of their chosen activities and the losses they incur when projects fail. The Cooperative Fund of New England, in Hartford, Connecticut, explains that its losses are low because of extensive loan review and oversight, availability of technical assistance, local involvement in each community where a loan is made, and shared responsibility with borrowers because all are part of a network of cooperative organizations.[12] Northern Community Investment Corporation manages losses by getting other financial institutions involved in its loans, monitoring its portfolio carefully, requiring financial reporting, providing technical assistance, diversifying its portfolio, and riding herd on borrowers.[13] Quitman County Federal Credit Union requires that potential borrowers be members in the credit union for ninety days, have fifty dollars in share accounts, and be gainfully employed. It makes credit checks on borrowers and requires security on its loans (other than unsecured personal loans).[14]

Credit risk is managed best by establishing and following explicit loan policies. Of the commercial banks that failed between 1979 and 1981, 81 percent had nonexistent or poorly followed loan policies; 69 percent had inadequate systems to ensure compliance with internal policies or banking statutes; 63 percent had inadequate controls or supervision of key bank officers or departments; and 59 percent had inadequate systems for identifying problem loans.[15] Simply having and following a written set of procedures on the basic mechanics of loan approval and documentation might have avoided many bank failures. While early development-finance programs found these procedures bureaucratic, the current crop of development banks is very serious about its loan policies. The banks commonly ensure that borrowers understand their obligations by requiring that every loan have a note, an agreement on terms and conditions, and, if applicable, a security agreement. These legal agreements prevent borrowers from unilaterally changing the risk of a loan through loan covenants restricting them from incurring more debt, changing management, or selling assets. The agreements, if they include a requirement for financial reporting, also permit lenders to learn about borrower problems as soon as possible.

Some loan losses are prevented by adopting loan policies that make it difficult for development-bank employees to commit fraud. Although it is a risk for very few development banks, the case of Franklin Community Credit Union in Omaha, Nebraska, shows that fraud can happen. The credit union was lauded for its development activities and raised millions of dollars in social investments. When the National Credit Union Administration closed it down in November 1988, it discovered that the credit union had assets of $2.5 million and certificate-of-deposit liabilities of $40 million—some thirty-seven million dollars were missing.[16] Because most efforts to commit fraud are disguised as loans to associates of the directors or managers of a financial institution where there is no intention of repaying the loan, development banks can avoid fraud by limiting loans to owners, managers, or their families or by reviewing these loans more closely.

Policies on collections, loan workouts, and loan foreclosures have also helped avoid loan losses. There is an above-average risk in development banking that borrowers will expect loans to be forgiven if times get tough. Development banks that demonstrate that their loans are serious obligations by staying in touch with slow payers, charging late fees, and foreclosing on loans are more likely to hear about problems from their borrowers.

Development banks have been very successful at managing risk by taking the time to understand the nature of their borrowers' businesses. Development bankers often identify less risk in their deals than do mainstream financial institutions, and they sometimes incur much lower losses than their more conventional counterparts would expect. The Institute for Community Economics (ICE) in Springfield, Massachusetts, has incurred lower loan losses than many commercial banks on its housing loans to low-income groups. Losses are kept low because loan managers understand the kinds of deals they review and proceed with the diligence needed to determine what will make the deals work and whether the people involved have the tenacity to see the projects to completion. Technical assistance is often offered as part of this process, especially by loan funds that work with new or marginal firms and by venture-capital funds that work with new or growing businesses. Such help can be very expensive, but it is essential if capital is to be offered to people who do not already have the capacity to use it well.

Development banks also manage risk by attracting good clients. This can be quite difficult for new banks, since they are more likely to attract good deals once they have become respected participants in economic development. According to Mary Houghton, a founder of Shorebank Corporation in Chicago, development-financing programs must be credible and responsive to attract good clients. Word-of-mouth testimonials by individuals who received professional treatment, as well as money, is the best way to reach them. Until it develops a reputation, a development bank must use other means to find good clients, including offering technical services or creating a project that demonstrates its capabilities. Development banks need visibility to generate a flow of good deals. Targeted marketing strategies—using media, publicity, direct mail, trade-association presentations, and contacts with housing, business, and financial professionals—also help.

Portfolio diversification is another important risk-management tool. Its purpose is to minimize the effect of any particular event on the stability of the financial institution by ensuring that borrowers are not all affected by the same events. Investing large amounts in a single borrower, industry, or community has been an important cause of failure in mainstream financial concerns. Savings institutions that invested only in mortgages in Texas have failed; commercial banks that invested heavily in oil companies in Oklahoma have failed. Development banks have fallen victim to the same error. A deciding factor in the 1989 collapse of Citizens' Coalition Federal Credit Union in Pontiac, Michigan, was the reliance of the community on General Motors for jobs and business sales. Even though the credit union had many small loans and a mix of consumer, real estate, and business loans, this could not protect it from plant shutdowns and layoffs.[17] Limiting the share of the loan portfolio lent to one borrower may not result in diversification. A sounder approach involves allocating risk exposure to a variety of economic sectors and locations. A very important method of expanding industrial and geographical diversification at relatively low cost is to buy and sell participations in loans with other development lenders. To pursue such a strategy, there must be other lenders who use similar or identical underwriting criteria for their loans and who have exhibited sound lending policies, good management, integrity, and honesty. For example, a group of savings and loan associations in California created the Savings Association Mortgage Company, Inc. (SAMCO), to sell interests in pools of loans to each other. The Northwest Bronx Coalition Federal Credit Union in New York City has a community-development loan program under which it asks other community credit unions to serve as co-lenders through loan participations.[18]

Financial institutions, whether mainstream or development banks, sometimes choose not to diversify because specialization allows them to develop expertise that lowers the cost of reviewing and originating loans. Balancing the gains from specialization and the gains from diversification is not simple. Diversification is especially difficult for development banks formed to serve a specific kind of borrower. One reason for the failure of Interfaith Loan Fund in Philadelphia was that its portfolio consisted only of loans to large producer cooperatives in the city. The Interfaith Loan Fund, started by the Philadelphia Association for Cooperative Enterprise (PACE), was dismantled after it suffered losses on both of its first two loans.[19] The Self-Help Credit Union, in Durham, North Carolina, which also targets worker cooperatives, has tried to diversify its portfolio by doing more small deals and by not limiting itself to making commercial loans to worker co-ops. It also makes first-mortgage real-estate loans and other kinds of loans. Establishing a mix of business and housing loans is one way to moderate the risk of business lending.

Development banks that have survived for a long time tend to pay a great deal of attention to loans after they are made. Loans are monitored to identify changes in the condition of borrowers, and the banks respond early and swiftly to resolve such problems. Loan monitoring also provides important information on patterns of delinquencies, which can be used to improve loan policies. The Industrial Cooperative Association

Loan Fund in Somerville, Massachusetts, receives monthly financial statements, comparisons of actual to budget performance, minutes of board meetings, annual audited financial statements and annual budget projections, and talks to borrowers monthly on the phone, as well as undertaking periodic site visits.[20] Some development banks have created overall monitoring programs that include a loan-classification system to help decide how to manage each loan in its portfolio. The ICE Loan Fund in Springfield, Massachusetts, places its loans in three risk categories—pass, internal guidance, and deficient.[21] For those loans categorized as pass, monitoring consists of acknowledging loan payments and reviewing regular financial reports. Contacts with the other two classes of borrowers are much more frequent.

Another aspect of effective loan management is creating incentives for borrowers not to default on loans. These may include requiring borrowers to commit their resources as equity contributions or collateral, creating peer pressure to repay loans, and requiring borrowers to build up their personal equity. Development bankers often use these tools differently than mainstream bankers do, but they find them just as important.

When borrowers have their own assets at risk, they are less likely to walk away from a loan. Borrowers can be put at risk by requiring them to make equity investments in their venture or to secure loans with important business assets. Losses are low at the Delaware Valley Community Reinvestment Corporation in Philadelphia because of careful loan structuring and review, but also because almost all loans are secured by first mortgages on property. Even though low-income people usually have few assets to commit or invest, some development lenders have found that securing loans with what business assets they do have is more effective than not requiring any security. If low-income people do not have resources to invest in new businesses, some development banks require that they make contributions to the business once they receive a loan (through payroll deductions or commitments to reinvest) in order to build up their personal stake in the business.

Many kinds of development banks use a personal sense of obligation as a tool to encourage loan repayment. Community-development credit unions use member education to remind participants that they own the credit union and are responsible for it. Potential borrowers must demonstrate that they understand their dual role at many credit unions.[22] Community-development loan funds also encourage borrowers to have a shared commitment to the funds' goals and make sure borrowers know that their defaults jeopardize the chances for other projects to receive loans.

Microenterprise loan funds sometimes rely more explicitly on peer pressure to encourage loan repayments. They require potential borrowers to join small borrower groups and make the availability of credit to any member of a group contingent on repayment of loans by every member. Many U.S. microenterprise loan programs are using peer groups, either alone or along with more traditional means of securing loans, such as taking a lien against general business assets. The Good Faith Fund in Pine Bluff, Arkansas, initially made loans only to peer groups. The Women's Self-Employment Project (WSEP) and the Self-Employment Circle fund, both located in Chicago, allow some people to borrow individually, while others join a peer group. The Micro Industry Rural Credit Organization (MICRO), in Tucson, Arizona, encourages borrowers to form peer groups, but it will give them the type of loan they choose. The Lakota Fund in Kyle, South Dakota, began operations making individual microloans of up to $1,000 (as well as small-business loans of up to $10,000) to members of the Lakota Tribe. It has reorganized its microloan component as the Circle Banking Project using a peer-group model. The U.S. microenterprise loan funds have adopted quite different structures for the peer-group loan. Most programs withhold additional credit to other group members unless they pay off a defaulting member's loan. The Women's Self-Employment Project allows groups to continue to borrow if they eliminate a member, bring in a new member, and go through the orientation program again. However, some programs also hold other members responsible for repayment by requiring them to cosign each other's loans. The policy of MICRO has been that members of a peer group all sign one promissory note, all thus becoming responsible for repayment.

The peer-group concept seems to work best when the groups range in size from five to eight members. According to Accíon International, which has initiated microenterprise loan programs in many countries, a group with less than five members, is less likely to be able to pay off the loan of one member who defaults and less able to maintain its group dynamic if one member resigns. If there are too many members, then it is difficult to build group solidarity. Programs in the United States generally require that groups have five members. According to the early experience of the Good Faith Fund, group members feel a greater sense of collective obligation if peer groups are formed on their own, take a long time to come together, and are accompanied by constant communication between the borrower groups and program staff.[23]

Development banks have used savings programs creatively to produce incentives and capacity to repay loans. Microenterprise loan funds in developing countries often tie credit to savings programs, which build an independent source of money for the fund and the borrower, as well as an additional source of repayment for loans. Requiring small, periodic deposits develops the habit of saving. This approach can also create an incentive to stay in the loan program, so long as it controls savings—that is, if it is understood that a borrower can only withdraw savings after repaying her loan. A savings program can also empower people. According to Mary Houghton, who is associated with the Good Faith Fund, such a program "changes the nature of your participation from being dependent on a big bank that might lend you money to participating in a movement to create capital."[24] Some community-development credit unions have also used savings programs to enhance repayment and to encourage borrowers to build equity.

Even when loan defaults are unavoidable, losses can still be limited if lenders stage loans based upon timely repayments of initial allocations, obtain loan guarantees, or secure their loans with collateral that they can liquidate to replace lost capital. Staging the availability of funds limits the size of loan losses when borrowers default. The Center for Community Self-Help Venture Fund in Durham, North Carolina, has used what it calls "staged financial commitments." It extends small loans and uses repayment performance to judge whether a borrower should be granted a larger loan. The Connecticut Product Development Corporation in Hartford stages its investments and reserves the right of termination if a business does not meet its development plan or does not report its progress.

Loan-guarantee programs can be set up in several different ways. In South Korea, India, and the Philippines, there are loan programs in which borrowers pay an extra fee of .5 to 1.2 percent of their loan; this is then pooled as an extra loan-loss reserve. Similarly, the state-run Michigan Strategic Fund has a program in which a loan-loss reserve is created by contributions made by a commercial bank, its borrower, and the state government. The borrower pays a one-time premium charge of between 1.5 and 3.5 percent into a loss reserve, the commercial bank matches this payment, and the state matches the combined contribution. Loan guarantees can also be sought from independent third parties who promise to repay all or part of a loan if the borrower defaults. The Santa Cruz Community Development Credit Union uses the California Coastal Agency guarantee program, which guarantees 60 to 90 percent of small-business loans.[25] Personal guarantees can be required from parties with a personal or financial interest in the loan. The experience of North Carolina's Center for Community Self-Help is that personal guarantees may be particularly important in securing the commitment of initial leadership in start-up businesses.[26] If managers have a personal risk, they may be less likely to walk away from a difficult situation. The Santa Cruz Community Development Credit Union requires that all community-development loans have a personal guarantee from the principal borrowers.[27]

Like mainstream financial institutions, development banks can liquidate marketable collateral to compensate for loan losses. Most development lenders find that they get fewer desirable assets than more traditional institutions to serve as collateral and that it is quite difficult to obtain collateral that has a liquidation value greater than the amounts of their loans. This is generally more of a problem for business loans than for housing loans. In either case, development lenders frequently use what collateral is available. The National Cooperative Bank Development Corporation, an affiliate of the National Cooperative Bank in Washington, D.C., which focuses on cooperatives serving low-income people, takes a general lien against business assets.

Interest-Rate Risk

Many development banks ignore (or are not aware of) interest-rate risk—uncertainty concerning the effect of changes in interest rates on the spread between what a financial institution earns on its funds and what it must pay for them. Financial institutions earn most of their money by charging borrowers more than they are charged by their own investors. If a financial institution can be forced by market conditions to change the rate paid to investors or charged to borrowers (but not vice versa), then it is accepting interest-rate risk. Many savings and loan associations were driven into bankruptcy in the late 1970s and early 1980s because the rates of interest they had to pay investors soared above what they were earning on their long-term loans. Even if a financial institution can live with a smaller spread, it cannot "sell" it to another investor. Even small development banks are selling, or looking for ways to sell, loans in secondary markets. If a development bank attempts to sell a loan that it made when interest rates were low at a time when interest rates are high, it will be paid much less than the outstanding amount of the loan. Because the purchaser could buy a new loan that paid the current higher rate, the old loan is simply not worth as much. Whenever funds attracted become more costly while borrower rates stay the same, a development bank suffers a loss. It can accept the loss immediately by selling the loan, or it can spread an equal amount over the remaining life of the loan by holding onto it and accepting lower spreads.

The effect of interest-rate risk on financial-institution spreads is demonstrated in the hypothetical example of "Community Bank" in Table 7-4. Community Bank has projected the impact on its operations of a 1 percent annual rise in interest rates under three different strategies for managing assets and liabilities. The bank initially has a 2 percent spread between its cost of funds and what it earns. In scenario three, Community Bank is able to maintain this spread because it matches assets and liabilities. In scenario two, the bank catches up to the change in rates every two years when its loan matures. In scenario one, it does not catch up until the sixth year, by which time the bank may have failed. If interest rates never changed, all three strategies would yield the same spread. If interest rates fell, Community Bank might achieve larger spreads and profits by taking on more interest-rate risk, as in scenario one.

Table 7-4
Community Bank's Interest-Rate Exposure (Assuming a Yearly 1% Increase in Cost of Funds)

	Scenario One	Scenario Two	Scenario Three
ASSET			
Maturity	5 years	2 years	1 year
Interest rate	7%	7%	7%
LIABILITY			
Maturity	1 year	1 year	1 year
Interest rate	5%	5%	5%
SPREAD			
Year 1	7 − 5 = 2%	7 − 5 = 2%	7 − 5 = 2%
Year 2	7 − 6 = 1%	7 − 6 = 1%	8 − 6 = 2%
Year 3	7 − 7 = 0%	9 − 7 = 2%	9 − 7 = 2%
Year 4	7 − 8 = −1%	9 − 8 = 1%	10 − 8 = 2%
Year 5	7 − 9 = −2%	10 − 8 = 2%	11 − 9 = 2%
Average spread	0%	1%	2%

However, unless it set a severe prepayment penalty against its borrowers, they would prepay their loans and Community Bank would still not reap a significant gain from rising interest rates. Development banks can easily assess the effect of changes in interest rates on net interest income through a simulation, where cash flows are projected on a monthly basis, including all flows of funds into and out of the bank, using various interest-rate assumptions.

Financial institutions are inexplicably resistant to managing interest-rate risk. Even though the interest-rate volatility that first appeared in the 1970s has irreparably damaged hundreds of them, thousands of savings institutions and credit unions remain unprotected from interest-rate risk. With some notable exceptions, development bankers generally are not more attentive than managers of mainstream financial institutions to interest-rate risk. Most have not found the time to analyze their exposure to it or to devise a strategy for managing interest rates.

Some financial institutions accept interest-rate risk because they do not think through the potential impact on their performance. At the moment it makes a loan decision, a financial institution is earning its target interest spread between sources and uses of funds. If it has never been caught with a mismatch that eliminated its spread (and it does not read the financial press), it may simply focus its resources on more immediate problems. This is the explanation for the poor interest-rate matches at many community-development credit unions.

A larger number of financial institutions accept interest-rate risks because they believe they can outguess the rest of the world by accurately predicting future changes in interest rates. If so, they can earn profits not only from taking credit risk but also from their skills in taking interest-rate risks. The incentive lenders have to increase income by mismatching assets and liabilities relates to the slope of the yield curve for investments. The yield curve is a graph plotting the interest rate earned on investments for each term to maturity (e.g., three months, six months, one year, etc.). Because there have been inflationary expectations for many years, and because investors ask for more compensation on long-term investments to protect them in case inflation is greater than anticipated, long-term interest rates have generally been higher than short-term rates in the 1980s. Thus, there has been an upward-sloping yield curve. If the curve never changed shape, lenders could maximize income by borrowing at its short end and lending at the long end. However, the yield curve does change shape, making this strategy very risky. In fact, even the notion of a permanently stable yield curve is contradictory. If interest rates were stable over a very long time, eventually the yield curve itself would grow much flatter, lessening the risk and the temptation to borrow short and lend long. Unfortunately, financial institutions have proven no better than anyone else at predicting interest rates, and, with few exceptions, any extra profits have been accompanied by equal amounts of extra risk.

Some development banks consciously accept interest-rate risk because they believe it is the only way to accomplish their goals. Development banks often want to lend for the long term, but their pool of investors will only provide short-term funds. Banks that accept this mix of liabilities and assets understand the risk they take. This approach is most common among loan funds and credit unions.

Development banks have at their disposal a wide array of techniques to reduce interest-rate risk or to increase the compensation they receive when they must accept it. Matching maturities of assets and liabilities is the most straightforward approach to minimizing interest-rate risk. It is commonly used by small savings and loan associations and commercial banks. Lending officers and deposit marketers know each week roughly what is in demand on the other side of the bank and try to make matches. It is often not reasonable or efficient to match each loan with a specific source of funds, but assets and liabilities can be categorized based upon when they are repriced, and these categories can be matched. The Institute for Community Economics Loan Fund in Springfield, Massachusetts, manages interest-rate risk by matching the overall terms of loans it makes with the loans it receives from investors.

For development banks with access to only very-short-term capital, maturity matching can be too constraining. Most investors are unwilling to accept the risk of providing long-term funds to development banks about which little public information is available and that can offer no liquidity. Charitable funders who finance many of the loan funds have been no more patient than the norm. Over time, we hope that development lenders with a sound operating history will be able to attract longer-term funds by offering additional security, demonstrating what the funds will allow them to accomplish, and, perhaps, offering a limited means for investors to exit their investment before maturity. Some loan funds have used an offer to repay investor loans on demand (if it is feasible) to attract longer-term funds. For now, maturity matching will not serve these lenders well unless they want to make short-term loans.

Development banks that are depository institutions can effectively match the maturities of their assets and liabilities. Depository institutions have better access to long-term funds because they can offer long-term investors safety. Regardless of their size, they can issue federally insured long-term certificates of deposit (CDs). However, few depository institutions offer CDs for terms longer than five years. The volume of thirty-year loans made by savings institutions demonstrates that this is not because there is little demand for long-term borrowing. The explanation may be that depositors/savers demand very high premiums to lock up their capital for long periods, and choose instead to purchase Treasury securities of long maturity that can be readily sold if cash is needed. If this is the explanation, then financial institutions that wish to make loans with maturities greater than five years should use another method of reducing interest-rate risk (particularly such hedging devices as swaps and futures, which are discussed below). However, it may also be the case that a development bank would be more successful in attracting longer-term CDs with a marketing approach based on development impact. Depository institutions also have a new means to attract long-term loans as a result of the Financial Institutions Reform, Recovery, and Enforcement Act of 1989, which allows commercial banks and credit unions, as well as savings institutions, to borrow from the Federal Home Loan Bank to make low-income housing loans.

Another way to limit interest-rate risk is to make variable-interest-rate loans. If the five-year loan made by the hypothetical "Community Bank" in Table 7-4 had an annually adjusted variable rate, the bank could have maintained its 2 percent spread. Most business loans made by commercial banks are variable-rate loans that float with the prime rate. A growing share of mortgage loans made by savings institutions are also variable-rate loans. This form of lending is commonly used by development-oriented commercial banks and by some credit unions. For example, one-third of the loan portfolio at California's Santa Cruz Community Development Credit Union is in variable-rate loans.[28] Almost all of the share loans held by NCB Savings Association the S&L purchased by National Cooperative Bank in Hillsboro, Ohio, to make and buy cooperative-housing loans, are variable-rate loans. These loans, such as adjustable-rate mortgages (ARMs), only eliminate interest-rate risk if certain conditions are met. The rates charged on loans must change with a financial institution's cost of funds. The shorter the lag between changes in fund costs and adjustments to loan rates, the greater protection variable-rate loans provide. In addition, the base to which loan rates are pegged must move coincidently with changes in the rates paid to investors. So, if loans to a loan fund increase in cost by 2 percent, then the base rate to which loans made by the fund are pegged must increase on close to the same date and by close to the same amount.

Variable-rate loans limit interest-rate risk for the lender solely by shifting it to the borrower, who must pay higher rates when interest rates rise. If they rise enough, borrowers may no longer be able to support loan payments. In such cases, interest-rate protection is gained at the expense of credit-risk protection. The ability of a borrower to operate profitably if interest rates rise somewhat should be part of the credit analysis by a development bank.

Cost increases associated with changes in interest rates on variable-rate loans can be passed on to borrowers without raising loan payments if current principal payments are reduced by the amount of the increase in interest payments and if the principal is repaid further in the future by extending the term to maturity. This approach, known as "rate indexing," allows a financial institution's income to rise with interest rates while its after-tax cash flow is reduced. Of course, all the bank has really done is to make the borrower an additional loan with which to pay the higher interest rates. This may be a higher-risk loan, and it is precisely the game played in recent years in making loans to certain Third World countries.

Instead of fully shifting interest-rate risk to the borrower, it is possible to share it by capping the increase in rates paid in any given period. This approach is common in mortgage lending and is widely available to large corporate borrowers in the interest-rate swap market, the financial market where parties swap payments on loans in order to reduce their interest-rate risk. Caps, or ceilings, on variable-rate loans give the borrower protection against rapidly rising interest rates. Caps can be offered to borrowers in exchange for a premium or a front-end fee. While the concept of a cap is straightforward, caps are difficult to price and leave the provider with some remaining risk to hedge.

Another common way to manage both interest-rate risk and liquidity is to sell loans. More and more development banks are investigating this option. For example, NCB Savings Association in Hillsboro, Ohio, sells all of its fixed-rate loans in the secondary-mortgage markets. Northside Community Credit Union in Chicago is currently looking into the potential for loan sales to formal secondary-market institutions.[29] The Community Reinvestment Fund in Minneapolis has created a secondary market for loan funds in Minnesota, Wisconsin, and Michigan, with additional states to follow. The National Association of Community Development Loan Funds in Philadelphia is also trying to develop opportunities for loan sales. Such sales can be a viable strategy for managing interest-rate risk if loans are sold quickly or are based upon commitments for sale at a particular price. If Community Bank in Table 7-4 had sold its five-year loan before interest rates changed, it would have received cash that could be used to pay off its short-term depositors. As discussed earlier, attempting to sell loans after interest rates change will expose the problem, not eliminate it. There are several entities that might be convinced to buy long-term development loans, including insurance companies and pension funds. They will probably only buy if they know the development bank or the borrower well or if the loan is supported by collateral or guaranteed in some way against default. Loans are sold most easily through the organized secondary markets described in the following section on managing liquidity risk.

Interest-rate risk can also be transferred without actually selling a loan by hedging with interest-rate futures or swaps. Hedging requires very specific technical knowledge and a large volume of loans. Thus, it is only useful for development banks that make many millions of dollars of loans each year. An interest-rate-futures contract is a standardized, transferable agreement to buy or sell a financial instrument on a specified future date at a set price. The buyer (the "long") agrees to purchase the item; the seller (the "short") agrees to deliver it. Each futures transaction is made through a clearinghouse. Participants rely on the creditworthiness of the clearinghouse and do not have to investigate individual buyers and sellers. A futures contract allows a lender to offset gains or losses that occur because of changes in interest rates in the cash market with losses or gains on the futures contract. Assume a development bank enters an interest-rate-futures contract where it agrees to buy a Treasury note at 8 percent from the seller in one year. Then the bank makes a long-term fixed-rate loan funded by one-year CDs. If, during the year, interest rates rise 2 percent, the development bank can offset its spread loss when it buys the Treasury note under the futures contract at a rate that is 2 percent below current rates and resells it at current market rates. If interest rates fall 2 percent, the development bank's loss on the futures contract (it must buy it at 2 percent above market rates) is offset by the increase in its interest-rate spread on loans.

Commercial banks are active participants in the futures markets; under special programs, other kinds of development banks can also participate. While most of the activity has been on the part of very large banks, some small banks have purchased and sold futures and forward contracts. Almost 2.4 percent of commercial banks with assets of less than $100 million used futures and forward contracts in September 1984.[30] If a development lender is willing to retain the credit risk, an organization such as Prudential Insurance, which has an interest-rate hedge and swap program, could take on the interest-rate risk. The program would need to be negotiated based upon its nonfinancial benefits to Prudential because most development lenders do not have a sufficient volume of loan activity or financial credibility to participate in futures programs otherwise. South Shore Bank of Chicago has participated in futures markets.

Although interest swaps are not yet a feasible tool for most development banks, they could be enormously useful. An interest-rate swap is an agreement between two parties to exchange interest payments on two separately made loans. One of the parties makes a fixed-rate loan; the other makes a variable-rate loan. The former exchanges its stream of fixed-rate interest payments for the latter's stream of variable-rate payments. There are risks in interest-rate swaps, but they are limited to the interest exchanges—no principal payments ever change hands. If the counterparty to the swap defaults on the agreement, the development bank receives the remaining interest payments on its own fixed-rate loan. The risk in this case is that interest rates will have risen in the meantime, leaving the development bank with an interest-rate mismatch. In addition, just as in the futures markets, there is a risk that floating-rate payments (payments on assets) will not perfectly match or move with funding costs (payments on liabilities). Because there are seldom perfect matches between any two loans' termination dates and settlement dates, swaps can be very complicated. In many cases a third party, such as the swap market, may be able to bear interest-rate risk at a lower cost than either lenders or borrowers. Unfortunately, the swap market is not accessible for small development lenders.

If a development bank cannot reduce or transfer interest-rate risk through one of the preceding techniques, it can still ensure that it is compensated for this risk. The potential losses due to interest-rate movements in a fixed-rate, long-term loan can be offset by charging a risk premium in the form of an additional interest charge or up-front fee. The risk premium is best calculated by reference to risk premiums being charged by participants in public fixed-income markets. For example, a development bank considering making a five-year fixed-rate loan could review the increase in interest rates between two publicly traded corporate bonds whose maturities differ by five years and whose ratings are identical (both BBB, for example). To have sufficient confidence in the results to actually base pricing decisions on them, a financial institution would have to examine the rates on a large number of bonds and construct a premium table that links an interest-rate premium for each additional year of maturity desired by the borrower.

A development bank should probably use several of the interest-rate-management tools described in this section, depending on its own expertise and funding base. For example, South Shore Bank in Chicago has used practically all of them.[31] It has a computerized budgeting and asset/liability management system that measures mismatches between assets and liabilities. It writes almost all commercial loans with interest rates that float with the prime rate and all real-estate mortgages with adjustable rates that change every two or three years. It uses a variety of secondary markets for loans, including the Federal National Mortgage Association, the Student Loan Marketing Association, and various state programs. It also sells mortgages to institutional investors and SBA-guaranteed loans to other investors, maintains a highly liquid securities portfolio, and has used financial-futures markets to hedge interest-rate risk where it could not avoid mismatches.

Liquidity Risk

Unless a financial institution holds an amount of cash at least equal to the maximum possible demand for cash by its investors on any given day, it has liquidity risk. Liquidity risk is the possibility that a financial institution will not be able to meet its obligations on time or that it will suffer a capital loss in order to meet them. Without sufficient cash on hand, a financial institution must sell other assets to raise the cash to meet its obligations. It may be forced to sell these assets at a lower price than it would obtain if it could be more patient in raising cash. If it cannot sell these assets quickly enough, investors may be able to push the financial institution into bankruptcy. This is why the Delaware Valley Community Reinvestment Fund in Philadelphia makes a point of knowing that it has liabilities due within a year equal to 31 percent of assets, while loans maturing within a year equal 16 percent of assets.

Financial institutions accept liquidity risk because liquidity has an obvious opportunity cost—they can earn more on loans than on liquid investments. Too much liquidity was one factor that led to the failure of the Lower East Side Federal Credit Union in New York City in 1978. It lent out a very small proportion of its assets and, as a result, had substantially lower earnings than it could have attained.[32] Development banks also accept liquidity risk in order to increase their development impact. A development bank that does not lend out its capital simply withdraws cash from circulating in the local economy.

Financial institutions traditionally measure the adequacy of their liquidity by comparing their ratios of loans/deposits, loans/liabilities, and liquid assets/liabilities to those of their peers or by reviewing changes in the ratios over time. These comparisons ignore the differences in loan portfolios and sources of funds between financial institutions. They also ignore opportunities to borrow or sell loans as means of obtaining additional funds. Because exposure to liquidity risk depends upon the structure, volatility, and maturity of the liabilities and assets of a financial institution, the best way to measure such risk is to project a financial institution's funds flows, incorporating various assumptions based upon past experience about whether investors in a loan fund will renew their loans or about the stability of a commercial bank's money-market accounts. For example, from its experience, the Cooperative Fund of New England in Hartford, Connecticut, assumes that up to 10 percent of its capital may be withdrawn by investors who hold demand notes.

Most financial institutions, after evaluating their liquidity needs, have chosen to keep a significant portion of their assets in liquid forms. In 1986, 50 to 66 percent of the assets of small commercial banks consisted of loans. Even though the best-earning assets are usually loans, securities are more liquid. Small savings and loan associations and credit unions also have a large share of their assets in securities (see Table 7-5). None of the three has loans greater than 70 percent of assets. They

Table 7-5
Balance Sheet Asset Compositions (as a Share of Assets)

	Small Commercial Banks	Small Thrifts	Small Credit Unions
Loans	.51	.66	.61
Investments	.45	.25	.38
Fixed assets	.02	.02	.01
Other assets	.02	.06	.00

Source: Federal Deposit Insurance Corporation, Commercial Bank Financial Statements (with adjustments to scale to $25 million from a range of $25–100 million), 1986; Functional Cost Analysis for 1986 Average Thrift Institutions, Federal Reserve Bank, Function Cost Section (data for thrifts with deposits up to $50 million), 1987; National Credit Union Administration, 1986 Yearend Statistics for Federally Insured Credit Unions (with adjustments to scale to $3 million from a range of $2–5 million), 1987.

all maintain substantially higher liquid reserves than they are required to by regulators to ensure that they can meet their obligations. Even so, some of these depository institutions are still not sufficiently liquid. Some securities (such as money-market securities) are easily converted to cash without a loss of value; others are more difficult to convert in this way. Long-term bonds, while frequently marketable, sometimes must be sold at a discount below their purchase price. Credit unions, in particular, have been holding very large bond portfolios that may not be convertible into cash without a loss.

It may appear that these banks are an inefficient way for investors to provide capital for economic development. After all, an investor can reasonably expect that the bank will not lend out much more than half of any investment. The rest simply goes into securities of the sort that the depositor might be able to invest in independently, such as Treasury securities and tax-exempt bonds. However, a development bank, by pooling investors, can afford to put a larger proportion of available capital into liquid development loans than each of the investors acting individually could prudently do.

Development banks have chosen quite different levels of liquidity. Table 7-6 shows the loan-to-asset ratio for a variety of development banks. Ones like the Mountain Association for Community Economic Development (MACED) Loan Fund in Berea, Kentucky, which have few and predictable debts, incur minimal liquidity risk and so need less liquidity. Although the MACED Loan Fund lends out about 80 percent of its assets, its goal is to lend more, and it is willing to live with a ratio of loans to assets of up to 100 percent.[33] Northern Community Investment Corporation in St. Johnsbury, Vermont, is also funded mainly by grants and therefore needs little liquidity. It tries not to lend out more than 80 percent of its loanable capital so that it always has capital to loan to deals in progress. It seeks additional capital whenever it approaches this 80 percent limit.[34] Kentucky Highlands Investment Corporation, a venture and loan fund in Kentucky supported almost entirely by grants, also reserves some capital for follow-on investments in its portfolio of companies.[35] Development banks that rely on short-term funding have much more potential liquidity risk and much lower ratios of loans to assets. For example, at mid-year 1988, Delaware Valley Community Reinvestment Fund, a community-development loan fund in Philadelphia, anticipated that its liabilities that had to be repaid within one year equaled 31 percent of assets. Because they rely heavily on share accounts that are very active, low-income credit unions generally have had about 64 percent of assets invested in loans.[36]

For some of the development banks, low ratios of loans to assets are explained, not by exposure to liquidity risk, but by rapid growth or lack of loan demand. The percent of capital lent out collectively by members of the National Association of

Table 7-6
Loan-to-Asset Ratios of Development Banks

Program	Ratio (%)
Institute for Community Economics Loan Fund[a]	83
MACED Loan Fund[b]	80
Quitman County Federal Credit Union[c]	78
Cooperative Fund of New England[d]	76
NCB Savings Association[e]	72
Northside Community Credit Union[f]	67
Kentucky Highlands Investment Corporation[g]	67
Santa Cruz Community Development Credit Union[h]	62
Shorebank Corporation[i]	60
Delaware Valley Community Reinvestment Fund[j]	44
Blackfeet National Bank[k]	40

[a]National Association of Community Development Loan Funds, *Statistical Profile of Member Fund Activity*, 30 June 1989.

[b]Figures provided by Paula Bowman, MACED Loan Fund, November 1989.

[c]Figures provided by Robert Jackson, Quitman County Federal Credit Union, December 1989.

[d]End-of-1988 financial statements.

[e]Figures provided by A. Lamont Mackley, NCB Savings Association, December 1989.

[f]Figures provided by Elaine Wricks, November 1989.

[g]Figures provided by Jerry Rickett, Kentucky Highlands Investment Corporation, January 1990.

[h]Figures provided by Karen Zelin, Santa Cruz Community Development Credit Union, December 1989.

[i]*Annual Report, 1988*.

[j]Prospectus, 30 June 1988.

[k]Figures provided by Jack Kelly, Blackfeet National Bank, November 1989.

Community Development Loan Funds in Philadelphia rose from 47 percent at the end of 1988, to 54 percent at the end of 1989, to 57 percent at the end of 1990 at least in part because loan activity caught up with liability growth.[37] Development banks need time to place their capital in sound loans. The Northside Community Credit Union in Chicago expects to raise its loan-to-asset ratio above 67 percent because it hired a new loan and marketing director.[38] The president of Blackfeet National Bank in Browning, Montana, believed that it had a small share of its assets in loans at the end of 1989 because there were few loans it could make on the reservation. The Santa Cruz Community Development Credit Union in Santa Cruz, California, which has a loan-to-asset ratio of 62 percent in 1989, will go as high as 85 to 90 percent if it succeeds in generating more business-loan demand.

Most development banks limit their ratios of loans to assets to manage credit risk. Those that make high-risk investments do it both to manage risk and to produce a more reliable revenue stream to repay creditors. Low-risk securities holdings can offset higher risk loan portfolios. Income earned on securities fills the gap when loans fail to produce expected income. Kentucky Highlands, which makes both loans and very-long-term venture-capital investments, sets aside a portion of its capital to generate short-term earnings to meet operating costs and to manage its risk. It reserves enough capital in certificates of deposit to ensure that large losses on equity investments will not lead to bankruptcy. Loan funds that make high-risk, low-interest loans often must hold more in securities than in loans to ensure that they will be able to repay investors. While the Industrial Cooperative Association (ICA) Loan Fund's loss rate is currently 25 percent of loans, its rate of loss on assets is a more manageable 5 percent because it does not lend out a large portion of its capital.[39] The ICA Loan Fund probably cannot prudently loan out more than 50 percent of its capital, even though most of its debt is made up of predictable three- to five-year loans. Low-income business-loan funds use a large part of the money provided by investors to manage their risk because they cannot attract the right kinds of capital. These loan funds could increase their loan-to-asset ratios if they had more equity capital.

The primary factor determining the level of liquidity a development bank must maintain is the kind of capital it attracts. If a development bank can attract investors on favorable terms, then it will need to maintain less liquidity in its asset mix. Financial institutions whose capital consists mostly of long-term debt or equity need less liquidity than those that have a great deal of demand debt. Black-owned savings and loan associations have needed more liquidity than their peers because they have had a lower ratio of certificates of deposit to total deposits, smaller average deposits, and a higher activity of accounts.[40] Liquidity needs for common stock are modest. For preferred stock, a financial institution must maintain sufficient liquidity to pay dividends. The timing of these payments is predictable, as is that of payments on debt with a fixed rate and maturity. Debt with variable rate and fixed maturity is slightly more difficult to manage. While the timing of payments is predictable, payment amounts change. Debt that must be repaid on demand requires the greatest level of liquidity. Financial institutions need to predict outflows on such debt and maintain sufficient liquidity to minimize the risk of estimation error.

Some development banks that cannot attract investors who will accept the same maturities as their borrowers instead obtain lines of credit to fill liquidity gaps. This approach leaves a bank with greater capacity to meet development goals than would holding a large portfolio of liquid loans or only making loans that can be sold in active secondary markets. However, the capacity to borrow money immediately when needed is not without cost. Setting up a line of credit usually involves paying a commitment fee and providing collateral (commonly a portion of the illiquid loans that are causing the liquidity-risk problem in the first place). If these costs are less than the gains from accepting and charging for illiquidity, then a line of credit is preferable. The Institute for Community Economics Loan Fund in Springfield, Massachusetts, obtained a line of credit with a commercial bank to assist in its liquidity management. As development banks are able to attain scale and demonstrate good financial condition, they should be able to obtain lines of credit from other financial institutions.

A development bank can also manage liquidity risk by making or holding loans that trade in active secondary markets. There are three quasi-governmental agencies that facilitate the sale of loans in secondary markets: Federal National Mortgage Association (Fannie Mae), Federal Home Loan Mortgage Corporation (Freddie Mac), and Student Loan Marketing Association (Sallie Mae). Each of these organizations buys, pools, and packages loans into securities that are sold to investors. The major secondary-market institutions have special programs that target the markets served by community-oriented depository institutions. The only well-developed secondary market for commercial lending to companies that are not publicly traded is the informal market in SBA-guaranteed loans provided by specialized brokers. Many business- and industrial-development corporations (BIDCOs) sell commercial loans in this market. California's Santa Cruz Community Development Credit Union has enhanced its liquidity by holding marketable mortgage loans acquired under an unusual arrangement. It has an agreement with a mortgage broker under which it sends members who need home-mortgage loans to the broker. The credit union buys the FHA-insured loans the broker makes in the secondary market. These loans can be sold again if the credit union needs liquidity.

Some development banks have found individual investors

willing to buy their loans. For example, South Shore Bank in Chicago has sold multifamily-mortgage loans without recourse to several insurance companies. In 1988, an insurance firm purchased an $8.3 million package of mortgage loans from the National Cooperative Bank in Washington, D.C., including $2.2 million of mortgages on properties owned by low- to moderate-income residents.[41] For loan funds in a few states, the Community Reinvestment Fund in Minneapolis will provide a secondary market. Otherwise, loan sales must be arranged with individual buyers. Such sales are rare, and they are unlikely to occur on short notice.

While many liquidity-management tools can enhance a development bank's effectiveness in meeting capital needs, secondary-market sales of loans are a particularly important tool for development banks to employ. Loan sales not only help manage interest-rate and liquidity risk but also enable development banks to expand their volume of lending with less capital and, sometimes, lower operating costs (at least the costs of attracting capital). For example, NCB Savings Association in Hillsboro, Ohio, the savings-institution affiliate of the National Cooperative Bank, only has assets of $25 million, but it has made and sold an additional $50 million of cooperative-share loans to Fannie Mae.[42] The power that better access to secondary markets could give development banking is considerable.

Development banks that manage risk well can perform on a par with their mainstream peers in loan losses, interest-rate exposure, and liquidity. They will still be different from more traditional institutions because only they have the incentive to experiment with innovations that reduce the risk of developmental lending.

8
Minimizing the Costs of Operations

TRADITIONAL BANKERS think of development banking as costing more than business as usual, and it can. For instance, loans tailored to the needs of a particular borrower or structured to be divided among a variety of funding sources are common for development lenders. These loans are more costly to make than standardized loans by one lender acting independently. Nonstandardized loans require more staff time to negotiate and settle. Hiring lawyers to draw up unique terms for a commercial loan at a commercial bank can cost $5,000 or more per loan (10 percent of a $50,000 loan). The transaction costs of a loan increase geometrically with the number of participants in its funding.[1] A low-income-housing loan that requires four or five sources of funding can take as much as five times longer to produce than a real-estate loan with one source of funding. According to South Shore Bank in Chicago, the transaction costs it incurs in making business loans to meet a development purpose are substantially higher than for its other business loans.[2]

More risky loans also require closer supervision, and development lenders tend to make more risky loans than other financial institutions. With the exception of venture capitalists (who seek the potential for high returns) and finance companies (who seek sufficient collateral), most lenders make loans only when borrowers have a strong enough cash flow to repay them with a margin for safety. Development lenders also require that borrowers demonstrate an ability to pay, but perhaps not by so wide a margin. Their customers typically have less collateral than those of a traditional lender. Thus, they must take more time to get to know the borrower on whose capabilities they are relying. In addition, development banks graduate many of their seasoned loan customers to mainstream financial institutions. Their costs of assessing risk are higher than those of institutions whose bread and butter is established customers.

Development banks tend to make smaller and, therefore, more costly loans than do more traditional lenders. The time it takes to make and manage a small loan is no less than for a large loan, and sometimes it is more. As a result, transaction costs make up a larger share of the loan amount for a small loan. A variety of studies have found that black-owned commercial banks operating in low-income areas have higher operating costs than their peers because they work with customers who require smaller-than-average loans and make smaller-than-average deposits. Thus, they need more employees per deposit dollar.[3]

The impact of loan complexity, risk, and size on operating costs for large commercial banks is illustrated in Table 8-1. Managing investments in liquid securities requires the smallest level of effort. The securities are standard, the level of risk is easily controlled, and the investment portfolio is likely to include a relatively small number of large investments. Building and maintaining a credit-card portfolio is far more costly than assembling a portfolio of Treasury securities. While the loans are highly standardized, there are thousands of small loans that are unsecured and high risk.

Table 8-1
Operating Costs for an Average Commercial Bank with
Assets of $600 Million

Product	Operating Costs as a Share of Volume (%)	Cost Rank
Investments	.170	1
Real-estate mortgages	1.154	2
Commercial and other loans	1.701	3
Installment loans	2.857	4
Credit-card loans	11.157	5

Source: Functional Cost Analysis, 1986 Average Banks, Federal Reserve System, Washington, D.C., 1987.

Development-oriented financial institutions are also likely to incur higher costs because they engage in activities considered peripheral to their financing function. Development banks that play an advocacy role in financial markets or offer technical assistance need more staff. Technical assistance is expensive— to provide intensive venture-development support, the National Rural Development and Finance Corporation (NRD& FC) in Washington, D.C., plans to spend one dollar on technical assistance for every three dollars it lends.[4]

Operating costs are especially high for development lenders that operate in the national arena or in rural areas because the deals they do are more distant from each other and take more effort to monitor. Technical-assistance costs also tend to be higher in rural areas because lenders must spend more time with borrowers to produce adequate deals in sufficient volume. The Institute for Community Economics in Springfield, Massachusetts, and the National Cooperative Bank Development Corporation in Washington, D.C., both try to reduce the cost of long-distance monitoring by looking for local partners with whom they can participate in loans, but someone bears the cost.

Operating expenses are also affected by the size of a financial institution. Dozens of studies have found that the benefits of economies of scale are principally enjoyed by commercial banks with assets greater than $50 million. Very few financial intermediaries can minimize operating costs until they have assets of $15 to $25 million. There are development lenders with sufficient assets to achieve scale economies, such as the World Bank, Economic Development Administration, Farmers Home Administration, National Cooperative Development Corporation, and Shorebank Corporation; however, most development banks, including community-development credit unions and loan funds, are too small.

The Cost Experience of Development Banks

Operating costs as a share of assets vary dramatically among both mainstream financial institutions and development banks (see Table 8-2). Money-market funds have relatively low operating costs because they buy commercial paper and certificates of deposit, which are standardized, low-risk investments, and they tend to achieve a relatively large size within a few years of starting up. Venture-capital funds have much higher operating costs because they make high-risk, nonstandardized investments that require a lot of time to arrange and manage. Operating expenses for venture funds would be even higher if labor costs were not held down by giving employees a big share of profits rather than high salaries. The operating costs of depository institutions generally fall in between, as do the level of risk and degree of standardization of their loans. The costs are closer to those for venture funds because depository institutions have much higher fixed costs than money-market funds.

Even financial institutions of the same type can have very different cost ratios relative to assets. The cost differences be-

Table 8-2
Operating Costs as a Share of Assets for Various Kinds of Financial Institutions

	Operating Expenses as a Share of Assets (%)
KIND OF INSTITUTION	
Money-market funds[a]	0.5
Savings and loan associations[b]	2.0
Credit unions[c]	3.1
Commercial banks[d]	3.2
Venture-capital funds[e]	2.5–5
Community loan funds[f]	4.5–12
SPECIFIC LENDERS	
J. P. Morgan[g]	2.3
Kentucky Highland Investment Corp.[h]	4.0
Bank of America[i]	4.1
Citicorp[j]	4.4
South Shore Bank[k]	4.7
Northside Community Credit Union[l]	5.7
Quitman County Federal Credit Union[m]	6.0
Industrial Cooperative Association Loan Fund[n]	7.5
Blackfeet National Bank[o]	8.0
Northern Community Investment Corporation[p]	10.0
Delaware Valley Community Reinvestment Fund[q]	18.0

[a]Investment Company Institute Reports on Money Market Fund Expenses.
[b]U.S. League of Savings Institutions, "'89 Savings Institution Sourcebook" (data for 1987).
[c]"Key Operating Statistics," *Credit Union Magazine*, April 1987, p. 8.
[d]Federal Deposit Insurance Corporation, *Statistics of Banking* (Washington, D.C., 1987), pp. 43, 53.
[e]Various venture-fund financial statements.
[f]Various loan-fund financial statements.
[g]*Annual Report, 1988.*
[h]Interview with Jerry Rickett, January 1990.
[i]*Annual Report, 1988.*
[j]*Annual Report, 1988.*
[k]*Annual Report, 1988.*
[l]Interview with Elaine Wricks, 1989.
[m]Interview with Robert Jackson, December 1989.
[n]Interview with Katherine Gross, November 1989.
[o]Interview with Jack Kelly, November 1989.
[p]*Annual Report, 1989.*
[q]Prospectus, October 1989, Philadelphia.

tween the commercial banks are explained by their customer orientation and the kinds of loans they make. Most of J. P. Morgan's loans are to very large, very credit worthy companies. As a result, Morgan's lending costs are much lower than those of Citicorp or Bank of America, which serve a wider variety of borrowers and make smaller loans. South Shore Bank's costs are only slightly above Citicorp's costs as a share of assets. Even though South Shore Bank is many times smaller and a development lender, it is very effective at managing its costs.

The development banks in Table 8-2 generally have higher cost ratios than the mainstream institutions. The community-loan funds have the highest ratios because they are more likely to make very customized loans to borrowers who are some distance away, to make small loans to new borrowers, and to operate at a level insufficient to achieve economies of scale. Size is a particularly important explanation for the high operating costs of the community-development credit unions and community loan funds listed in Table 8-2. Northside Community Credit Union in Chicago had assets of $1.8 million at the end of 1989, while Delaware Valley Community Reinvestment Fund in Philadelphia had assets of $1.3 million in the middle of the same year. It is impressive that operating costs at these financial institutions are not a substantially higher share of assets, particularly given the nonfinancial services they offer. For example, Delaware Valley Community Reinvestment Fund provides extensive technical assistance to a third of its borrowers in financial packaging, strategic planning, community-land-trust development, or business planning.[5] The operating costs as a share of assets for Blackfeet National Bank in Browning, Montana, were also higher than for the other commercial banks because it only had assets of $4.7 million, too low an amount to absorb the substantial fixed costs in commercial banking.

How Development Banks Minimize Costs

Development banks generally do a better job than mainstream financial institutions in managing their overall costs. Much of the decline in profitability of commercial banks in the mid-1980s was due to poor cost management, including purchasing unnecessary computer technology and hiring large management staffs. Private development banks have generally not made these mistakes. They cannot afford to make them.

Development banks have been able to lower the transaction costs of development lending somewhat by becoming experts at it. Some development banks experiment constantly with new techniques for lowering costs. For example, Shorebank Corporation of Chicago is considering a major new initiative in Michigan that will investigate whether it is possible to reduce the cost of development banking in rural areas by sharing outreach staff among multiple financing entities. Microenterprise loan funds have paid particular attention to finding innovative ways to minimize transaction expenses. They cut costs on their very small loans by eschewing traditional banking procedures, such as requiring extensive financial reviews and a great deal of paperwork, and relying instead on character references and ability to form a peer lending group. Peer-group lending also reduces the costs of providing technical assistance and servicing loans because the staff work through a group of businesses, rather than with individual businesses.

Development banks have offset some of the higher transaction costs associated with development lending with lower costs elsewhere on their income statements. For an average commercial bank, employee compensation is 45 percent of operating expenses.[6] Even if the cost of having employees review and structure deals cannot be cut, the other 55 percent of costs usually can. While South Shore Bank's staffing costs as a share of loans are 35 percent higher than the average for commercial banks of similar size, the bank has been able to keep other ex-

penses below the average. Overall, South Shore Bank's costs—
and its profitability—are in line with industry averages for
commercial banks of its size.[7] Most development banks have
more modest facilities than mainstream financial institutions,
smaller numbers of administrators, and no more technology
than they can use effectively. The Cooperative Fund of New
England in Hartford, Connecticut, keeps its costs low because
trustees, members, and even staff volunteer their services.

Many development banks underpay staff, although this is
not in their long-term best interest. Development banks need
highly motivated and competent staff. Expenses can be moder-
ated by hiring those who share the development bank's "sense
of mission," but pay must be high enough to retain experienced people. As pointed out by Steven Dawson, a founder of
the Industrial Cooperative Association (ICA) in Somerville,
Massachusetts, "If we are not to repeat the 1960's loss of leadership, funders and development funds must face squarely the
question of staff compensation. The skills and experience required to manage development funds command $40,000 to
$100,000 salaries in private finance and consulting firms. While
competitive salary ranges for low-income development funds
are out of the question, we must nonetheless establish realistic
salary standards that will help ensure retention of our experienced technicians and staff leaders."[8] The president of the
Kentucky Highlands Investment Corporation, a rural, nonprofit venture-capital firm, agrees that the corporation has only
been able to attract and keep good people because its salaries
are competitive with those of private lenders (although they are
substantially lower than the income of venture capitalists).[9]

Development banks can hold down salaries without sacrificing employees by compensating them with stock and using financial incentives. The Blackstone Bank, of Boston's Roxbury
neighborhood, which lends primarily to area businesses, pays
its loan originators on commission and provides equity to key

management staff.[10] Even nonprofit development banks can and should link compensation with performance. For example, the Grameen Bank in Bangladesh is developing a system to evaluate and possibly compensate branch offices based upon their success in attracting clients and keeping losses low. Asociación para el Desarrolo de Microempresas (ADEMI), a microenterprise loan program in the Dominican Republic, offers bonuses to staff for monthly success in keeping loan delinquencies low.[11] Even after paying bonuses, overall costs can still be lower than they would have been if loan losses were not controlled as well. Of course, incentive strategies must be designed so that the incentive is not to make bad loans (or to only make very safe loans).

Hiring the best people for the job can also reduce staff costs. The best person to manage loans at a development bank is more likely to be a community-organization loan packager or a Small Business Administration loan reviewer than a commercial banker who has experience managing Fortune 500 business loans. The Bank of America State Bank in Concord, California, a commercial bank capitalized by the Bank of America to finance economic development in California, hired as its field specialists a person who had worked for a housing-development organization and a person who had run San Francisco's Office of Economic Development.[12] Choosing people based upon the relevance of their experience has kept staff costs at many credit unions and loan funds far below salaries on Wall Street.

Shifting the cost of technical assistance elsewhere is another common way in which development bankers improve their cost structure. Development banks can transfer the high cost of technical assistance to a separate tax-exempt organization. Isolating the technical-assistance function also can make it easier to attract grants to finance such a program. A commercial bank can form a bank community-development corporation (CDC).

Shorebank Corporation has the Neighborhood Institute in Chicago. A savings and loan association can form a service corporation, alone or with other S&Ls. A credit union can form a companion 501(c)(3) organization. California's Santa Cruz Community Development Credit Union began to pursue this option in 1989. A community loan fund that is a 501(c)(3) organization can form a separate organization or solicit restricted funds for technical assistance.

Creating a development bank under the wing of an existing organization can reduce costs (through shared overhead and expertise) and shift costs (if the parent absorbs more than its share). Sand County Venture Fund in Palo Alto, California, has very low operating expenses because its affiliate, Sand County Ventures, is an investment bank that bears much of the cost of deal underwriting and review. Sand County Ventures' fee for these services is spread among all of the investors in a deal. Of course, the venture fund can cover its costs only if its affiliate is successful in finding additional investors in its deals who pay the fees. The Industrial Cooperative Association Loan Fund benefits from being part of ICA by sharing administrative staff.[13] At the Mountain Association for Community Economic Development (MACED) in Berea, Kentucky, the two loan-fund staff members have other responsibilities with MACED, and part of their time is funded by grants to the broader organization.[14] Some credit unions, most often those with an occupational or associational bond, receive significant sponsor subsidies. Such support is sometimes available in more limited form to low-income credit unions. Quitman County Federal Credit Union shares staff with the Quitman County Development Organization and receives operating subsidies from it.[15]

Standardizing loan terms can also lower transaction costs, and it can be done without sacrificing development impact. A great deal of time is spent negotiating loan terms, and more time is spent keeping track of loans that require different times for payment and forms of payment. It can be less costly in the long run to spend more money up front to develop a few standard agreements and then, at least for small loans, refuse to negotiate the terms. If a loan agreement is structured carefully to meet the needs of a particular class of borrowers, fine adjustments to terms usually will not improve the performance of the borrowers. In the Mt. Auburn Associates study of revolving-loan funds supported by the Economic Development Administration, the investigators found very little relationship between the performance of borrowers and only small differences in the maturity of loans or monthly payments by borrowers. Even if a standard agreement discourages some borrowers, the cost savings will allow a development bank to serve more borrowers and make more loans to them. Standardization that suits the characteristics of customers should not deter development. Microenterprise loan funds have adopted standard documents and terms for loans precisely to reduce lending costs. Many funds offer only one term to maturity and one payment plan. This makes collections and tracking easy. Standardization of loans will also increase the marketability of development of loans and thereby improve the chances for developing secondary markets.

Costs can also be reduced through the selective use of partnerships, where the partners absorb some part of the information and technical-assistance costs. Development bankers can use community-based organizations (CBOs), community-development corporations (CDCs), and technical-assistance organizations to seek and screen applicants, provide loan counseling, package loans, or make referrals. Partnerships can also be formed with other financial institutions to participate in loans and share transaction costs. The Native American Self-Employment Program contracts elements of its loan administration to a local bank.[16] The Institute for Community Economics (ICE)

Loan Fund in Springfield, Massachusetts, has participated in several loans of other community-loan funds that did not have sufficient capital or technical expertise to meet loan demand. The Center for Community Self-Help in Durham, North Carolina, has a "Partnership Lending" program.[17]

Development banks usually find it necessary to make small compromises in their development goals in order to manage their costs. One common compromise is to make larger loans than is preferred. Community groups frequently cite very small loans as the most urgent unmet capital need in their communities. Because it is precisely these loans that are the most costly to make, most development banks find it necessary to establish a minimum loan size. California's Santa Cruz Community Development Credit Union requires that community-development loans involve at least $5,000. It does not make personal loans of less than $1,000, except through its VISA card program, nor does it pay dividends on share accounts of less than $100.[18] Kentucky's MACED Loan Fund lends amounts of $5,000 and up, but looks for loans larger than $20,000 because it has found that smaller loans are also more risky.[19] Some development banks eschew size cutoffs, but they seek some larger borrowers to average out transaction costs. The ICE Loan Fund has continued to seek deals regardless of size, but fund managers also recognize the savings involved in doing larger deals. The Center for Community Self-Help has found that its loan fund must be able to operate in the $200,000 to $500,000 range to offset the costs of small-business lending.[20] Mixing small and larger loans is not an answer for all development banks. It may be inappropriate, for example, for microenterprise loan funds, which have created a very specific mechanism for delivering credit in small amounts.

Development banks that are depository institutions are forced to choose between maximizing their development lending and responding to all the basic banking needs of a community. If it chooses to offer customers low-cost checking accounts, a depository institution may need to offset the high costs of many small accounts by investing the proceeds in the cheapest way, that is, marketable securities. If it wants to maximize its capacity to lend, the institution may need to restrict its depository services, perhaps by setting a minimum account size. South Shore Bank's branch in the Austin neighborhood of Chicago makes loans, but it does not offer retail deposit services. The Self-Help Credit Union in Durham, North Carolina, targets its deposit services to social investors while lending to cooperatives with low-income members. As a result, it has lower overhead costs (no teller windows or tellers) and needs less staff.

Some development banks lower their costs by making a mix of development and nondevelopment loans. They fund 100 percent of a loan where they are only needed to provide a subordinated loan for part of the funding. By providing the complete loan package, their operating costs per loan are reduced, and their risk may fall, too. Development banks also try to hold on to some of their seasoned customers who would be considered credit worthy by mainstream financial institutions. Other development banks serve customers who need funds for purposes consistent with the goals of the institution, but who might be able to obtain capital elsewhere. Development lenders that are 501(c)(3) organizations cannot do conventional lending, but they can form affiliates for this purpose and help subsidize the development lender.[21] After a start-up period, Elkhorn Bank (Southern Development Bancorporation's commercial bank subsidiary) will pass substantial sums to Arkansas Enterprise Group, its nonprofit affiliate. This strategy mimics that of Shorebank Corporation: South Shore Bank's profits from conventional lending subsidize the activities of its nonprofit affiliates. It may even be possible to offset completely the higher costs of development loans if lenders can earn above-average profits on other products.

There are times when costs can neither be reduced nor passed on to customers, as when a development bank enters a new development market, adds new programs for which there is little experience, or serves a market that offers substantial social benefits but cannot pay its way. In these cases, development banks must seek external subsidies.[22] If such funds are not available, then development banks must turn down deals. This is another reason that financial innovation is an essential part of development banking.

9
Capital Ins and Outs

DEVELOPMENT BANKS need capital to make loans and to finance start-up costs, initial working capital, and reserves. A development bank's capital structure—the mix and terms of its equity and debt—determines what markets it can serve and establishes the minimum it can charge borrowers. Capital structure also determines to what degree it can undertake complementary development activities and who will ultimately set its goals. Two of the difficult decisions development banks face are how much they should be willing to pay for capital and how much they should charge borrowers for the use of their capital. The latter issue, loan pricing, is discussed later in this chapter.

The Importance of Capital Structure
A development bank can only provide financial products that are consistent with its capital structure. It can provide equity capital only if it obtains a large proportion of its capitalization from grants or the sale of stock. It can make long-term loans only if it has sources of long-term funds or can use other tools to hedge interest-rate and liquidity risk. It has been difficult for development banks to attract patient capital, and, as a result,

some of them do not provide borrowers with financial products that best meet their needs. For example, because they can only attract short- and medium-term debt to do equity-like financing, some business-loan funds that lend to new, low-income enterprises burden their clients with debt service.[1] Only a small minority of development banks provide equity capital. They all have been funded primarily with grants or stock.

The level of risk in a development bank's portfolio must also match its capital structure. Such a bank can only accept high levels of credit risk if it has sufficient equity to absorb the losses. Highly leveraged institutions (those whose equity is very small compared to their debt) must be conservative in the credit risks they assume. According to Katherine Gross, the Industrial Cooperative Association Loan Fund's "lending is constrained by the size of our loss reserve (a form of equity), not by the size of the fund." The fund cannot prudently lend out its loan capital unless it attracts sufficient equity to cover anticipated losses.[2] Most loan funds try to manage the risk of their lending by attracting equity reserves to absorb their losses. Ten of the twelve business-loan funds surveyed for a Ford Foundation workshop on low-income business lending had a funded loan-loss reserve of from 4 to 40 percent of outstanding loans.[3] Commercial banks sell stock to raise the funds that act as their reserves for loan losses. These reserves are small, as are the losses they can absorb. Royalty-investment funds can take on much more risk because they have a capital base that is almost entirely equity capital.

What a development bank pays for its capital sets the absolute floor on the rate it can charge to customers. Even if staff work for free and avoid all losses, investors must be repaid. Development banks that serve markets where borrowers can pay market rates of return generally pay the average in their market for loan capital. Development lenders that make low-income housing loans or that make loans to business cooperatives in low-income communities try to attract very-low-cost capital. The Self-Help Venture Fund in Durham, North Carolina, declines funds offered at more than 4 percent because it makes high-risk, low-interest loans.[4] To make sure that earnings are sufficient to cover the cost of funds, many development banks do not accept debt at rates above the current rate earned on idle funds. The Institute for Community Economics (ICE) Loan Fund in Springfield, Massachusetts, does not accept loans above the current rate on money-market accounts because that is where it puts its idle funds. Development banks that seek very-low-interest capital seem to have been able to tap into a pool of investors with social motivations (who are in any event to be preferred to yield-chasers).

Its cost of capital also affects what complementary activities a development bank can undertake. All development banks seek out the lowest-cost sources of capital because it gives them more flexibility to undertake complementary development activities whose costs cannot always be passed through to borrowers, such as technical assistance and development of new products and markets. The federally supported loan funds of the "war on poverty" era were best equipped to undertake development activities without impairing their sustainability. Most have ratios of donated equity to assets of 50 percent or more. The Mountain Association for Community Economic Development (MACED) Loan Fund in Berea, Kentucky, only has assets of $3 million, but $2.5 million is in capital grants and $500,000 is in 1 percent, thirty-year loans. Northern Community Investment Corporation in St. Johnsbury, Vermont, has almost 60 percent equity in its capital structure, and most of its debt is also in the form of thirty-year, 1 percent loans from the Farmers Home Administration. Because federal funding has all but disappeared, the newer loan funds have ratios of equity to assets of 10 to 20 percent. It is more difficult for them to meet their development goals.

The type of capital raised by a development bank can also determine who will ultimately control its activities. The holders of a majority of the voting common stock of a development bank can vote to change directors, management, or goals. Holders of debt do not have an ownership interest, but lenders can require loan covenants that still limit the discretion of management. Some debt comes with restrictive covenants that are more severe than the control exerted by minority shareholders. Along with selling a minority share of voting stock, ways to issue stock without loss of control include selling nonvoting stock and selling preferred stock. Nonvoting stock is more difficult to sell than voting stock because the potential control provided by ownership of voting stock reduces the risk of the investment. Thus, nonvoting stock usually sells at a higher price. While preferred stock yields control only in extreme situations, it usually involves an agreement to pay investors dividends, which reduces the flexibility of a new development bank to use income for development activities. Which form of capital is most consistent with the goals of a development lender depends on who the owners of equity would be and what the covenants required by lenders might be.

How Capital-Structure Decisions Are Made

Most financial institutions use equity capital to fund start-up costs, initial working capital, and reserves to see them through periods when performance is poor. This equity capital ensures that they can avoid bankruptcy. For-profit financial institutions issue stock, and nonprofit financial institutions attract grants, because equity capital is patient. There are no interest payments that must be paid whether a development bank earns income or incurs a loss. Furthermore, equity reserves can be relied on to pay off debt investors when a development bank incurs a loss. Equity capital gives a financial institution time to

Table 9-1
Foresight Loan Fund's Cash-flow Projections

Year	Start-up Costs	Revenue	Costs	Cash Flow	Cumulative Cash Flow	Equity	Debt	Assets	Minimum Equity Target	Equity/Assets (%)	Minimum Target Equity/Assets (%)
0	100,000	—	—	—	—	500,000	0	500,000	NA	100	100.00
1		220,000	250,000	(130,000)	(130,000)	370,000	1,630,000	2,000,000	202,500	18.50	10.13
2		550,000	570,000	(20,000)	(150,000)	350,000	4,650,000	5,000,000	242,500	7	4.85
3		770,000	780,000	(10,000)	(160,000)	340,000	6,660,000	7,000,000	335,000	4.86	4.79
4		1,100,000	1,000,000	100,000	(60,000)	440,000	9,560,000	10,000,000	450,000	4.40	4.50
5		1,100,000	1,000,000	100,000	140,000	540,000	9,460,000	10,000,000	450,000	5.40	4.50

reach the scale where its revenues cover its costs and absorbs the risk of doing business even after it reaches this scale.

The hypothetical example in Table 9-1 of "Foresight Loan Fund" illustrates how initial equity capital needs for a loan fund are determined. The loan fund anticipated start-up and fixed costs of $100,000, assets of $10 million by the end of four years, revenues equal to 11 percent of assets, and costs (including operating costs, funding costs, and loan losses) that would be 12.5 percent of assets in year one, 11.4 percent in year two, 11 percent in year three, and 10 percent in years four and five. As a result, the fund projected it would incur a cumulative cash shortfall of $160,000 in its third year and would not generate any net income until its fourth year. Thus, Foresight needed to raise at least $160,000 of patient capital to finance its cumulative negative cash flow, in addition to the capital it planned to raise to fund its loan portfolio ($1,630,000 in the first year, growing to more than $9 million by year four). The loan fund also wanted a working-capital cushion equal to three months of its operating costs and an additional equity reserve for unexpected events equal to 2 percent of its assets. Taking all of these objectives into account, Foresight chose to raise $500,000 in equity in addition to loanable funds. As a result, when its cumulative shortfall was greatest (in year three), Foresight still had equity reserves ($340,000) sufficient to provide its desired working-capital cushion and reserve for unexpected losses ($335,000).

In reality, loan funds frequently start up with only enough equity capital to make it through their first or, perhaps, first two years of operations, betting that they will be able to attract additional grants in the future. Because funders are reluctant to make multiyear commitments, the loan funds have little choice. Nonprofit development banks would have a better chance to survive if funders were more willing to make long-term commitments. Funders could protect themselves from funding poor programs by providing multiyear commitments based upon attainment of explicit goals each year.

While equity capital is crucial to development banking, debt capital also has its place. With the exception of venture-capital funds, financial institutions have a much larger share of debt in their capital structure than all other kinds of companies. They can survive with a higher proportion of debt because they have more predictable revenues and because they can attract debt at reasonable prices. Investors often charge them less for their debt than nonfinancial corporations must pay because their assets are of higher quality and marketability. Depository institutions—commercial banks, savings and loan associations, and credit unions—have the most debt in their capital structure because they offer deposit insurance. Investors who stay within the insurance limits do not need to worry at all about asset quality or leverage. If Citibank could sell debt as cheaply as it collects deposits, it would give up its commercial-bank charter today. Deposit insurance offers an enormous incentive to issue debt. Community-development loan funds are as highly leveraged as depository institutions, but this is only because they have attracted social investors who are willing to accept uncompensated risk. These loan funds could not achieve such high leverage if they were borrowing using traditional avenues, nor could any other financial intermediary.

Financial institutions choose to be highly leveraged because leverage can improve performance—that is, increase net income available to compensate equity investors, augment reserves, or allow them to make more loans. Leverage increases net income as long as a financial institution is able to generate sufficient revenues from the additional debt to compensate for the additional interest costs, risk, and transactions costs. At the same time, leverage increases the likelihood that a financial institution will fail if it judges risk poorly. The chance of bankruptcy often increases with leverage. Current U.S. tax policy

reinforces reliance on debt as a means of improving performance. Interest payments are deductible expenses when figuring
income-tax liability, but dividends paid to equity investors are
not. As long as the tax benefits of debt are greater than the
expected cost of bankruptcy (i.e., the cost of bankruptcy times
the probability of bankruptcy), financial institutions that are
not exempt from taxation will use as little equity and as much
debt as they can.

Taking on a large share of debt is rational behavior for financial institutions as long as their cost of debt can be recovered through additional activity and they can effectively use the
assets to pursue their lending goals (i.e., they do not have to
make poor-quality loans to invest the debt proceeds). For development banks, an even less stringent standard may be justified.
Even if an increase in leverage hurt performance, it might be
appropriate for a development bank as long as net income did
not fall below a level sufficient to compensate equity investors
and to fund growth or if the worsening of its financial performance was offset by a greater development impact.

Development banks often end up with less equity than they
would like because there are few equity investors willing to accept the terms that most of them offer—a small return and a
small likelihood of ever getting their capital back. Only a few
grantmakers are interested in community-development banking, and the average grant they are willing to make to an
emerging development bank is modest. The member funds of
the National Association of Community Development Loan
Funds (NACDLF) average equity as a share of total capital of
12.2 percent; NACDLF urges members to work toward 30 percent.[5] Loan funds try to make up for low levels of external equity investment by attracting low-interest debt. Interest savings
on large amounts of low-cost loans can, over time, replace small
amounts of grant capital, but it is too slow a process to be desirable. Nevertheless, the supply of investors willing to make low-

interest loans is much larger than is those willing to give money away.

While commercial banks are more able to compensate equity investors, their access to equity investments is also constrained because they cannot offer equity investors a means to exit from their investments. The investors who provided equity for the original purchase of Shorebank Corporation in Chicago have not been able to liquidate their investment. Thus, while the bank has achieved a certain level of financial success, its equity investors have neither shared in that success nor even been able to get their initial capital back for other development investing. This has affected Shorebank's ability to raise additional equity capital for new ventures.

The traditional methods for achieving liquidity in equity investments—an initial public offering of stock into one of the stock exchanges or a sale for cash to a larger company—cannot completely serve the needs of a development bank. A public stock offering could enhance liquidity for a development bank, but it would also subject it to the short-term-trading mentality of the public markets. A publicly traded development bank could cease to be a development bank in short order. The same outcome might be expected if a development bank were purchased by a mainstream financial institution. It is the general failure of traditional financial institutions that provided the impetus to create development banks in the first place. However, in this age of increasing pressure under the Community Reinvestment Act, a large bank could do far worse than to purchase a reasonably successful development bank in its own region with promises of additional capital and support for its development goals.

Financial innovation is required in the area of liquidity for development-bank investors, even for nonprofit funds that cannot issue stock. A traditional debt structure involves debt that is convertible into equity. It may be possible to solve the development-bank liquidity problem by creating equity convertible into debt. It is in its early years that a development bank most needs external equity capital. A successful development bank should be able to operate profitably, retaining earnings and building internal equity. In such a case, it should be possible to allow for equity that would convert to debt and be repaid once the development bank's retained earnings allowed it. Each year, as retained earnings increased, additional equity could convert to debt that would be amortized and eventually liquidated. In fact, many commercial-bank holding companies have issued preferred stock that can be redeemed after seven years or more or else converted to debt. Such "reverse conversion" would slow the growth of a development bank once conversion began, since the bank would be increasing its leverage to buy out investors rather than to acquire additional assets or make loans. However, this may be an acceptable trade-off if it dramatically widens the pool of potential equity investors in development banks. In a special case of "reverse conversion," an employee-stock-ownership plan (ESOP) could also provide both a source of debt for acquisition of a bank holding company and an exit strategy for initial investors in the holding company. Using this technique, investors who wanted to exit from a holding-company investment could sell their stock to an employee trust.

Development-Bank Investors

Development-bank capital comes most often from socially motivated investors, and most development banks rely heavily on them. Even community-development credit unions, which must raise the vast majority of their capital from members of their communities, count on nonmember deposits from social investors. These investors are motivated to invest primarily by the goals of the development bank, such as assisting women and minorities to start businesses or helping low-income residents to buy homes. They usually also require some financial return on their investments, but frequently will accept below-market rates of return. Development bankers have found that they also care a great deal about the safety of their investments (Institute for Community Economics in Springfield, Massachusetts), whether they know someone who is associated with a development bank (the West Philadelphia Community Federal Credit Union), professional and responsive dealings with development banks (the Central Appalachian People's Federal Credit Union in Berea, Kentucky), and expertise (Industrial Cooperative Association in Somerville, Massachusetts). While even social investors prefer debt to equity investments, they are more likely to provide equity investments than are other investors.

The most active institutional social investors are religious organizations and progressive foundations. Religious groups were some of the first social investors, and, in spite of initial bad experiences in the 1960s with social investment, they are still the most strongly represented group among institutional investors in development banks. Religious organizations provide 23 percent of the capital invested in community-development loan funds.[6] All of the $1 million invested in the Chicago-based Anawim Fund of the Midwest comes from religious orders and organizations in that area. The Institute for Community Economics Loan Fund has received 12 percent of its loans, or $1.7 million from religious organizations.[7]

Foundations have been particularly important sources of more sizable chunks of capital for the largest development banks. The decision of the Ford Foundation to fund the Center for Community Self-Help in Durham, North Carolina, over the years has enabled it to expand into a diverse development institution. Without the multimillion-dollar investment made by the Winthrop Rockefeller Foundation, there might not be a Southern Development Bancorporation in Arkansas. Foundations are also an important source of capital for smaller development funds. The member funds of the National Association of Community Development Loan Funds (NACDLF) attract about 20 percent of their capital from foundations.[8]

Individual social investors are a more important source of capital than is generally believed. The ICE Loan Fund receives 83 percent of its loans from individuals. Overall, the member funds of the NACDLF attract about 27 percent of their capital from individuals.[9] The investors in the San Francisco–based Working Assets Money Fund (with assets of more than $200 million at the beginning of 1990) and the other socially screened mutual funds are also predominantly individuals. A large share of the deposits in development-oriented depository institutions also comes from such investors.

Because the pool of socially motivated investors is still small, development banks also look to their broader community for capital. Members of the area where a development bank is located sometimes become investors as a way to support community economic development or to enhance their public image. These individuals and organizations can be harder for a development bank to attract than social investors who have no stake in a local community. They tend to be more skeptical about the potential for development banking to succeed and more attracted by the trimmings at mainstream financial institutions. Chicago's South Shore Bank has raised the majority of its capital from outside social investors, as has the Self-Help Credit Union in North Carolina.

Local groups that have invested in development banks include nonprofit organizations like hospitals and universities, financial institutions, civic groups, local businesses, and government organizations. The Blackfeet Indian Tribe invested almost $1 million in the stock of Blackfeet National Bank based upon its expectations of economic-development benefits for the tribe rather than direct financial return. Commercial banks have, as part of negotiated agreements, purchased certificates of deposit in a variety of community-development credit unions. For example, People's Settlement Associates Federal Credit Union of Wilmington, Delaware, negotiated $300,000 in deposits from local banks.[10]

There are also individual mainstream investors concerned about social justice who have put their money in development banks that offer market rates of return. They generally have invested in the insured deposits of commercial banks or credit unions or in mutual funds. Many investors are not willing to give up financial return but enjoy having some progressive social impact along with their interest. The socially screened mutual funds have grown to almost $1 billion through serving these investors in addition to social investors.

Low-income communities are usually not viewed as a source of development-bank capital, but there are some resources in these communities that have been tapped by credit unions. Community-development credit unions must attract local depositors (who are unlikely to be social investors, since 80 percent of the deposits in a low-income credit union must come from members). Because it is hard for low-income members to save, credit unions have established savings programs. At First American Credit Union in Window Rock, Arizona, 85 percent of member savings have been accrued through payroll deductions. First American requires that members pay off loans through a payroll-deduction plan. To develop a savings habit, the credit union stipulates that borrowers agree to an additional payroll deduction that is deposited in a share-savings account.

How much financial institutions pay for their capital generally depends upon the overall level of interest rates and the investment characteristics presented to investors (i.e., risk, transaction costs, and illiquidity). Most of the differences in required rates of return in Table 9-2 can be explained by level of risk,

Table 9-2
Average Required Return on Capital for Various Investors in December 1989

Source	Rate (%)	Rate Relative to Market
Grants	0	Below
Foundation PRI	3–10	Below
Community-loan-fund investors	0–7	Below
Commercial-bank savings accounts	5	Market
Commercial-bank money-market accounts[a]	6.37	Market
Commercial-bank 6-month CD[a]	8.01	Market
Commercial-bank federal funds[b]	8.25	Market
Commercial-bank 5-year CD[a]	9.36	Market
1- to 10-year medium-quality bond[c]	9.42	Market
10+ year medium-quality bond[c]	9.75	Market
Commercial-bank prime rate[b]	10.5	Market
Junk bond[c]	14.29	Market
BIDCO stock[d]	15–20	Market
Venture-capital-fund stock[d]	20–30	Market

[a]"Banks vs. Money Funds," *Wall Street Journal*, 6 December 1989, C-20.
[b]"Money Rates," *Wall Street Journal*, 26 December 1989, C-15.
[c]"Yield Comparisons," *Wall Street Journal*, 26 December 1989, C-15.
[d]Derek Hansen, "BIDCOs," unpublished paper, August 1985.

liquidity, and term to maturity. For example, commercial banks paid less for short-term deposits than for five-year certificates of deposit. Business- and industrial-development corporations (BIDCOs) paid much more for their risk capital than commercial banks paid for liquid, insured deposits. However, the rate paid by investors in community loan funds can only be explained by the existence of investors willing to accept below-market returns. The rate of interest paid to loan-fund investors is close to what is paid to buyers of money-market accounts in commercial banks, even though loan-fund investments are less liquid than money-market accounts and do not have federal deposit insurance. Loan-fund investors are willing to accept a below-market financial rate because they value social returns.

The presence of social investors in the marketplace adds an additional factor that figures heavily in what development banks pay for their capital. Social investors willing to accept below-market returns have been very important for loan funds and credit unions, but all development banks have relied on them to some extent. Even so, development banks have not been completely sheltered from the market's demand for higher compensation when the overall level of interest rates is higher or the investment characteristics presented (risk, trans-action costs, and illiquidity) are undesirable.

Social investors willing to accept returns below the market rate are a valuable source of capital, but they are unlikely to provide all of the capital that development banks need. The pool of investors in loan funds that rely on below-market rates is still quite limited. The members of the National Association of Community Development Loan Funds in Philadelphia to-gether have attracted $75 million; adding in the other commu-nity-development loan funds that are not members of the asso-ciation might double the amount. There is no doubt that the total would be larger if higher rates were paid. In fact, many small community-development credit unions have seen their growth thwarted—and their future clouded—because they were only able to pay below-market dividends to their mem-bers.

Development banks that have offered rates of return that are at or slightly below market rates have been able to attract the largest amount of capital. While Shorebank Corporation has paid very low returns to its equity investors, most depositors have earned market rates of return. As of the end of 1988, South Shore Bank in Chicago had attracted $150 million in deposits (including $70 million in development deposits, attracted based upon commitment to community development by the investors), on which it offered the average rate prevailing on similar deposits in the Chicago area. The Calvert Social Investment Fund of Washington, D.C., a mutual fund that screens investments for social criteria, has attracted more than $200 million in investments, on which it has paid returns matching the average for similar mutual funds. California's Working Assets Money Fund has attracted $200 million, on which it has paid returns slightly below average for money-market funds. Vermont National Bank attracted $35 million (80 percent from Vermonters) in social-investment deposits in a few months by offering market rates and generating some publicity. In California, Bank of America State Bank organizers believe they can achieve less ambitious results quickly by appealing to the same kind of investors.

Some development banks have offered both market-rate and below-market-rate investment alternatives, using the former to broaden their base and the latter to deepen their social impact. South Shore Bank in Chicago is a prime example. While 93 percent of its deposits at the end of 1988 were paying market rates, the remainder was attracted to Rehab CDs, which paid rates from 1 to 4 percent below comparable market rates for certificates of deposit. Real-estate developers who want to rehabilitate local buildings are offered market-rate loans, plus interest-free loans from the fund as necessary to keep any subsequent rent increases affordable to tenants.[11] The lower rates paid on Rehab CDs allow Shorebank to play a bigger development role. In 1981, Santa Cruz Community Development Credit Union in California began offering "Bread and Roses" accounts through which members were given the option to return dividends.[12] When it had $1 million in assets, 25 percent was in these accounts. Today, the credit union pays most of its members market rates of return. The lower rate it received on "Bread and Roses" accounts allowed it breathing room to build up reserves and grow to a scale where it could afford to match the rates paid by other financial institutions.

There is evidence that many kinds of development banks can afford to pay market rates for at least part of their funds. Commercial banks, savings and loan associations, credit unions that have achieved assets of at least several million dollars, and royalty-investment funds (RIFs) all have the capacity to pursue development goals and generate sufficient profits to offer market rates of return, at least, to debt holders. For depository institutions, the cost of market-rate debt capital is quite low. For RIFs, the upside potential is high, and it can be shared with investors. Loan funds, which serve the smallest, poorest, and highest-risk borrowers, generally cannot pay market rates for capital. Their borrowers cannot afford the higher rates, and the funds need the subsidies to generate the equity that is so hard to attract from funders.

Whether development banks choose to return earnings to investors is a different matter from whether they can generate market-rate returns. Southern Development Bancorporation in Arkansas has an agreement with its investors to contribute any income above the inflation rate to a tax-exempt affiliate that will use the funds for related job-creation activities, at least until the affiliate has an endowment of $5 million.[13] It attracted twenty-four equity investors (including Arkansas businessmen, such as the founder of Wal-Mart Stores, and foundations, such as the Winthrop Rockefeller Foundation) who were willing to accept these terms.

Table 9-3
Required Loan Pricing for a Development Bank
(as a Percent of Year-end Assets)

Expected and unexpected losses (cost of risk)	1.0
Operating expenses (cost of operations)	2.5
Target net return on assets (income objective)	.5
Interest expenses (cost of debt)	8.0
Total costs	12.0
Required average gross return on assets	12.0

A Framework for Pricing Development-Bank Loans

The flipside of what to pay for capital is what to charge for its use. The best price a sustainable development bank can offer its customers for capital is what it needs to cover its costs of capital, losses, and operations. The costs that must be recovered are presented in the hypothetical example in Table 9-3, where the cost of risk is shown as expected and unexpected losses. A development bank needs to be compensated for both kinds of losses.[14] In the table, target net return on assets is substituted for the more common target return on equity so that all of the costs are shown as a share of assets.[15] The development bank in the example must price its services so that its gross return on assets is at least 12 percent.

Pricing must take into account what a development bank earns on assets that are not loaned out. Assets for the development bank in Table 9-3 include earning assets, such as loans and investments, and nonearning assets, such as cash and furniture and equipment. Because the development bank in the example earns nothing on nonearning assets, it must earn more than 12 percent on its assets that generate revenue to achieve its required overall rate of return on assets. If it earns

Table 9-4
Net Loan Yields for Commercial Banks (Assuming Assets of
$40 Million)

Type of Loan	Gross Yield	Expenses	Loan Losses	Net Yield
Investments	10.96	.293	0	10.667
Real-estate mortgage	12.271	1.389	.430	10.452
Installment	14.682	3.679	.908	10.095
Commercial and other	12.564	2.145	1.516	8.903

Source: Federal Reserve System, Functional Cost Analysis, 1986.

little on its investments, it must price its loans higher. If it does not charge fees for depository services, it must earn more on investments and loans. A development bank that minimizes its nonearning assets, maximizes its investment earnings, and charges reasonable fees for services has the most flexibility in pricing loans. One way in which Union Savings Bank of Albuquerque, a labor-controlled savings institution in New Mexico, has managed its spread between costs and revenues is to buy few fixed assets and thereby keep nonearning assets very low.[16]

Because losses and expenses vary by type of loan, pricing on each loan should depend on its characteristics. In Table 9-4, differences in prices, costs, and loan losses are shown for various kinds of commercial-bank loans. Gross yields (the price charged borrowers) are much farther apart than are net yields because the loan prices capture the differences in anticipated losses and transactions costs between various kinds of loans. The one exception is "commercial and other" loans. Based upon the net yields in the table, it appears that these loans were priced too low. The commercial-loan market has become very competitive, and commercial banks have not been adequately compensated for the credit risk of such loans.[17] If a development bank had to lower its prices to compete with other lenders, it would not be doing its job.

Many development banks do not individually price their loans. For example, many loan funds and community-development credit unions charge an equal markup on all loans. While this approach is simple, it is not necessarily fair or effective. Borrowers who entail lower costs or risk implicitly subsidize those who impose higher costs and risk. Unless higher cost and risk are always correlated with social benefits, this is not an effective or efficient way to allocate capital resources. Some development banks, including California's Santa Cruz Community Development Credit Union, charge a premium based upon their risk or transactions costs and offer a discount based upon economic-development benefit. If a social-benefit discount can realistically change the viability of a project, it is justifiable.

Part of structuring a development-bank loan is figuring out the terms that make it most affordable for a borrower to pay the required price. There are a variety of ways in which the affordability of a loan can be improved without lowering its yield. The goal is to find the mix of terms—such as interest rate, fees, compensating balances (for depository institutions), period to maturity, and frequency and level of payments—that works best for the development bank and the borrower. Many development banks are experimenting with ways to recapture their costs from customers while maximizing affordability to the borrower.

Borrowers can compensate a development bank not only through interest payments but also through fees and, for depository institutions, profits from deposit relationships. Borrowers from depository institutions are sometimes asked to deposit set amounts of money in accounts that bear no interest. These amounts are referred to as "compensating balances" because the interest earned by the depository institutions is part of its compensation for making a loan. If an organization must maintain large bank accounts for other reasons, it may be cheaper for it to agree to compensating balances in exchange for lower rates or fees from a development bank that is a commercial bank.

Fees are becoming a more common way for development banks to seek compensation for their transaction costs. Sometimes borrowers who cannot afford higher loan payments are able to pay up-front fees. Some development banks pass on their costs fully, while others charge fees based upon ability to pay. Fees are charged up front, charged when the loan matures (backend fees), or rolled into the loan. Northern California Community Loan Fund in San Francisco charges fees for out-of-pocket expenses, payable at closing, of up to a maximum of 1.5 percent of a loan amount. Expenses above that figure can be added to the loan amount and amortized over the term of the loan. New Hampshire Community Loan Fund in Concord has considered charging borrowers points, setting up a technical-assistance fee structure, and charging backend fees equal to one or two points for very small, short-term, or complicated loans. Santa Cruz Community Development Credit Union in California charges a loan fee of the greater of $75 or 2 percent on community-development loans of less than $10,000; it charges $75 or 1.5 percent on larger loans.[18] Blackfeet National Bank in Browning, Montana, manages its costs on very small loans by charging origination fees of $50 per loan and minimum interest of $25 per loan.[19]

The number of years for which a loan is made and the timing and level of payments also can have a large impact on its affordability (and its collectibility). By lengthening the term of a loan, the periodic payments can be lowered (even though the total payments are higher). However, the risk of the loan may also rise, requiring a higher rate of interest. Loan payments that are less frequent may put less of a burden on borrowers.

They can also increase risk because they provide less timely information on whether the borrower's ability to repay has been impaired.

Adjusting loan-payment terms to increase affordability is most common in residential-mortgage lending. If what is needed is mortgages for moderate-income residents with smaller payments in the early years, lenders like NCB Savings Association in Hillsboro, Ohio, offer graduated-payment mortgages. In the future, more lenders may offer price-level-adjusted mortgages (PLAM). A PLAM allows a lender to protect itself from inflation without charging borrowers a substantial inflation premium from the beginning. Borrowers are initially charged only a real rate of interest. Each year, their loan balances increase by the amount of inflation, and their payments for the next year are recalculated based upon this new balance. If the need is to keep rent payments low on multifamily real-estate mortgages, the Local Initiative Support Corporation has offered five-year loans with no interest for several years, amortized the loans over twenty years, and required payment of 140 percent of principal at maturity.

Rate indexing has been used to maintain the affordability of variable-rate business loans. Cost increases associated with changes in interest rates on variable-rate loans can be passed on to borrowers without raising loan payments by reducing current principal payments by the amount of the increase in interest payments and allowing the principal to be repaid further in the future by extending the term to maturity.

When the required loan price is more than a borrower can afford to pay out of current earnings, there are ways a development bank can defer some income. One alternative for business financing is to substitute royalty financing, as does Connecticut Product Development Corporation, where businesses agree to pay a share of their sales revenue. Another approach is to offer mezzanine financing, usually in the form of subordinated debt with fixed interest plus warrants, convertibility of the debt to stock, or preferred stock. A third alternative is to provide loans with conditional equity-participation agreements (equity kickers). The kickers can be stock-purchase warrants or incremental cash payments above the basic interest rate that are based upon stock performance, net worth, sales, or profit. Erie County Industrial Development Authority, a loan fund in Buffalo, New York, makes loans with warrants for a company's stock.[20]

The Arguments in Favor of Market-Rate Pricing

To be sustainable financial institutions, development banks need to charge market rates of return whenever it is feasible. Unless a development bank has lower costs or attracts funds more cheaply than other financial institutions, the rate of return that will cover its costs is going to be the market rate. Lower operating costs or loan losses are unlikely. Funding costs are often lower, but not low enough to make up for higher costs.

As demonstrated in Chapter 3, many of the business borrowers from development banks should be able to afford to pay market rates for capital under some combination of terms. Financial subsidies are likely to change the viability of businesses in only a very few cases. More often, firms that cannot afford market-rate loans either need more patient capital, such as equity financing, or are simply not viable businesses. Financial subsidies are much more significant for low-income housing, but they are not important to every deal, particularly when the financing is very short term.[21] Even when subsidies are needed to ensure the affordability of housing, there are sometimes government and private programs that are explicitly intended to bear these costs. For example, out of forty-four home loans the Self-Help Credit Union of Durham, North Carolina, made in the first half of 1990, nine were part of a turn-key loan program with the Charlotte Housing Authority and nine were through the Durham Bond Program, both of which enhance affordability.[22]

Adopting a goal of charging market rates of interest actually helps ensure that a development bank makes the largest possible contribution to economic development. A development bank charging market rates is less likely to attract borrowers who do not need its services, but would understandably accept interest-rate subsidies if they were available. More important, market pricing forces a development bank to search aggressively for deals with sufficient economic potential to afford market rates and to develop new markets and products that can generate such returns. Finding ways to structure development loans that allow a development bank to charge market rates also provides the greatest encouragement to other financial institutions without specific community-development goals to make similar loans.

Charging market rates also allows a development bank to stretch its resources farther. When most loans cover their costs, scarce charitable resources can be used for technical assistance to generate new loan customers and for product development to serve them better. The additional income can also be used to increase the volume of loans made, to make some higher-risk loans, or to subsidize some borrowers for whom the subsidy really makes a difference. Because it reduces the number of clearly untenable deals attracted by the possibility of capital grants, publicizing a goal of providing market-rate business loans can also reduce deal-review costs. Moreover, charging market rates for loans reinforces the message to borrowers that development loans are serious obligations. Charging for services has the same benefits and, in addition, it builds in responsiveness to customers. If the services are not worth it, customers will not use them.

Many development banks have adopted market-rate pricing,

but more have not. Commercial banks, such as South Shore Bank in Chicago, have found that borrowers can afford to pay market rates if loans are properly structured. By charging market rates, the bank has ensured its ability to be there for its constituencies for the long haul. Many of the microenterprise loan funds assert that the need they are responding to is not one for capital subsidies, but, rather, for access to capital. These funds charge interest rates that are closer to market rates than most other loan funds. Some credit unions also do market-rate pricing. For example, Santa Cruz Community Development Credit Union in California sets the interest rate on each loan by taking into account the strength of the borrower, the loan amount and term, the collateral, previous credit history, management experience, deposit relationships, risk, and market rates for similar loans in the local market.[23]

Among most small development banks, there is still too little support for market-rate pricing. Loan funds that concentrate on low-income housing tend to charge rates far below market. On their housing deals, this is justified because interest costs dramatically affect affordability. However, many business-loan funds charge low prices without a similar justification. According to the Mt. Auburn Associates study of 116 revolving-loan funds supported by the Economic Development Administration, close to 50 percent of the borrowers paid interest rates greater than three points below the prime rate in 1986.[24] The study goes on to say that the interest-rate subsidies did not correlate with improved economic impact of the loans or lower loan defaults.

Some development lenders charge low rates of interest less to preserve affordability than because they consider market rates usurious and charging them unethical. This is a good argument for holding down development-bank costs in order to minimize required returns. However, as long as the availability of capital for development projects is limited, it is not clearly an ethical decision to deprive some viable borrowers of funding by providing funds at a lower cost than necessary to other borrowers. A few development banks also give up the opportunity that market-rate financing provides to increase income and, therefore, lending capacity because they have been able to obtain very cheap capital, and they want to pass the benefits of lower costs on to their borrowers.

For development banking to achieve its potential, development bankers need to pay more attention to pricing. To make sure that scarce resources are not wasted and that the flow of capital continues to grow, they must seek out projects that offer the highest possible financial returns from among the pool of deals that meet their social goals. They must find ways to structure loans that allow them to capture upside potential. When they decide projects need subsidies to achieve their community-development goals, the subsidies must be explicit so that they can evaluate the financial viability of the projects and assess whether social benefits justify the subsidies.

10
The Future of Development Banking

THE NEED for development banking has not diminished in the 1990s. Capital for community development, innovative businesses, and affordable housing is still in great demand. Federal, state, and local governments are not fiscally prepared to provide the necessary capital, and the financial powerhouses of the banking, thrift, venture-capital, and securities industries are increasingly distracted by their own difficulties and layoffs and are unlikely to focus proactively on community development.

The challenge for community-development finance is to create a financial system for promoting development that allows room for judgment, tolerates the unconventional manager without initial capital, and is sufficiently patient to achieve the desired results. There are specific steps development bankers, mainstream financial institutions, government agencies, and foundations can take in the 1990s that will allow us to meet the challenge.

Development Bankers

The essential task for successful development banks in the 1990s is to maintain their social content. Constant vigilance is required to continue the social mission of development institutions as they age. Such banks can lose their edge if they do not adjust their programs when the glaring social problems that called them into being are solved or ameliorated. They can lose direction when the founding entrepreneurs grow weary or move on to new social challenges. When a development bank attains financial success, it can become less adventurous and more protective of its existing gains. It should be the conscious task of the board of directors to update a development bank's social mission frequently and revive the founding passions.

A second task for successful development banks is to replicate themselves in new geographical areas. For all of the perceived success of South Shore Bank in Chicago, the replication of its bank-holding-company model by others has been exceedingly slow. There are few other commercial banks with similar goals, and it has, in most cases, been quite painful to start them. The start-up and capitalization of Community Capital Bank in New York City took more than four years. The Institute for Community Economics in Springfield, Massachusetts, the parent of the community-loan-fund model, has been far more successful in replicating small loan funds around the country. However, while their proliferation has resulted in more funding for difficult and small deals, loan funds cannot alone build the new financial system needed to promote community development. The barriers to entry for a small loan fund are low, but, given the absence of deposit insurance, the barriers to growth and sustainability are much higher.

What is needed is more development banks of a sustainable scale that have deposit insurance. The pool of investors willing to provide uninsured loans is growing each year, but it is still very small and, given how most investors make decisions, likely to stay small. In contrast, the market for insured deposits at development banks appears to be essentially unlimited. The extraordinary flow of deposits (more than $30 million in the first nine months of existence) into the Vermont National Bank Socially Responsible Banking Fund is a clear indication of the availability of such capital. While community-development credit unions can meet many community-capital needs, commercial banks and savings institutions and, in particular, holding companies are generally more flexible and stable.

The third task for development banks is to broaden their investor base. The greatest barrier to the creation and growth of development banks is poor access to equity capital. Loan funds and credit unions need more grants, which they should be able to justify by the economic-development benefits they provide. For commercial banks, what is missing is investors willing to commit to investments in permanent preferred stock or common stock. The single step most likely to enhance the availability of equity capital is improving the liquidity of equity investments. The original equity investors in South Shore Bank in Chicago have not been able to sell their stock after sixteen years of operation. It is a very rare investor who is able to sustain such illiquidity. A worthwhile experiment would be for one of the leading development banks to sell equity (or appropriately configured debt) into the social-investment market via a public offering. The purpose of the experiment would be to determine if there are enough investors willing to purchase the security in small amounts and hold it for a reasonable time. If there are, then the same technique could be used to raise equity capital for other development banks. The security offering would be explicit about below-market returns. It would offer to maximize liquidity by facilitating a market for the stock. It would be distributed by brokers who have ready access to social investors. In fact, the combined securities arms of the social-investment organizations (particularly Calvert, Working Assets, and Progressive Asset Management) should be able to raise a fair amount of capital in $1,000 increments for equity in an organization such as South Shore Bank.

Mainstream Financial Institutions

Mainstream financial institutions could do a great deal to assist development banking as part of their response to growing pressure to serve their communities. Community Reinvestment Act (CRA) ratings for depository institutions became publicly available in July 1990. The effect of public access to the ratings will eventually be quite dramatic. The four possible ratings include outstanding, satisfactory, needs to improve, and substantial noncompliance. It is difficult to imagine any major public investor (states, cities, counties, and similar bodies) being willing to place deposits with a financial institution with a rating of "needs to improve" or "substantial noncompliance." If public investors are joined in their boycott of organizations with low ratings by foundations, social mutual funds, churches, and informed consumers, these financial institutions will have a compelling reason to change their behavior.

In regions where effective development banks already exist, the fastest method for improvement will be for mainstream financial institutions with poor ratings to form lending partnerships where they purchase loans originated by a development bank or lend a development bank additional capital. It may also be appealing for poorly rated financial institutions to provide liquidity, at a premium price, to the original shareholders of successful development banks. In cases where community loan funds are prevalent (and without shareholders), poorly performing banks could provide grants or subordinated loans for use as loan-loss reserves. They could also make deposits in community-development credit unions.

Where a development bank does not exist, mainstream financial institutions could provide the equity capital and staffing to create one. Small-lending programs at large banks will never achieve the focus and commitment of, or address development needs as well as, a local development bank that is adequately capitalized. It is interesting to contemplate the formation of a series of development banks fully capitalized through equity investments by major banks, each of whom began 1990 with poor CRA ratings. While this may not be the set of investors that the organizers of a development bank originally envisioned, such shareholders, who also agree to make a commitment to participate in loans originated by the development bank, may be perfectly adequate.

Government

In the fiscally constrained 1990s, the most important agencies of government to development bankers will be the financial regulators. In the past, they have not given special consideration to applicants for charters who have development goals. In fact, regulators have regarded them with particular suspicion. Without compromising their goals of safety and soundness, regulators could provide a helping hand to development banks. Development loans, when compared to Third World loans or to some of the leveraged-buyout loans of the 1980s, look pretty tame.

Regulators could make the application process for forming a depository institution less daunting. They could assist development banks by accepting draft applications for informal comment, waiving application fees for banks with primary development goals, and helping to match development banks in formation with experienced executives from larger banks who might want more-meaningful work. These activities could provide a welcome break from efforts to deal with the savings and loan debacle and prevent commercial banks from following the same path.

The government could play a major role in the expansion of development banking by granting banks the privileges they seek to expand into new areas and services based upon their performance in meeting community-credit needs. Banks are actively seeking legislation that would allow them to underwrite securities and sell insurance. They are also seeking full interstate banking privileges. These opportunities could be made available only to banks that are committed to community development; one way of demonstrating such commitment would be to make serious investments of money and time in local development banks.

Of course, an increase in state and federal funding for development banking, particularly under programs that provide patient capital, share risk, or enhance liquidity for private development banks, would be extremely valuable. There are existing programs that could be slightly modified to serve development banks, such as the Special Impact Program of the U.S. Department of Health and Human Services, Office of Community Services, which provides planning and venture funds to community-development corporations. There are also state models for motivating private investors to provide higher-risk capital that could be extended to broader regions, such as the Michigan Strategic Fund's business- and industrial-development corporation (BIDCO) program.

Foundations and Other Funders

For the most part, major foundations have not provided reliable support to development banking. One exception is the Ford Foundation, which also led a group of foundations that have banded together with the Local Initiative Support Corporation to create a liquidity mechanism for affordable housing. In the 1990s, foundations should be replaced by banks and thrifts as a source of secondary-market purchases of loans and should reorient themselves toward providing equity capital. Foundations—and other funders—previously uninvolved with development banking may simply wish to purchase equity from an existing development-bank investor. Funders that have already made development loans should think about becoming initial equity investors and active, informed board members in new development banks.

All funders making debt investments in development banks should consider extending the term of the debt to match the needs that the banks serve. They should also target their investments to help development banks achieve a sustainable scale, rather than helping many tiny programs to compete for limited capital. They should support innovations that improve the ability of borrowers to afford market rates of return. They should invest their cash in insured depository institutions that have community-development goals.

In addition to their investment function, foundations should strongly support activist organizations using the Community Reinvestment Act (CRA) to force major financial institutions to be more responsive to community needs. With the disclosure of CRA ratings already beginning, a major increase in funding monitoring and activist organizations could pay dramatic dividends in the form of new capital for community development.

Community Activists

Someone must hold the federal regulators' feet to the fire to make sure that the CRA ratings accurately reflect the performance of financial institutions. There are community organizations across the nation that have challenged financial institutions on their community-reinvestment performance. Their continued efforts are necessary to encourage mainstream financial institutions to support development banking. We hope that at least one organization will keep a scorecard tracking each kind of rating the regulators award. If there are too many good ratings, then the judges are probably being too easy.

What would make the 1990s a successful decade for development banking? If in the year 2000 there are insured depository institutions (banks, savings and loans, or credit unions) in each of the twenty-five largest metropolitan areas that are effective development banks operating at a sustainable scale. If any financial institution that is given a "substantial noncompliance" CRA rating quickly loses 25 percent of its deposits. If someone from the development-banking world is appointed a state banking commissioner or member of the board of governors of the Federal Reserve Board. If the community-development loan funds maintain their exemplary loss record and can use it to attract several hundred million dollars for their work with the most difficult and smallest borrowers. If at least one successful model for lending to high-risk development businesses emerges and is found suitable for replication. Then, the 1990s will be an extraordinary decade for development banking and community-development finance. Such a decade is well within reach.

Notes
Glossary
Index

Notes

Chapter 1

1. Paul Starobin, "Thanks a Lot, Joe!" *National Journal,* 23 June 1990, p. 1568.

2. *Going for Broke: Fixing the Bank Insurance Fund,* p. 1 (Financial Democracy Campaign fact sheet, Durham, N.C.).

3. Data describing who owns capital resources and who invests them are summarized in the tables at the end of Chapter 1.

4. *Flow of Funds Accounts, Financial Assets and Liabilities Year End, 1965–1988* (Washington, D.C.: Federal Reserve Board, 1989).

5. Social Investment Forum, 711 Atlantic Ave., Boston, Mass. 02111, (617) 451-3252.

6. "Banking on the States," *Ways and Means,* April 1989, p. 3.

7. Informal tabulation compiled by the Federal Reserve Bank of Philadelphia, Office of Community Investment, 1988.

8. Calvin Bradford, *Impact of Neighborhood Lending Programs in Chicago, Partnerships for Reinvestment: An Evaluation of the Chicago Neighborhood Lending Programs* (prepared for the National Training and Information Center, 1989).

9. Calvin Bradford, "Reinvestment: The Quiet Revolution," *Neighborhood Works* 12, no. 4 (August–September 1989): pp. 22ff.

10. William A. Duncan, "Strengthening a Rural Economy," *Economic Development and Law Center Report,* January–February 1985, pp. 7 and 8.

11. Large-scale housing lending has a higher chance of success within the public sector.

12. Peter Plastrik and Steve Rohde, "The Michigan Strategic Fund: Roots and Results," *Entrepreneurial Economy Review,* October 1988, p. 6.

13. Oral presentation by Chuck Matthei at a meeting on development finance sponsored by the Woodstock Institute of Chicago in November 1989; interview with Steve Rohde, August 1992.

14. Interview with Stephen McConnell, Northern Community Investment Corporation, St. Johnsbury, Vt. November 1989.

15. Of this total, community-development credit unions have assets of about $500 million. Member funds of the National Association of Community Development Loan Funds have assets of approximately $75 million, with other local and regional loan funds controlling at least another $250 million. Small-business investment companies (SBICs) have assets of $2.35 billion, and minority-enterprise small-business investment companies (MESBICs) have assets of $443 million (Shorebank Corporation in Chicago alone has assets of $200 million). Other commercial banks and savings and loan associations formed to promote community development together account for another few hundred million dollars. Marvin Beaulieu, "The Need for Capital and the Sustainability of Capital Funds," pp. 9–16 (papers commissioned for Business Development and Self-Employment Loan Fund Workshops, Center for Management and Community Development, Tufts University, Medford, Mass., March 1988; available from the Ford Foundation, New York).

16. When talking about development-oriented financial institutions, some practitioners argue that only commercial banks should be called development banks since, with few exceptions, only commercial banks are allowed to have the word "bank" in their names. However, many kinds of financial institutions, including investment banks, are described as banks, even if they cannot technically use the word. In addition, in the literature on developing countries, financial institutions that facilitate development are referred to generically as development banks.

Other practitioners differentiate between development banks and development funds, arguing that the term *bank* should refer to financial institutions that are regulated and can accept deposits. They call financial institutions that accept deposits (commercial banks, savings and loan associations, and credit unions) *development banks* and refer to financial institutions that solicit nondepository loans and investments (such as venture funds and loan funds) as *development funds.* These practitioners believe that the term *bank* has connotations of strength not applicable to many loan funds. Even though they do not appear in this book, it is useful to recognize that these distinctions may be made.

17. The community-development loan fund model that is used in this book adopts many of the features of the one developed by the Institute for Community Economics. In the case of microloan funds, the book incorporates much of the approach proposed by Acción International, taking into account the brief experience of existing U.S. programs. In the case of royalty-investment funds, the book relies heavily on the experience of the Connecticut Product Development Corporation.

18. Mt. Auburn Associates, *Factors Influencing the Performance of U.S. EDA Sponsored Revolving Loan Funds,* vol. 1, p. 4 (report prepared for U.S. Department of Commerce, Economic Development Administration, Research and Evaluation Division, Washington, D.C., August 1987).

19. National Association of Community Development Loan Funds, "NACDLF Member Fund Statistical Profile as of 12/31/90" (brochure, Philadelphia, 1990).

20. Jeff Ashe, *Development Credit to Assist Small-Scale Enterprise,* p. 25 (Southern Development Bancorporation supplemental report, September 1986; available from Shorebank Corporation, Chicago).

21. Jason Brown, *Small Scale Bank Lending in Developing Countries: A Comparative Analysis,* p. 12 (Washington, D.C.: U.S. Agency for International Development, February 1985), and Katherine E. Stearns, *Assisting Informal-Sector Microenterprises in Developing Countries,* pp. 25–32 (Cornell/International Agricultural Economics Study, Department of Agricultural Economics, Cornell University, Ithaca, N.Y., August 1985).

22. Peter S. Fisher, "Product Development Corporations and State

Economic Development," p. 2 (presented at the annual meeting of the Association of Collegiate Schools of Planning, Graduate Program on Urban and Regional Planning, University of Iowa, October 1987).

23. Udayan Gupta, "Enterprise," *Wall Street Journal*, 18 December 1990, B-2.

24. Shorebank Corporation, *1988 Annual Report*, p, 1.

Chapter 2

1. Michael Kieschnick, *Venture Capital and Urban Economic Development* (Washington, D.C.: Council of State Planning Agencies, 1979); Council for Northeast Economic Action, *Empirical Analysis of Unmet Demand in Domestic Capital Markets* (prepared for the U.S. Economic Development Administration, Washington, D.C., February 1981); Interagency Task Force on Small Business Finance, *Studies of Small Business Finance: A Report to Congress* (Washington, D.C., February 1982); and Interface, *Where Credit Is Due: A Study of Small Business Access to Capital* (New York, June 1988).

2. "Progressive News," *Ways and Means*, April 1989, p. 8, and Katherine L. Bradbury, Karl E. Case, and Constance R. Durham, "The Geographic Patterns of Mortgage Lending in Boston, 1982–1987," *New England Economic Review* (Federal Reserve Bank of Boston, 1989).

3. Council for Northeast Economic Action, *Empirical Analysis of Unmet Demand in Domestic Capital Markets*, p. 4 (prepared for the U.S. Economic Development Administration, National Technical Information Service, Washington, D.C., February 1981).

4. Laura Henze, Nancy Nye, and Dick Schramm, *Roundtable Workshop for Business Development and Self-Employment Loan Funds Serving Low Income People: Summary Report*, p. 10 (Tufts University, Medford, Mass., 1 October 1989; available from the Ford Foundation, New York).

5. And, even in this area, the overwhelming majority of ESOPs that receive loans are tax-avoidance schemes offering few, if any, real benefits to employees.

6. Federal Reserve Board, "Quarterly Survey of the Terms of Lending," *Federal Reserve Bulletin*, December 1989.

7. James A. White, "The Decade of Phenomenal Growth for Institutions," *Wall Street Journal,* 26 December 1989, C-1.

8. Indexing has not spread further because there is heavy marketing of various stock-selection techniques. Of course, if everyone used it, indexing would not work. Indexing is a freeloader problem—indexers take advantage of all the information obtained by other investors. For it to work well, there must be many investors who do not index.

Chapter 3

1. Mt. Auburn Associates, *Factors Influencing the Performance of U.S. Economic Development Administration–Sponsored Revolving Loan Funds,* vol. 2, *Case Studies,* p. O-13 (report prepared for the U.S. Department of Commerce, Economic Development Administration, Research and Evaluation Division, Washington, D.C., August 1987).

2. National Federation of Community Development Credit Unions, *An Analysis of the Role of Credit Unions in Capital Formation and Investment in Low- and Moderate-Income Communities,* p. 89 (presented to the Executive Office of the President, Office of Policy Development, 17 December 1986).

3. Ronald Grzywinski, "The New Old-Fashioned Banking," *Harvard Business Review,* (May–June 1991): p. 95.

4. Kathryn Tholin, *Putting It All Together: The Birth of the Austin/West Garfield Federal Credit Union* (Chicago: Woodstock Institute, 1989), p. 17.

5. Institute for Community Economics, *The Community Land Trust Handbook* (Emmaus, Pa.: Rodale Press, 1982).

6. Interview with Mary Houghton, Shorebank Corporation.

7. Interview with Jerry Rickett, president, Kentucky Highlands Investment Corporation, January 1990.

8. Interview with Andy Lamas, PACE, November 1989.

9. Interview with Robert Jackson, Quitman County Development Center, Marks, Miss., November 1989.

10. Institute for Community Economics, *The Community Loan Fund Manual* (Springfield, Mass. 1987).

11. Dennis R. Marino et al., "Evaluation of the Illinois Neighborhood Development Corporation: Background Report" (Chicago: Woodstock Institute, 1980).

12. Mt. Auburn Associates, *Factors Influencing the Performance of U.S. Economic Development Administration–Sponsored Revolving Loan Funds,* vol. 1, p. X (report prepared for the U.S. Department of Commerce, Economic Development Administration, Research and Evaluation Division, Washington, D.C., August 1987).

13. Center for Community Self-Help, *Sustainability of Nonprofit Loan Funds,* p. 10 (papers commissioned for Business Development and Self-Employment Loan Fund Workshops, Center for Management and Community Development, Tufts University, Medford, Mass., March 1988; available from the Ford Foundation, New York).

14. While the financial data in this example are for a manufacturing company, the results are very similar for retail and wholesale service organizations.

15. Center for Community Self-Help, *Sustainability of Nonprofit Loan Funds,* p. 10.

16. Mt. Auburn Associates, *Factors Influencing Performance,* vol. 2, p. C–10.

Chapter 4

1. Mt. Auburn Associates, *The Design and Management of State and Local Revolving Loan Funds,* p. 25 (prepared for U.S. Department of Commerce, Economic Development Administration, Research and Evaluation Division, Washington, D.C., August 1987).

2. Council for Community Development, Inc., *The Community Development Finance Corp.: A Review and Action Plan Final Report* (Cambridge, Mass., June 1982).

3. Laura Henze, Nancy Nye, and Richard Schramm, *Roundtable Workshop for Business Development and Self-Employment Loan Funds Serving Low Income People: Summary Report,* p. 18 (Tufts University, Medford, Mass., 1 October 1988; available from the Ford Foundation, New York).

4. National Federation of Community Development Credit

Unions, *The Lower East Side Community Financial Center: A Prototype for Inner City Banking,* p. 18 (New York, 29 March 1985).

5. Interview, December 1989.

6. Henze, Nye, and Schramm, *Roundtable Workshop for Business Development,* p. 1.

7. Interview with Katherine Gross, Industrial Cooperative Association, Somerville, Massachusetts, November 1989.

8. Richard Schramm, *Loan Fund Evaluations: Developing Information Needed to Assess Loan Fund Benefits and Costs,* pp. 2–8 (papers commissioned for Business Development and Self-Employment Loan Fund Workshops, Center for Management and Community Development, Tufts University, Medford, Mass., March 1988; available from the Ford Foundation, New York).

9. Mt. Auburn Associates, *Design and Management,* p. 105.

10. Ibid., pp. 100–106.

Chapter 5

1. Conference of State Banking Supervisors, *State of the State Banking System,* May 1988.

2. Practicing Law Institute, *The Thrift Industry in 1985,* p. 559.

3. "Congress OKs Sweeping Bill to Save Thrift Industry," *Congressional Quarterly,* 12 August 1989, pp. 2147–51.

4. Practicing Law Institute, *The Thrift Industry in 1985,* p. 552.

5. A qualified thrift lender has qualified thrift investments greater than 70 percent of total tangible assets. Qualified thrift investments are loans, equity, or securities held by the institution or its subsidiaries that are related to residential real estate or manufactured housing, plus the book value of property for its own use, plus up to 10 percent of tangible assets (consisting of liquid assets, 50 percent of sold loans, investments in FHLB, deposits in thrifts, FHLMC, FNMA, or GNMA mortgage securities, and other mortgage-backed securities). Tangible assets are defined as all assets, less goodwill and other intangible assets.

6. Part 12, Code of Federal Regulations, Banks and Banking, revised 1 January 1988.

7. Certain loans, even though they are used for a commercial, corporate, business, or agricultural purpose, are not considered business loans for the purposes of the 20 percent restriction. These are loans that are (1) fully secured by residential property, (2) fully secured by share deposits of the borrower, (3) insured or guaranteed by a federal or state agency, or (4), when aggregated with other business loans to the same borrower, are less than $25,000.

8. Interview with Kathy Thompson, Credit Union National Association, Washington, D.C., January 1990.

9. Part 12, Code of Federal Regulations, Chapter 7, Section 701.27 (NCUA), 1 January 1988 edition.

10. Commercial banks and savings and loan associations, however, can have affiliates that participate in profits, such as small-business-investment corporations.

11. Interview with Richard M. Saul, former chief of Consumer Action and Cooperative Programs, Office of Economic Opportunity, December 1989.

12. Interview with Robert Jackson, Quitman County Development Center, Marks, Miss., December 1989.

13. Prospectus, Delaware Valley Community Reinvestment Fund, Philadelphia, October 1989.

14. National Federation of Community Development Credit Unions, *An Analysis of the Role of Credit Unions in Capital Formation and Investment in Low- and Moderate-Income Communities*, pp. 27–28 (presented to the Executive Office of the President, New York, 17 December 1986).

15. Part 12, Code of Federal Regulations, Chapter 7, Section 701 (NCUA), 1 January 1987 edition.

16. Institute for Community Economics, *The Community Loan Fund Manual* (Springfield, Mass., 1987), pp. 4–17.

17. The National Credit Union Administration proposed to tighten its requirements for economic feasibility by increasing minimum membership to 2,000 people. While this proposal was not implemented, it sends a signal that NCUA will prefer applicants with larger memberships.

18. Interview with Kathy Thompson, January 1990.

19. It may take some legal assistance to structure this approach.

Organizers of commercial banks must be five individuals, who usually are required to finance organizing expenses. However, the corporation formed with investor capital to become a bank holding company could enter into an agreement with the organizers to reimburse them for these costs.

20. Federal Home Loan Bank Board, Office of District Banks, Applications Procedures Memo, Washington, D.C., 25 February 1987.

21. As with every step, organizers should consult an attorney before proceeding.

22. Harry Schibanoff, "So You Want to Start a Bank? A Look at Some of the Hurdles," *American Banker,* 8 January 1988, p. 4.

23. Loan funds are subject to federal truth-in-lending disclosure laws and to state usury laws. Even if they are exempt from registration, they still must comply with SEC disclosure laws.

24. Ronald Grzywinski, "A Proposal to Create Permanent Neighborhood Development Banks," *The Entrepreneurial Economy,* Corporation for Enterprise Development, Washington, D.C., December 1984, pp. 6–7.

25. Regulators try to limit this practice for large commercial banks by requiring that bank holding companies (BHCs) and their banks maintain the same ratio of capital to total assets. However, banks with less than $150 million in assets are permitted to have 300 percent "double leverage"—that is, the ratio of equity in banks and nonbank subsidiaries to the equity in the parent BHC can be 3.

26. Stanley M. Huggins, *Effective Utilization of a Bank Holding Company,* pp. 488–504 (proceedings of a conference on Bank Structure and Competition, Federal Reserve Bank of Chicago, 14–16 May 1986).

27. Office of the Comptroller of the Currency, Interpretive Ruling 7.7480, Banking Circular BC-185.

28. Dennis R. Marino et al., *Evaluation of the Illinois Neighborhood Development Corporation Background Report* (Chicago: Woodstock Institute, 1980), p. 54.

29. Jean Edelhertz, *Credit Union Formation* (unpublished report, 26 July 1988).

30. Gary C. Zimmerman, "Growing Pains," *FRBSF Weekly Letter,* 11 December 1987, p. 1.

31. National Federation of Community Development Credit Unions, *An Analysis of the Role,* p. 4.

32. Ibid., p. 11.

33. *Low income* is defined by the lower living standard income level (LLSIL), published semiannually by the Employment and Training Administration of the Department of Labor.

34. Interview with Elaine Wricks, Northside Community Credit Union, Chicago, November 1989.

35. Interview with Robert Jackson, November 1989.

36. Marcie Oppenheimer, "Open a Credit Union," *Community Finance,* Spring 1989, p. 5.

Chapter 6

1. Mary Houghton, South Shore Bank, Chicago, notes on conference speech, Self-Employment Conference, Toronto, October 1989.

2. Steve Dawson, "Funding Development Finance: The Case for a New Relationship between Funders and Development Funds," p. 9 (papers commissioned for Business Development and Self-Employment Loan Fund Workshops, Center for Management and Community Development, Tufts University, Medford, Mass., March 1988; available from the Ford Foundation, New York).

3. Commercial banks and credit unions were selected because there are industry averages available for them, they illustrate some important differences, and they are two of the six models given special attention in the book. The source of the data in the summary table for commercial banks is FDIC commercial-bank financial statements with adjustments to scale to $15 million from range of $25–100 million. The source of the data for credit unions is NCUA 1986 Yearend Statistics for Federally Insured Credit Unions with adjustments to scale to $3 million from a range of $2–5 million.

4. The professional association of certified public accountants has asserted that credit union share accounts are debt, but credit union regulators are fighting this interpretation, arguing that share accounts are equity. Debt involves a contract to make predetermined payments on borrowed funds. The dividends paid on share accounts are not

predetermined but, rather, determined by the earnings of the credit union. However, share accounts are treated like bank deposits by those who hold them. For the purpose of this accounting discussion, share accounts are treated as debt.

5. Robert Morris Associates, *Statistical Supplement,* A Semiannual Supplement to RMA's Commercial Lending Newsletter, July 1989, Philadelphia, and National Credit Union Administration, 1989 Mid-year Statistics for Federally Insured Credit Unions, Washington, D.C.

6. Federal Deposit Insurance Corporation, *Annual Report,* Washington, D.C., 31 December 1982.

7. Booz-Allen and Hamilton, *Managing Delivery System Economics: A Branch Study* (for the American Bankers Association, October 1987).

8. Based upon figures taken from Credit Union National Association, *Credit Union Report, 1986,* and checked in interviews.

9. Gary C. Zimmerman, "Growing Pains," *FRBSF Weekly Letter,* 11 December 1987, p. 1.

10. "Volunteers," *Credit Union Magazine,* December 1976, pp. 8–12, and February 1977, pp. 28–31.

11. Ibid.

12. Laura Henze, Nancy Nye, and Richard Schramm, *Roundtable Workshop for Business Development and Self-Employment Loan Funds Serving Low Income People: Summary Report,* p. 26 (Tufts University, Medford, Mass., 1 October 1988; available from the Ford Foundation, New York).

13. Interview with Stephen McConnell, Northern Community Investment Corporation, St. Johnsbury, Vermont, November 1989.

14. Even though an $8 million microloan fund must administer a much larger number of loans than a community-development loan fund of the same size, the microloan fund's administrative costs are not proportionally higher and it seeks a much larger spread between what it pays for capital and what it charges borrowers. Microenterprise loan funds are better able to contain administrative costs by having borrowers promote the program, form their own groups, collect their own loan payments, give each other advice, and help each other make payments. Technical-assistance requirements are also smaller.

15. This statement cannot be made with certainty since many of the figures provided by CPDC are approximations.

16. Harry Schibanoff, "So You Want to Start a Bank? A Look at Some of the Hurdles," *American Banker,* 8 January 1988, p. 4.

17. Brian Nixon, "Chicago's Shorebank: The National Model," *Independent Banker,* April 1987, pp. 6–13.

18. Interview with Burton Jonap, Connecticut Product Development Corporation, March 1987.

19. Interview with Fran Tata, president of Union Savings Bank of Albuquerque, Albuquerque, New Mexico, January 1990.

20. *Community Finance: News of the New York Community Financial Network,* January 1990, S-1.

21. The exact number of years will depend on the level of confidence of organizers of the development bank concerning its ability to attract operating subsidies.

22. Interview with Karen Zelin, Santa Cruz Community Development Credit Union, Santa Cruz, California, December 1989.

23. James N. Clark, *The Lower East Side Community Financial Center: A Prototype for Inner City Banking* (New York: National Federation of Community Development Credit Unions, 1988), p. 24 (consulting report).

24. Interview with Karen Zelin, December 1989.

Chapter 7

1. John Weiler and Jeff Nugent, "The Art and Science of Community Development Lending," *Community Investments,* 3, no. 2 (Spring 1991): p. 2.

2. The best measure of loan losses is the rate of loss from the average proportion of loans defaulting over some long period. This measure can be calculated either by computing (1) cumulative losses from loans that have matured as a share of the total of these loans or, if program managers want to capture changes in loss experience over time, (2) cumulative losses on a set of matured loans made during a particular period as a share of the total of these loans. The measures include only loans that have matured because repayment is assured only after that point. While they offer the most accurate picture of loss experience, these measures are rarely calculated because they cannot

be computed until a program has a substantial history, they demand a planned data-collection effort, and no one requires them.

3. Interview with Marvin Cohen, president, Chicago LISC, 1988.

4. Harold Black, *The State of Minority Savings and Loan Associations* (Department of Finance, University of Tennessee, Knoxville, prepared for the Federal Home Loan Bank Board, Washington, D.C., 1989).

5. Cumulative-loss rates can understate or overstate a development bank's level of credit risk. Including loans that are still outstanding in ratios of cumulative loan losses can underestimate loan-loss potential, particularly for a program with many new loans. Cumulative-loss rates are likely to be much higher when loans are three or more years old. A cumulative measure can overstate current loss potential for a development-finance program that has found ways to reduce its loss rates over time. Since mainstream financial institutions quote annual losses, while development banks generally report cumulative losses, it is hard to make comparisons. Direct comparisons of these two very different measures are likely to overstate development-bank losses.

6. Center for Community Self-Help, *Sustainability of Nonprofit Loan Funds*, p. 11 (papers commissioned for Business Development and Self-Employment Loan Fund Workshops, Center for Management and Community Development, Tufts University, Medford, Mass., March 1988; available from the Ford Foundation, New York).

7. Interview with Julia Vindasius, Good Faith Fund, Pine Bluff, Arkansas, November 1989.

8. Interface, *Where Credit Is Due: A Study of Small Business Access to Capital*, p. 89 (New York, June 1988).

9. Interview with Robert Jackson, Quitman County Federal Credit Union, Marks, Mississippi, November 1989.

10. Mt. Auburn Associates, *Factors Influencing the Performance of U.S. EDA Sponsored Revolving Loan Funds*, vol. 2, *Case Studies*, p. A-12 (produced for the U.S. Department of Commerce, Economic Development Administration, Washington, D.C., August 1987).

11. Michael Bernick, "The New Inner City Loan Funds: Financing Mechanisms for Inner City Entrepreneurship," *San Francisco Renaissance,* Winter 1986, pp. 1–3.

12. "Information for Social Investors," p. 5 (Hartford, Conn.: Cooperative Fund of New England, no date; prospectus).

13. Interview with Stephen McConnell, Northern Community Investment Corporation, St. Johnsbury, Vermont, November 1989.

14. Interview with Robert Jackson, November 1989.

15. "Bad Management Named Cause of Most National Bank Failures Since 1979," *Banking Report* 50 (25 January 1988): p. 114.

16. Robert L. Rese, "Fallen Hero: A Credit Union Fails and Omaha Wonders: Was It Bamboozled?" *Wall Street Journal,* 8 February 1989, A-1.

17. Interview with Herbert Price, Citizens' Coalition Federal Credit Union, Pontiac, Michigan, December 1989.

18. Marcie Oppenheimer, "Open a Credit Union," *Community Finance,* Spring 1989, p. 2.

19. Interview with Andy Lamas, PACE, Philadelphia, December 1989.

20. Interview with Kathryn Gross, Industrial Cooperative Association Loan Fund, Somerville, Massachusetts, November 1989.

21. Interview with Greg Ramm, Institute for Community Economics, Springfield, Massachusetts, 1988.

22. Margaret J. Stone, "Delinquency Problems of Community Development Credit Unions," *Economic Development and Law Center Report,* April–June 1981, p. 9.

23. Interview with Julia Vindasius, November 1989.

24. Quoted in Mary O'Connell, "Learning from the Third World," *Neighborhood Works,* July–August 1986, p. 4.

25. Interview with Karen Zelin, Santa Cruz Community Development Credit Union, Santa Cruz, California, December 1989.

26. Center for Community Self-Help, *Sustainability of Nonprofit Loan Funds,* p. 16 (papers commissioned for Business Development and Self-Employment Loan Fund Workshops, Center for Management and Community Development, Tufts University, Medford, Mass., March 1988; available from the Ford Foundation, New York).

27. Interview with Karen Zelin, December 1989.

28. Ibid.

29. Interview with Elaine Wricks, Northside Community Credit Union, Chicago, November 1989.

30. Stanley C. Silverberg, *Deposit Insurance and the Soundness of Banks,* Proceedings: A Conference on Bank Structure and Competition, Federal Reserve Board of Chicago, 1–3 May 1985, pp. 447–52.

31. Illinois Neighborhood Development Corporation, *Offering Circular,* p. 26 (Chicago, 1 June 1985).

32. James N. Clark, *The Lower East Side Community Financial Center: A Prototype for Inner City Banking* (New York: National Federation of Community Development Credit Unions, 1985), p. 24.

33. Interview with Paula Bowman, MACED Loan Fund, Berea, Kentucky, November 1989.

34. Interview with Stephen McConnell, November 1989.

35. Interview with Jerry Rickett, Kentucky Highlands Investment Corporation, London, Kentucky, January 1990.

36. National Federation of Community Development Credit Unions, *An Analysis of the Role of Credit Unions in Capital Formation and Investment in Low- and Moderate-Income Communities,* p. 14 (presented to the Executive Office of the President of the United States, New York, 17 December 1986).

37. National Association of Community Development Loan Funds: *Statistical Profile of Member Fund Activity as of June 30, 1988* (Philadelphia, 1988); *Statistical Profile of Member Fund Activity as of June 30, 1989* (Philadelphia, 1989); and *NACDLF Member Fund Statistical Profile as of December 31, 1990* (Philadelphia, 1990).

38. Interview with Elaine Wricks, November 1989.

39. Interview with Katherine Gross, November 1989.

40. Black, *State of Minority Savings and Loan,* p. 5.

41. *Bank Notes* 6, no. 4 (December 1988): p. 1.

42. Interview with A. Lamont Mackley, NCB Savings Association, Hillsboro, Ohio, December 1989.

Chapter 8

1. Center for Community Self-Help, *Sustainability of Nonprofit Loan Funds,* p. 14 (papers commissioned for Business Development and Self-Employment Loan Fund Workshops, Center for Management and Community Development, Tufts University, Medford, Mass., March 1988; available from the Ford Foundation, New York).

2. Interview with Mary Houghton, South Shore Bank, Chicago, 1988.

3. Harold A. Black, *The Status of Minority Savings and Loan Associations,* pp. 4–5 (Department of Finance, University of Tennessee, Knoxville, paper prepared for the Federal Home Loan Bank Board, Washington, D.C., 1989).

4. National Rural Development and Finance Corporation, *Technical Assistance Plan* (Washington, D.C., 1988); provided by Neal Nathanson.

5. Brochure and Prospectus, Delaware Valley Community Reinvestment Corporation, Philadelphia, October 1989.

6. Federal Reserve Bank, *1986 Functional Cost Analysis* (New York: Federal Reserve Bank of New York, Bank Services, 1987), p. 6.

7. *Annual Report,* South Shore Bank and Affiliates, Chicago, 1986; Federal Reserve Board, *Functional Cost Analysis, Average Banks* (New York: Federal Reserve Bank of New York, 1987), p. 6.

8. Steven Dawson, "Funding Development Finance: The Case for a New Relationship between Funders and Development Funds," p. 7 (papers Commissioned for Business Development and Self-Employment Loan Fund Workshops, Center for Management and Community Development, Tufts University, Medford, Mass., March 1988; available from the Ford Foundation, New York).

9. Interview with Jerry Rickett, Kentucky Highlands Investment Corporation, London, Kentucky, January 1990.

10. Joseph P. Kahn, "The Money Game," *Inc.,* October 1988, p. 109.

11. Mary Coyle, Jean Pogge, and Julia Vindasius, *Practitioners' Workshop on Micro-enterprise Credit Methodology Summary Report,* p. 9.

12. Interview with Mike Mantle, Bank of America State Bank, Concord, California, November 1989.

13. Interview with Katherine Gross, Industrial Cooperative Association Loan Fund, Somerville, Massachusetts, November 1989.

14. Interview with Paula Bowman, MACED Loan Fund, Berea, Kentucky, November 1989.

15. Interview with Robert Jackson, Quitman County Federal Credit Union, Marks, Mississippi, November 1989.

16. Coyle, Pogge, and Vindasius, *Practitioners' Workshop,* p. 8.

17. "Center to Start Self-Help Home Ownership Program," *Self-Help Update,* Fall 1989, p. 3 (Center for Community Self-Help/Self-Help Credit Union).

18. Interview with Karen Zelin, Santa Cruz Community Development Credit Union, Santa Cruz, California, December 1989.

19. Interview with Paula Bowman, November 1989.

20. Center for Community Self-Help, *Sustainability of Nonprofit Loan Funds,* p. 12 (papers commissioned for Business Development and Self-Employment Loan Fund Workshops, Center for Management and Community Development, Tufts University, Medford, Mass., March 1988; available from the Ford Foundation, New York).

21. Lenders that are 501(c)(3) charitable organizations probably can make entire loans rather than providing only the unsecured subordinated portion of the financing that projects require.

22. For a recent description of subsidy programs, many of which can also address credit risk and interest-rate risk, see Charles E. Riesenberg and Carolyn P. Line, *Principles and Practices of Community Development Lending: A Five-Step Investment Model to Strengthen Bank Community Development Programs* (Minneapolis, Minn.: Federal Reserve Bank of Minneapolis and First Bank System, 1989).

Chapter 9

1. Steven Dawson, *Funding Development Finance: The Case for a New Relationship between Funders and Development Funds,* p. 3 (papers commissioned for Business Development and Self-Employment Loan Fund Workshops, Center for Management and Community Development, Tufts University, Medford, Mass., March 1988; available from the Ford Foundation, New York).

2. Laura Henze, Nancy Nye, and Richard Schramm, *Roundtable Workshop for Business Development and Self-Employment Funds Serving Low Income People: Summary Report,* p. 18 (Tufts University, Medford, Mass., 1 October 1988; available from the Ford Foundation, New York).

3. Ibid., p. 31.

4. Center for Community Self-Help, *Sustainability of Nonprofit Loan Funds,* p. 11 (papers commissioned for Business Development

and Self-Employment Loan Fund Workshops, Center for Management and Community Development, Tufts University, Medford, Mass., March 1988; available from the Ford Foundation, New York).

5. National Association of Community Development Loan Funds, *Building the Foundation for Economic, Social, and Political Justice: A Five-Year Profile of the Membership of the National Association of Community Development Loan Funds, 1986–1990,* pp. 20, 21 (Philadelphia, July 1991).

6. National Association of Community Development Loan Funds, *Membership Report,* p. 2 (Philadelphia, August 1991).

7. National Association of Community Development Loan Funds, *Revolving Loan Fund Fact Sheet* (Philadelphia, 30 June 1989).

8. National Association of Community Development Loan Funds, *Membership Report,* p. 2 (Philadelphia, August 1991).

9. Ibid.

10. *Community Finance,* "Viewpoint: Northeast Regional Conference," January 1990, S-4.

11. South Shore Bank, *Watch Your Interest Build* (brochure).

12. "A Short Walk Down Memory Lane," *Santa Cruz Community Credit Union Newsletter,* Spring 1987, p. 4.

13. Southern Development Bancorporation, *Offering Memorandum* (obtained from Shorebank Corporation, Chicago, September 1986).

14. While no firm rules exist to guide a development bank in charging for unexpected risk, evidence from the practice of securities markets in pricing this risk indicates that a risk premium equal to about half the rate of unexpected loss is appropriate (Dimensional Corporate Loans, San Francisco, Calif., *Risks and Return in Corporate Lending,* unpublished paper, 1986).

15. Return on equity (income/equity) can be separated into return on assets (income/assets) multiplied by leverage (assets/equity).

16. Interview with Fran Tata, Union Savings Bank of Albuquerque, Albuquerque, New Mexico, January 1990.

17. Dimensional Corporate Loans, *Risks and Return.*

18. Santa Cruz Community Development Credit Union, *Community Development Loan Policies* (Santa Cruz, Calif., 16 June 1987).

19. Interview with Jack Kelly, Blackfeet National Bank, Browning, Montana, November 1989.

20. Mt. Auburn Associates, *Factors Influencing the Performance of*

U.S. Economic Development Administration Sponsored Revolving Loan Funds, vol. 2, *Case Studies,* p. I-7 (report prepared for the U.S. Department of Commerce, Economic Development Administration, Research and Evaluation Division, Washington, D.C., August 1987).

21. Institute for Community Economics, *The Community Loan Fund Manual,* pp. 7–25 (Springfield, Mass., 1987).

22. "Loans Grow in 1990," *Self-Help Update,* Fall 1990, p. 2 (Center for Community Self-Help, Durham, N.C.).

23. Santa Cruz Community Development Credit Union, *Community Development Loan Policies.*

24. Mt. Auburn Associates, *Factors Influencing Performance* vol. 1, *Research Methodology and Findings,* p. 18.

Glossary

Numbers in parentheses refer to Sources for the Glossary, following.

Accounts-receivable (A/R) financing   Short-term loans that use accounts receivable as collateral; or sales of receivables at a discount to raise cash (1).

Amortization   The gradual reduction of a debt or obligation by making periodic principal and interest payments over the term of the loan agreement (1).

Annual percentage rate (APR)   The cost of a loan from the borrower's point of view, including finance charges and any other mandatory charges. It is based on the amount financed, the finance charge, and the term of the loan. The APR is expressed by the effective annual simple-interest rate (1).

Annuity   A series of periodic payments for a fixed future period or for life (6).

Appraisal   An evaluation of the market value of some asset by an independent expert (1).

Asset   Anything owned by a business that has commercial or exchange value. It may be tangible (physical in character), such as land, buildings, or machinery, or intangible (characterized by legal claims or rights), such as patents or amounts due from customers (15). In the case of a financial institution, assets are the financial instruments and real property it owns.

Asset/liability management The process of planning, organizing, and controlling asset and liability mixes, volumes, maturities, yields, and rates to achieve a specified interest margin. Interest margin is the difference between interest income and interest expense (13).

Balance sheet A financial statement that summarizes the resources, or financial position, of a financial institution by listing its assets and how assets are funded, either by liabilities or equity. Assets must equal liabilities and equity.

Balloon payment The last payment on a loan, where the required payments are not all equal and the last payment is substantially larger than the others (1).

Banker's acceptance A draft on a commercial bank that is paid when funds are deposited in the bank by the borrower on the maturity date of the banker's acceptance. The draft is secured by goods that are being traded; in addition, the commercial bank guarantees payment.

Bank holding company In general usage, any company that owns or controls one or more banks. However, a bank holding company as defined by the Bank Holding Company Act of 1956 is any corporation controlling 25 percent or more of the voting shares of at least two banks, or otherwise controlling the election of a majority of the directors of two or more banks (15).

Bond A long-term interest-bearing certificate of debt by which the issuer obligates itself to pay the principal amount at a specified time and to pay interest periodically (15).

Break-even point The volume of sales required so that total revenues and total costs are equal (15). For a financial institution, total costs consist of loan/investment losses, operating costs, and the cost of funds.

Broker A member of a securities firm who handles orders to buy and sell securities and commodities for a commission (14).

Business- and industrial-development corporation (BIDCO) A financial institution licensed by several state governments to increase the flow of risk capital to small, growing businesses.

Buydown program A plan that allows builders to purchase loans at less-than-market interest rates through front-end discounts.

Capital adequacy (rules) Regulations that require depository institutions to maintain capital at least equal to a certain percentage of their assets (15).

Capitalization The total investment in a financial institution, consisting of debt, stock, and retained earnings, which finances its operations and asset purchases (1).

Capital markets (or financial markets) The marketplace where funds are channeled from investors to borrowers. There are a variety of markets that deal in specific financial instruments, such as the over-the-counter market, the spot market, and the futures market.

Certificate of deposit (CD) A time deposit on which a depository institution usually allows withdrawal only at a stated maturity date and pays interest at agreed-upon dates (11).

Charge off To treat as a loss an amount originally recorded as an asset when a lender recognizes that a borrower will not fully repay a loan (15).

Charter A document issued by a federal or state supervisory agent granting a depository institution the right to do business. The terms and conditions of operations are enumerated in the charter (1).

Chattel   Articles of personal property used as collateral (1).

Collateral   Assets pledged by a borrower to a creditor that will be given up if the loan is not paid (1).

Commercial bank   A for-profit corporation owned by stockholders that provides depository services to individuals and organizations and uses the proceeds to make personal, commercial, and real-estate loans to individuals and organizations through secured and unsecured lending.

Commercial loan   A loan made to a business for commercial purposes that is not secured by a pledge of real estate.

Commercial paper   Short-term IOUs issued by large corporations.

Commitment   An advance agreement by a lender to provide funds for a loan at a later time and under certain conditions. The commitment is usually limited to a specified period and designates a dollar amount and yield (16).

Common stock   Those securities issued by a corporation—representing ownership in it—that have the lowest-priority claim to the corporation's assets, but share directly in profits and usually carry voting rights (11). Common stock has no maximum limit on dividend payments to holders, but common-stock dividends can only be paid after preferred-stock dividends have been paid in full (10).

Community-development corporations (commercial bank)   Subsidiaries of commercial banks or bank holding companies that can serve low- and moderate-income areas or small businesses by acquiring property, making equity investments, and providing loans with flexible terms, grants, and technical assistance.

Community-development credit union (CDCU)   Federal credit unions (and some state-chartered ones) whose members have a residential or associational common bond and where a majority of the members are low income.

Community-development loan fund (CDLF)   A privately

owned, nonprofit organization that makes loans to assist low- and moderate-income people, women, and minorities in obtaining housing and jobs; lends to businesses and other organizations rather than to individuals; and seeks loans from individual and institutional investors who are sympathetic to the goals of the loan fund.

Community land trust (CLT)   A nonprofit corporation whose purpose is to remove land permanently from the speculative market by buying the land and then leasing it for long-term private use.

Community Reinvestment Act (CRA)   A federal law enacted in 1977 to counteract the practice of geographic discrimination in lending.

Construction loan   A loan that finances the erection of a building, secured by a pledge of the proposed structure and the land on which it will be built; disbursements are made in stages as the construction progresses (9).

Consumer loan   A loan made to an individual for any non-business purpose except the construction or purchase of real estate. Consumer loans are sometimes used by the borrower for business purposes.

Core deposits   Deposits in a depository institution made by individuals or institutions who are unlikely to move their funds frequently in search of higher yields. "Hot" deposits, on the other hand, move to instruments that offer higher interest rates when the opportunity exists (3).

Corporation   A body formed and authorized by law to act as a single person even though it is constituted by one or more people who own shares of the corporation. Each investor is only liable for its actions to the extent of his or her investment.

Correspondent bank   A bank that carries on an account relationship with another bank, or that engages in an exchange of loan or operating services with another bank (1).

Credit   The ability or right to buy or borrow in return for a promise to pay later (1).

Credit life insurance   Life insurance that repays borrowers' loans if they die.

Credit risk   The uncertainty concerning whether returns will be different than expected; the probability that a debtor will be unable to repay a debt (1).

Credit union   A nonprofit cooperative depository institution owned and controlled by members who have some common bond.

Credit Union National Association Mortgage Corporation (CUNA Mortgage)   The mortgage corporation owned by the national trade association for credit unions, which pools credit-union mortgages and sells them in the secondary markets.

Dealer   An individual or firm that purchases securities and holds them (taking title) until sold to another (1).

Debenture   An obligation that is backed only by the integrity of the borrower and not secured by a specific lien on property; an unsecured note of a corporation (1).

Debt   A claim on the earnings of the organization issuing the debt (the issuer) that entails scheduled repayment of interest and principal and has repayment priority over equity investments if the organization declares bankruptcy. Failure to pay the promised interest on schedule forces the issuer to declare bankruptcy. Debt holders do not participate in management, except in the case of bankruptcies. Common forms of debt include money-market instruments (such as Treasury bills and certificates of deposit), which are short-term securities, and capital-market instruments (such as Treasury notes, corporate bonds, and mortgages), which are longer-term securities (10).

Default   Failure to meet a financial obligation previously committed. With regard to a bond or promissory note, the failure to make a payment either of principal or interest when due (1). Many loan agreements also place the borrower in default if specified financial conditions are not met, even if required payments are made.

Delinquent   A loan payment that is overdue but within the grace period allowed before actual default is declared (1).

Depository institution   A financial intermediary that accepts savings or demand deposits from the public.

Development bank   A financial institution that has the twin goals of fostering economic development and conserving its capital.

Development finance   The provision of capital to viable projects that contribute to economic development.

Disintermediation   The withdrawal of deposits from such financial intermediaries as savings institutions and commercial banks for reinvestment in debt securities that offer higher interest rates—Treasury bills or bonds, for example (15).

Diversification   The process of holding a portfolio of assets of diverse type, size, location, or sector in which the effect of any particular event on the stability of the financial institution is minimized.

Dividend   The share of profits distributed to shareholders or stockholders of a company, which may be paid in cash (cash dividend), stock (stock dividend), property, or other securities (dividend in kind) (8); the interest paid on share accounts held in a credit union.

Economic development   A quantitative or qualitative increase in economic activity that results in a wider distribution of the quantities being measured and is capable of being sustained in the future from the economy's own resources.

Effective interest rate   The actual interest rate earned or paid, taking into account compounding (15).

EFT (Electronic Funds Transfer) System   The transfer of payments by electronic means. Defined by the Electronic

Funds Transfer Act as any transfer of funds, other than a transaction that is originated by a paper instrument, that is initiated through an electronic terminal, telephone, or computer or magnetic tape and that orders or authorizes a financial institution to debit or credit an account (8).

Equity The residual value of a firm that remains after deducting its liabilities from its assets; the net worth of a firm; or funds invested by stockholders plus retained earnings. Equity is an ownership claim—that is, a claim on all earnings of the issuer remaining after debt claims are satisfied. Equity has no maturity or repayment date. Equity holders, who participate in management by electing the board of directors, are compensated with dividends (which must be approved by the board of the issuing firm) or with appreciation in value of their equity claim if they can sell it for more than their original equity investment.

Equity kicker An additional return in the form of stock-purchase warrants or incremental cash payments above the basic interest rate that is based upon stock performance, net worth, sales, or profit.

Equity securities Investors who participate in the earnings of a corporation do so by purchasing its equity securities. The two types of equity securities are preferred stock and common stock.

Factoring The short-term financing obtained by selling accounts receivable to a factor. A factor is a financial organization whose business is purchasing the accounts receivable of other firms, at a discount, and taking the risk and responsibilities of making collection (1).

Federal Deposit Insurance Corporation (FDIC) The federal agency that insures depositors at commercial banks and serves as the lead supervisory agency for state-chartered commercial banks that are not members of the Federal Reserve System.

Federal funds   Funds that commercial banks lend to one another for short amounts of time, usually overnight.

Federal Home Loan Bank Board   Until 1989, the system that chartered and supervised federal and state thrifts through a three-member board and twelve district banks. The Federal Home Loan Bank Board has been restructured into two agencies: the Office of Thrift Supervision, under the treasury secretary, which charters and supervises federal savings associations, federal savings banks, and thrift holding companies; and the Federal Housing Finance Agency, which oversees the credit operations of the twelve regional Home Loan Banks.

Federal Home Loan Mortgage Corporation (Freddie Mac)   A federally sponsored private agency that purchases mortgage loans that are not insured by the Federal Housing Administration or guaranteed by the Veterans Administration from originating financial institutions, packages them into securities, and sells them to other investors.

Federal National Mortgage Association (Fannie Mae)   A federally sponsored, private organization that purchases FHA/VA and conventional mortgage loans from originating financial institutions, holds a large portfolio of these mortgages, and packages other mortgages into securities for sale to investors.

Federal Reserve Board   The federal agency that sets U.S. monetary policy, controls the U.S. payment system, and regulates state-chartered commercial banks that are members of the Federal Reserve System and bank holding companies.

Federal Savings and Loan Insurance Corporation (FSLIC)   Until 1989, the fund run by the Federal Home Loan Bank Board to insure depositors at savings institutions. The FSLIC has been abolished and replaced by the Savings Association and Insurance Fund (SAIF), which is controlled by the FDIC.

Fiduciary   Any person or corporation with the responsibility to act on behalf of another party, in their best interest (9). For example, pension-fund trustees act to protect the pension investments of participants.

Finance company   A state-licensed financial institution that issues debt to the public and uses the proceeds to make consumer or commercial loans.

Financial institution   An institution that uses its funds chiefly to purchase financial assets (deposits, loans, bonds), as opposed to tangible property (plants, machines, inventories) (15).

Financial intermediary   An institution that borrows on its own behalf and invests the proceeds in a variety of securities.

First mortgage   A real-estate loan that creates a primary lien against a specified piece of real property (1).

501(c)(3)   A section of the Internal Revenue Code that exempts organizations from federal taxation if they are organized and operated exclusively for charitable purposes, no part of the net earnings of which benefits any private individual, no substantial part of the activity of which is carrying on propaganda, and which does not participate in any political campaign on behalf of any candidate (5).

Fixed-rate loan   A loan in which the interest rate remains constant over the term of the loan (1).

Floating-rate loan (or variable-rate loan or adjustable-rate loan)   Debt in which the interest rate is tied to a selected money-market indicator, such as Treasury bills, and moves up and down with that market indicator (12).

Futures contract   The right to buy or sell a financial instrument at a specified price on a specified future date (15).

Gap management   The identification and management of interest-rate risk created by differences between the maturities of a bank's assets and liabilities.

Government National Mortgage Association (GNMA)   An

organization that is part of HUD, which purchases mortgages guaranteed or insured by a federal agency and guarantees the timely payment of interest and principal on long-term securities formed from pools of these mortgages.

Graduated-payment mortgages   Mortgages where payments are lower than those for average mortgages in the early years, but grow each year.

Guaranteed/guaranty loan   Loans made by a lender in which a third party, the guarantor, intervenes in an agreement between two persons by becoming responsible to one for all or part of the debt of the other (12).

Hedge   Any purchase or sale of a good or security having as its purpose the elimination of possible profit or loss arising from price fluctuations (1).

Home Mortgage Disclosure Act (HMDA)   A federal law enacted in 1985 requiring commercial banks, savings and loans, and credit unions that operate in an SMSA and have more than $10 million in assets to report by census tract their annual volumes of housing-related loans.

Housing cooperative   Multifamily real estate owned and controlled by member–occupants who each receive one share vote and have a share interest in the cooperative and a proprietary lease that entitles them to occupy a particular living unit.

Impact   The effect of a development bank's outputs on community economic development.

Income statement   A financial statement that summarizes a financial institution's financial performance by listing revenues, expenses, and net income. Revenues less expenses equal net income.

Indexing   The practice of constructing a portfolio that includes a small piece of every stock without regard to its individual merit in order to attain the same performance as the overall market.

Insurance company A financial intermediary that contracts with individuals or businesses to reimburse them for financial losses due to death or accidents in return for established premium payments.

Interest-rate risk Uncertainty concerning the effect of changes in interest rates on the spread between earnings on funds and what a financial institution must pay for its funds.

Interim loan A short-term mortgage loan, often for the construction of a building (9).

Investment bank (or security firm) A financial institution that locates funds for borrowers (securities underwriters), matches savers with borrowers (brokers), and buys and resells securities of borrowers (dealers).

Leverage The use of borrowed funds by a business. The expectation is that the interest charged on borrowed funds will be lower than the earnings on the money borrowed (1); the relationship of a firm's debt to its equity, as expressed in the debt-to-equity ratio or in the ratio of assets to equity.

Liability A debt or obligation of a company; all claims against a corporation (15); for example, the main liability of a depository institution is its deposits.

Limited-equity cooperative A housing cooperative where the co-op organization bylaws limit the amount of dividends that can be paid on funds invested in the co-op and the amount of return allowed when shares are sold.

Limited partnership A form of business organization in which members of the partnership give up an active role in management and, in exchange, are not personally liable for the incurred debts of the partnership beyond their own investment. By law, at least one partner, called the general partner, must be fully liable (15).

Line of credit An advance approval of a specified level of credit that can be borrowed against as needed, usually in return for a commitment fee (11).

Liquidity   The ability of a financial institution to meet its current debts without selling assets at a loss (1); the ease with which investors can cash out of the investment if they need their money back.

Liquidity premium   Additional interest charge or up-front fee to compensate a financial institution for illiquidity.

Liquidity risk   The risk that a financial institution may not have adequate cash or other liquid assets to meet demands for cash withdrawals and loan requests, requiring it to sell assets at a loss (7).

Loan   A sum of money "rented" by a lender to a borrower, to be repaid with or without interest (12).

Loan-loss rate   The rate of loss on loans, which is calculated as: cumulative losses from loans that have matured as a share of the total of these loans; cumulative losses on a set of matured loans made during a particular period as a share of the total of these loans; annual loans charged off to losses as a share of loans outstanding; or cumulative losses as a share of cumulative loans made.

Loan-loss reserve   A financial account established based on a financial institution's loss experience to compensate for expected losses from the loans extended (1).

Loan-to-value (L/V) ratio   The ratio between the amount of a given mortgage loan and the appraised value of the security for that loan, expressed as a percentage of the appraised value (1).

Market rate of return   The financial return required by individual investors and financial institutions (who together comprise the capital markets) for a borrower with certain attributes.

Maturity   The due date on which full final payment on a loan must be made (1).

Mezzanine financing   Privately placed intermediate-risk capital, usually in the form of subordinated debt with fixed interest plus warrants, convertibility of the debt to stock, or preferred stock.

Microenterprise loan fund   A not-for-profit corporation that makes very small, short-term loans for working capital to "microentrepreneurs."

Minority-enterprise small-business investment company (MESBIC)   An SBIC that is limited to investing in small businesses that are at least 50 percent owned, controlled, and managed by minority or socially or economically disadvantaged individuals.

Money-market funds   Mutual funds that only invest in money-market securities, such as certificates of deposit, commercial paper, government bills and notes, and banker's acceptances.

Mortgage bank   A financial institution that issues short-term debt and uses the proceeds to orginate, sell, and service residential and commercial mortgages.

Mortgage loan   A loan secured by the pledge of real estate (15).

Mutual fund   A financial corporation that invests funds obtained from the sale of shares of its own stock in the securities of other corporations. Investors have the right to resell their shares to the fund at their pro rata share of the current market value of the fund's investments. Dividends paid to shareholders are based on the earnings of the securities, minus expenses (9).

National Credit Union Administration (NCUA)   The federal agency that charters and supervises federal credit unions and insures federal and state credit unions through its National Credit Union Share Insurance Fund (NCUSIF).

Negative amortization   Increases in loan balances as a result of less-than-interest-only payments.

Nonmember deposits   Deposits made by individuals and organizations that are not members in low-income credit unions.

Nonperforming loan Loans where the lender judges that the borrower fails to have the ability to fulfill the original contractual terms of the loan or where payments of interest or principal are overdue by ninety days or more (15).

NOW account A savings account that allows checklike drafts to be drawn against the interest-bearing deposit.

Office of the Comptroller of the Currency A branch of the Treasury Department that charters and supervises national banks.

Output The quantity of services provided by a development bank and the efficiency with which the services are provided.

Patient capital Funds obtained from investors who are willing to wait to be repaid and compensated far longer than the norm. Patient capital is needed to fund business start-ups and expansions because it can take years before these investments bear fruit.

Permanent financing Mortgage financing for real estate.

Personal guarantee A guarantee of loan repayment provided by an individual, usually on a business loan.

Pooling (of risk) The process whereby each member of a large group of investors purchases small shares of an investment. If the investment fails to produce income, each investor loses only his or her share, rather than the whole investment.

Preferred stock Those securities issued by a corporation—representing ownership in it—that have a claim upon the earnings (and sometimes upon the assets and control) of a corporation ahead of common stock (12). Preferred stock has an established dividend rate that is the maximum amount of dividends that its holders can receive (10).

Price-level-adjusted mortgages (PLAMs) Graduated-payment mortgages that allow a lender to protect itself from inflation without charging borrowers a substantial inflation premium up front by adjusting loan balances each year to take into account inflation in the previous year.

Private returns on investment Financial compensation, such as interest, dividends, appreciation in the value of assets, or royalties.

Provision for loan losses A charge against loan revenues made to capture the effect of all projected loan losses for which there are not already loan-loss reserves.

Qualified thrift lender A thrift with qualified thrift investments greater than 70 percent of tangible assets. Qualified thrift investments are real estate–related loans. Out of the 70 percent, a 15 percent basket can include consumer, education, small-business, and nonprofit construction loans.

Rate indexing The technique of passing through cost increases associated with interest-rate changes on variable-rate loans to borrowers (without raising loan payments) by reducing current principal payments by the amount of the increase in interest payments and allowing the principal to be repaid farther in the future by extending the term to maturity.

Rate sensitivity The amount that the net interest margin changes for a given change in overall interest-rate levels (3).

Real estate Tangible land and all physical property, including all physical substances below, upon, or attached to land. Thus houses, trees, and fences are classified as real estate; all else is personal property (16).

Real-estate-investment trust (REIT) An organization, usually corporate, established for the accumulation of funds for investing in real-estate holdings or for extending credit to others engaged in construction. The funds are usually accumulated by selling shares of ownership in the trust (1).

Real-estate-mortgage trust (REMT) An organization that buys and sells real-estate mortgages (usually short-term junior instruments) rather than real property (2).

Reserve requirements Requirements of depository-institution supervisory agencies that require a percentage of deposits to be set aside (3).

Retail bank A depository institution that offers retail services, such as consumer loans and deposit services for small savers.

Retained earnings Net income that is not distributed to investors as dividends.

Return on assets The ratio of income to assets.

Return on equity The ratio of income to equity.

Risk Uncertainty that returns will be different than expected on a loan or investment (1).

Risk pooling A strategy to reduce risk, where investors hold portfolios including fractional claims on a large number of investment projects in order to reduce the variability of their overall return below the average variability of each component investment standing alone.

Risk premium Additional interest charge to compensate a financial institution for risk.

Royalty Compensation for the use of a person's property based on an agreed percentage of the income arising from its use (15).

Royalty-investment fund (RIF) A for-profit or not-for-profit limited partnership or corporation whose purpose is to advance capital to businesses to finance the start-up of a new firm or the expansion of an existing one in return for a royalty on specified sales.

Savings and loan association A for-profit corporation that has many of the same characteristics as commercial banks. However, only some savings and loan associations are owned by stockholders. Others, known as mutual savings and loan associations, are owned by depositors and borrowers, who elect the board and share in profits.

Secondary market Markets such as the securities-dealer market or the stock exchange, where ownership of assets is transferred from one owner to another (1); there are active secondary markets for money-market securities, bonds, stocks, and securitied mortgages.

Securitization The process whereby loans are pooled and packaged into securities that are sold to investors.

Security A legal contract indicating a debt or ownership interest that specifies the amount of the transaction and the terms and conditions for repayment (10); the property or asset that is pledged to a creditor as an assurance against default on a claim (1).

Security credit Credit that is backed by securities.

Self-sufficient financial program A financial program that generates revenues from investments and loans at least equal to its loan losses, operating costs, and the cost of funds from its investors.

Senior debt A debt ranking ahead of other debts in repayment in the case of bankruptcy (15).

Shared-appreciation mortgages (SAMs) Mortgages where an outside investor provides part of the down payment in return for sharing in any appreciation in the value of the home when it is sold in the future.

Share drafts Interest-bearing "checking" accounts in credit unions.

Shares The partial ownership of a corporation or the stock certificate evidencing ownership (11); member deposits in credit unions.

Small Business Administration (SBA) A federal agency that guarantees small-business loans issued by commercial banks, savings institutions, and BIDCOs, and licenses SBICs.

Small-business investment company (SBIC) A special type of venture-capital firm that is licensed and regulated by the U.S. Small Business Administration and, as a result, can borrow from the SBA.

Special (or specific) reserve   A balance-sheet account containing funds set aside to absorb possible losses on a specific loan.

Spread   The difference between two prices (15).

Stock options   Rights to purchase shares of stock in the future at a price set in the present.

Student Loan Marketing Association (Sallie Mae)   A federally sponsored private organization that purchases guaranteed student loans from financial institutions (and makes loans to financial institutions) and issues securities to public financial markets to finance its purchases.

Subordination   Acknowledgment by a creditor in writing that the debt due him or her from a specified debtor will not be paid until all senior, unsubordinated debt has been paid (15).

Surplus (for depository institutions)   The amount by which the price of shares of stock exceeds their par value plus undistributed earnings held either as undivided profits or unallocated reserves.

Sustainable financial program   A financial program that may earn revenues less than its costs, but having a reliable source of external subsidies that makes up the difference.

Swap   An agreement between two parties to exchange interest payments on two separately made loans.

Sweat equity   Equity created by the labor of a purchaser or borrower that increases the value of the property (15).

Syndicate   A group of investors, each of whom invests in a project and takes some share of ownership.

Term loan   A loan scheduled to run for more than a year and usually repayable in annual or more frequent installments (1).

Thrift holding company   An organization that owns one or more savings institutions.

Total returns on investment   Social returns, including both private returns and externalities (costs and benefits external to the investor).

Transaction cost   The cost to review and structure an investment.

Unconventional mortgages   Mortgages that are federally insured by HUD/FHA or VA.

Underwriting   The process of evaluating borrower creditworthiness, collateral, performance potential, and risks involved in making an investment.

Unexpected losses   The variability in losses that is likely to occur from year to year.

Unimpaired capital (for depository institutions)   The difference between assets and liabilities.

Unsecured debt   A debt for which no collateral has been pledged (15).

Valuation reserve (for thrifts)   An allowance set aside to cover the risk that a loan or investment will not be repaid in full.

Venture capital   Funds invested in a high-risk enterprise, usually in the form of equity (1).

Venture-capital fund   A financial intermediary that raises capital from individual or institutional investors and uses the proceeds to invest in equity, debt with equity features, or rights to royalties from businesses.

Wholesale banking   The function of providing bank services, loan security, and loans mostly or solely to businesses (1).

Working capital   Current assets minus current liabilities. The capital immediately available for the continued operation of a business (15).

Yield   The rate of return on an investment, expressed as a percentage of the investment (1); or the total money earned on a loan for the term of the loan, computed on an annual-percentage basis (1).

Yield curve   A line drawn to connect the observations in a graph, where the horizontal axis plots the years to maturity of a particular kind of security and the vertical axis plots the corresponding market yield to maturity at each date (10).

Sources for the Glossary

1. American Bankers' Association. *Banking Terminology.* Washington, D.C.: American Bankers' Association, 1981.

2. Bagby, Joseph. *Real Estate Dictionary.* Englewood Cliffs, N.J.: Institute for Business Planning, 1981.

3. *The Bank Director's Handbook.* 2d ed. Dover, Mass.: Auburn House, 1986.

4. Brownstone, David. *The VNR Real Estate Dictionary.* New York: Van Nostrand Reinhold, 1981.

5. *The Complete Internal Revenue Code.* July 1990 ed. New York: Research Institute of America, 1990.

6. Davids, Lewis E. *Dictionary of Banking and Finance.* Totowa, N.J.: Littlefield Adams, 1978.

7. Graddy, Duane B., Austin H. Spencer, and William H. Brunsen. *Commercial Banking and the Financial Services Industry.* Reston, Va.: Reston Publishing, 1985.

8. Hanson, Derrick G. *Dictionary of Banking and Finance.* Marshfield, Mass.: Pitman, 1985.

9. Institute of Financial Education. *A Glossary of Savings Association Terminology.* Chicago: Institute of Financial Education, 1976.

10. Kaufman, George G. *The U.S. Financial System: Money, Markets, and Institutions.* Englewood Cliffs, N.J.: Prentice-Hall, 1980.

11. McCaffrey, Bill. *Language of Business.* Cambridge, Mass.: Cambridge Business Research, 1988.

12. Munn, Glenn G. *Encyclopedia of Banking and Finance.* Boston: Bankers, 1983.

13. Olson, Ronald L., Harold M. Sollenberger, and William E.

O'Connell, Jr. *A Model for Commercial Banks: Asset/Liability Management.* Greenbelt, Md.: Ivy Press, 1984.

14. Pessin, Allan H., and Joseph A. Ross. *Words of Wall Street: 2000 Investment Terms Defined.* Homewood, Ill.: Dow Jones–Irwin, 1983.

15. Rosenberry, Jerry M. *Dictionary of Banking and Financial Services.* 2d ed. New York: John Wiley & Sons, 1985.

16. Rosenberry, Jerry M. *Dictionary of Business and Management.* 2d ed. New York: John Wiley & Sons, 1983.

17. Rosenberry, Jerry M. *The Investor's Dictionary.* New York: John Wiley & Sons, 1986.

Index